Graphics Programming with Java™

SECOND EDITION

Graphics Programming with Java™

SECOND EDITION

Roger T. Stevens

CHARLES RIVER MEDIA, INC.
Rockland, Massachusetts

Publisher: Jenifer L. Niles
Interior Design/Comp: Publishers' Design and Production Services, Inc.
Cover Design: Sherry Stinson
Printer: InterCity Press, Rockland, Ma

CHARLES RIVER MEDIA, Inc.
P.O. Box 417, 403 VFW Drive
Rockland, MA 02370
781-871-4184
781-871-4376(FAX)
chrivmedia@aol.com
http://www.charlesriver.com

This book is printed on acid-free paper

GRAPHICS PROGRAMMING WITH JAVA™
SECOND EDITION
Roger Stevens
  ISBN 1-886801-91-6
  Printed in the United States of America

99 00 01 02 7 6 5 4 3 2 1

CHARLES RIVER MEDIA titles are available for site license or bulk
purchase by institutions, user groups, corporations, etc. For additional
information, please contact the Special Sales Department at
781-871-4184.

Contents

1

Introduction

In the early 1990s, a team at Sun Microsystems led by James Gosling and Patrick Naughton was attempting to create a new computing environment that would make it simple for ordinary people to use a variety of electronic devices. In writing code for this environment, Gosling began by using the C++ language. He soon found that some of the features that provided flexibility to C++ when it was used by experienced programmers, such as the use of pointers and addresses for direct memory management, added an undesirable degree of complexity. So he began to develop a whole new language, which came to be called "Java." The approach was to use as much of the syntax of C++ as possible so as to make the language easy to use by experienced C++ programmers, but at the same time, to remove or modify those features of C++ that often led to troubles that required sophisticated debugging, even when implemented by experienced programmers. At the same time, Naughton was developing the visual capabilities for the language so that it might provide a simple graphic implementation of the environment. However, the first practical application of Java turned out to be in developing Web pages. The result is that the first releases of Java contained a number of well designed methods that could be used for simple development of Web pages, but that many other methods needed for full-fledged program development were rather primitive or not even developed at all. However, it was soon realized that the capability of Java to run the same program on a number of different platforms and operating systems would vastly simplify the development of many computer applications. Consequently, Java 1.1 and Java 2 have added or expanded many of the programming capabilities that were minimized in the first released versions. While Java is not yet as complete as a commercial programming language, it is fast reaching the point when you will be seeing a lot of commercial programs written in Java. Furthermore, if you are writing a program in C++, you not only have to write the basic program in this language, you have to make additional provisions for graphics on the platform of your choice. For example, to make your program display on Windows 95/98, you need to learn a number of arcane instructions for this particular platform and include their code in your program. On the other hand, if you use Java, you can do everything you want using just the Java language, and the program will work not only on Windows 95/98, but also on any other platform for which a Java interpreter exists.

Java Features

Sun sums up Java as "a simple, object-oriented, distributed, interpreted, robust, secure, architecture-neutral, portable, high-performance, multithreaded, and dynamic language." This covers a lot of territory in a single sentence. Let's see how these characteristics affect us. The simplicity of Java comes from two sources. First, the syntax of Java is almost the same as that of C and C++, so if you are an accomplished C or C++ programmer who wants to work with Java, you'll find that almost always if you write statements for a task in C or C++ terms, the program will work with Java. The few exceptions are quickly learned and easy to remember. The second source of simplicity is that aspects of C and C++ that have been a source of trouble in the past have been eliminated. A major problem with C has always been the passing of parameters between functions. Any number of parameters could be passed to a C function, but what was passed were copies of values of the actual parameter values. After the function got through working with these parameters, only one could be returned to the calling program; the values of the others retained their original values, no matter what the function had done to them. To get around this restriction, the notion of pointers was introduced. It then became possible to pass pointers (addresses of variable locations) to a function; the function could work with the contents of these addresses so that they were permanently changed by the actions of the function. This introduced all sorts of possible complications, such as getting or returning data from or to the wrong address, working with an address when you meant to work with its contents, or vice versa. The introduction of classes and objects in C++ made the use of pointers unnecessary, but they were kept in the language to maintain backward compatibility with C. In Java there are no pointers; in fact, there aren't even any functions. Everything is done through classes and objects, working with methods that are within the objects. This is one of the differences between Java and C and C++ that you'll have the most trouble getting used to, especially if you haven't been making full use of C++'s object-oriented capabilities.

Similarly, when you set up an array in C or C++, the compiler stores the address of the beginning member of the array. (Usually the compiler allows a block of memory sufficient to store all array members, but it is possible to define a pointer location only, without the needed memory being assigned.) If your program, when running, wants to work with an array member outside the array memory block, C and C++ don't object at all. They just blindly count down the proper number of members from the start of the array and work with the contents of the new memory location. If this is outside the array and actually contains some program instructions, you are in for some weird results that are often difficult to track down. In Java you must define the size of an array before using it; if you try to go outside the defined limits, the program quits with a warning message.

We've already pretty well covered the fact that Java is object oriented. To sum up, instead of calling functions to perform various mathematical operations, we send a message to an object, which then responds in an appropriate way. According to people who are object-oriented programming boosters, it is a more natural way of thinking about problems. Whether this is true or not, you better get used to thinking this way, because this is the only way that Java can work.

Java is both a compiled and interpreted language. When you write a Java program, it is first compiled by the *javac* compiler. The result is a set of bytecodes that represent a virtual computer, one that doesn't really exist yet. Then, when you run a compiled Java program, a Java interpreter designed especially for your machine converts the bytecodes to something your computer can understand on the fly. (There is no reason why one couldn't develop a microprocessor that understands Java bytecodes directly, without an intervening interpreter, but that hasn't been done yet.) This characteristic of Java allows it to work in a distributed environment, where it can work with classes that reside at different locations on the Net, for example. It also accounts for the fact that Java is architecture neutral, since various architectures are handled by the various interpreters. This neutrality is what makes Java highly portable from one machine to another. Interpreters currently exist for Windows 95/98, the Mac, Unix machines, Linux, and the Sun Solaris workstation.

Because Java does not allow direct memory addressing, because of its tightened controls over type-checking, and because the interpreter approach results in dynamic linking, Java is a robust language, which dramatically reduces chances for program failures. These features, particularly the insertion of the interpreter between Java bytecodes and the computer, make the system secure, with no opportunity for things such as software viruses, to do low-level mischief in your machine.

Finally, we need to point out that Java has multithreaded capabilities. This does not mean that Java can actually run several tasks simultaneously. Rather, Java allocates time slices to various tasks so that they appear to be working at the same time, although they are actually working one at a time and interleaving their actions. All of the internal actions needed to determine the order in which instructions are performed and in which memory locations are accessed are performed by Java without your external intervention. You only need to define the threads and Java takes care of the rest.

Java Expansion

The very core of Java is the simple programming language, but the key to Java's expansion is the object-oriented nature of the language. A Java object consists of a stand-alone section of code, which has certain designated inputs that cause the object to produce particular outputs. This makes it easy to add new objects to expand the capabilities of the Java language. The initial releases of Java provided graphics extensions to Java in the form of the Java AWT. These were oriented primarily toward Java's first use as a producer of Web pages. Thus, there were very fast and sophisticated methods for reading GIF and JPEG files (which are the two graphic format files most used on the Web) and some fairly primitive methods for drawing lines, rectangles, and ellipses. The first edition of this book described these methods and showed how to create more complex drawing methods to do things that couldn't be handled directly by the AWT. Java 2 has added a new two-dimensional drawing package. It will now handle directly most of the things that we had to generate our own code for in the previous versions. Java 2 also incorporates the Java swing set of components, which have a lot of simplified techniques for creating windows, displays, and complicated applications. Sun calls these "lightweight" components, meaning that they are written completely in the Java language. Finally, there is the Java 3D package, which provides all of the tools for creating images in three-dimensions and then displaying them in two-dimensional form. This package is not an official part of the Java 2D package, but it can easily be added. When you download and run the file java3d|_|-win32opengl-jdk.exe the compressed Java 3D files will be expanded and placed in the proper Java sub-directories.

Getting, Setting Up, and Using Java

The latest version of Java 2 (as of the time of publication of this book) is included on the CD-ROM. You can easily load it onto your hard drive. Chapter 2 shows you how to install it on your system, and how to compile and run a few simple programs. If you want the very latest release of Java, it is available to you at no charge by downloading the Java Developer's Kit from the Sun Microsystems homepage at *http:\\www.sun.com*.

The Java Language

Chapter 3 is a quick overview of the Java language. It tells you how the language works, the expressions that are used, how to work with classes and objects, operators that are available, mathematical functions, and the contents of some useful classes. If you're an accomplished C or C++ programmer, a quick reading of this chapter should get you ready to program with Java. If you've never used C or C++, you'll need to study the chapter more carefully to become familiar with the syntax. As you begin to program, you can reference back to this chapter if you have any questions about how to perform a particular task.

Java Swing Components

The new Java 2 contains the swing components, which form a whole catalog of new methods for Java operation. Throughout this edition of the book, we'll continually make use of these new methods. Chapter 4 provides a brief description of the swing components and gives some information on why and how they are used.

Components, Containers, and Layout Management

The programs in Chapter 2 display their results in a DOS window. Chapter 5 shows how to create a window and produce a graphics display within it. It also explains the difference between setting up and running a Java program and creating a Java applet that can be viewed with an applet viewer or with a Net browser. Finally, Chapter 5 describes the components that are used to create a window layout and shows how to put them together. Several sample programs show the results of these operations. We've used the new swing components for most of these layouts. Among other things, they now make it possible to write a program that can be used either as an application or as an applet. In addition to the layout techniques described in the first edition, there is a new layout called the BoxLayout that makes it easier to lay out many complicated pages. It is also described in Chapter 5.

Checkboxes, Lists, Menus, and Scrolling

These are a few of the classes for user interface that are included with Java. Chapter 6 tells how to use these in actual programs. Once you've become familiar with the techniques, you should be able to use most Java user interface classes with little additional instruction. Most of these classes have an improved form in the Java swing components. For one thing, classes such as the checkbox, may not only have a text title but may in addition or instead have an associated icon. It is these new versions that are described in the new version of Chapter 6.

Colors

The Java 2D package provides for high-quality color output that can provide very sophisticated use of color by advanced users and yet has easy-to-use color handling for the ordinary user. The Java 2D use of Color Space, Color Model, and Color are described in Chapter 7. This chapter also provides details of how Java defines colors using its default model, describes the Java predefined colors, and shows how to define your own colors that are equivalent to the VGA 16-color mode colors or 256-color mode colors. The use of color gradients is also described.

Display Text in a Graphics Window	Chapter 8 shows how to use text in a Java Graphics window. Java doesn't preserve a pointer to the current text location; instead, every string must have its coordinates specified. The chapter shows how to select fonts, type styles, sizes, and positioning of text strings under these constraints. In addition to these basic text handling capabilities, Java 2D has a number of sophisticated techniques for handling text and an additional group of text handling capabilities are included as part of the Java swing package. These are described in Chapter 8 and some examples are given.
Working with Images	Java has an excellent capability for displaying JPEG and GIF graphics files. Chapter 9 describes these file formats and shows a very simple way in which Java swing can be used to view such a file. It then shows how to create and display your own graphics file. It also shows how to use swing components to display a directory of graphics files, display a thumbnail, and then display a selected file full size. It also considers double buffering and storage of graphic images.
Viewing BMP Graphics Files	The BMP graphic file format is used extensively by Windows, but is not supported by Java. You can write a Java program that will display such files, although it won't be quite as fast as Java's programs to show GIF and JPG files. Chapter 10 gives you details of the BMP file format and shows you how to select a BMP file from any directory and display it.
Animation	Multiple-frame GIF files have become the de facto standard for providing small animations on the Web. Chapter 11 shows you how to write programs that display animated images and tells you where you can get information on writing your own GIF animation files. The use of sprites is also described. The CD-ROM contains Anfy Java by Fabio Ciucci, a set of animated backgrounds with text moving through them in various ways. These are extremely well done. You can use these to create your own custom Web pages, or as models for writing your own Java applets.

Creating Your Own Web Page	Chapter 12 shows you how to create your own Web page. A simple program is shown to demonstrate the technique for creating a Web page. The required steps to transfer your page to the Web are described.

Plotting Points, Lines, and Rectangles	Chapter 13 shows how to use Java methods for drawing lines, rectangles, and round rectangles. The first edition of this book provided programs to draw wide lines and patterned lines (such as dashed lines, dotted lines, center lines, etc.) that were not directly supported by Java 1.0 and 1.1. The Java 2D package now has all these line drawing capabilities as well as anti-aliasing, translation, rotation, and shape distortion. Chapter 12 shows you how to use all of these techniques.

Clipping	Many computer languages include clipping capabilities because there can be catastrophic damages to the program when graphics are specified to be drawn outside the display boundaries. Java will not allow this kind of damage, so clipping is not required for that reason. However, Java provides the capability for limiting drawing of graphics to within a defined shape boundary, and this capability can be useful in many graphics situations. Chapter 14 describes how to use this.

User Interfaces	Often we need to enter data in a window that will control the production of a graphic. Chapter 15 shows how to establish communication between buttons, text areas, and so forth. and the graphics drawing program. One example program allows the user to insert bounds for a Mandelbrot set and then draws the resulting figure. Another program displays a Mandelbrot set and allows the user to select a point on it for the origin of a Julia set, which is then drawn.

Drawing and Filling Polygons	Java includes methods for drawing and filling polygons. In addition, the new Java 2D package of Java 2 allows you to rotate, translate, or scale such a polygon. The procedures for doing this are described in Chapter 16.

Drawing Circles, Ellipses, and Arcs

Java includes methods for drawing and filling ellipses. Chapter 17 shows how to use these. Originally, Java only allowed ellipses whose major and minor axes coincided with the *x* and *y* axes of the display. The new Java 2D drawing package allows for the rotation, translation, and scaling of ellipses, which permits a display that contains tilted ellipses that may be either drawn or filled. These are also covered in this chapter.

Using Threads with Java

Chapter 18 shows you how Java uses threads to run several programs at essentially the same time. A sample program is provided that shows how this is done and allows you to examine the results. Another program shows how threads can be used to provide animated displays.

Parametric Cubic Curves

Java doesn't support any advanced methods for defining complex curves without specifying them in terms of each of a large number of small line segments. Chapter 19 describes how parametric cubic methods may be used with Java to draw Bezier, or B-Spline curves and also shows how to use Java 2D's own Bezier curve method.

Three-Dimensional Modeling

Chapter 20 shows how to model various solids such as cones, spheres, cubes, cylinders, and various solids of revolution and how to display them on a two-dimensional screen. The Java 3D package is used to perform these operations.

More Advanced Web Pages

Now that you know how to create graphics with Java and how to create your own simple Web page, you'll want to learn more about Web page production. Chapter 21 tells you how to determine when to create a graphic directly on a Web page and when to simply load a graphics file. It also shows how to obtain information from a visitor to your Website.

Commercial Java Packages

Although you can easily get by with the free Java Developer's Kit and documentation, Chapter 22 describes some more sophisticated Java software that you might be interested in purchasing. Some useful shareware programs are also described.

CHAPTER

2

Getting, Setting Up, and Using Java

Unlike C++, where compilers such as Microsoft's Visual C++ compiler cost hundreds of dollars, the Java compiler is available at no cost. At the time this book was published, the latest Java compiler was Java 2, which is available in the *Java* directory on the accompanying CD-ROM as the file *jdk12-win32*. The associated documentation is in *jdk12-doc*. Java 2 includes the Java 2D package for drawing two-dimensional graphics and the Swing component package, which provides applications with a unique look and feel. In addition, the three-dimensional graphics drawing package is in the file *java3D1_1-win32-opengl-jdk.exe* in the *Java* directory. Java is not a static language; it is being improved almost daily. If you want to keep up with the latest versions of Java, you can download them from Sun's Java Website. Usually you have your choice of the latest released version of Java or a beta version that is further improved but not completely debugged. You can also order (either from the Website or by mail) a CD-ROM called *Java Jump Start* from Sun Microsystems. This contains not only the latest released version of Java but also several books on all facets of Java. Whatever method you use to get the version of Java that you want, it is a simple matter to get it up and running on your computer. This chapter tells you just how this is done.

Downloading the Java Developer's Kit

The CD-ROM includes the latest version of the Java Developer's Kit (JDK) at the time this book was published. Sun is now calling this Java 2, although at this writing, the JDK is called jdk1.2. You may want to update from time to time by downloading the latest version from Sun's Website at *http://www. javasoft.com*.

When the homepage comes up, navigate to *Download* and then select the version of the JDK that you want. You will get a self-extracting file for the JDK for the platform you have selected. (Note that the CD-ROM furnished with this book contains the JDK version for Windows 95/98, but versions for other operating systems are available at the Website.) If your computer is storing the file in some obscure directory, it may be a good idea to note the path and file name while you're downloading; this will save having to hunt for the file later.

You'll also want to download jdk12-doc, which contains the documentation for all of the Java classes. The pages at the Sun Website will tell you how to do this. The documentation will come in handy if you are going to delve deeply into how Java works. Many documentation pages are in the form of *html* files and need a Net browser to read and print them. You may want to download the *HotJava* browser from the above source to do this. I have found that if I try to print long html files, often all pages after page 11 are printed blank. I tried loading such html files to Corel Word Perfect and to Microsoft Word, but neither could both load and print them satisfactorily. There is, however, an office suite called Star Office Suite that can be downloaded from the Web without charge. It's quite a download, since the file contains 60 megabytes, but its word processor is capable of loading and printing long html documents, so if you think you're going to need hard copies of a lot of Java documentation, you may want to download it.

Expanding the JDK On Your System

The latest versions of the JDK come as a compressed, self-extracting file. Once you run this file, you must also run one of the extracted files called *SetUp* in order to get all of the Java files separated and into the right directories. Java will end up in a subdirectory called *JAVA* under the directory or subdirectory that contained your self-extracting JDK file. Thus, if you want all your Java installation to be in a primary directory called *JAVA* you need to start the process with the self-extracting file in your root directory. If you haven't used any version of Java before, you have no problem. If you've used a previous version of Java and are upgrading, you need a completely empty directory for the new Java version. Move everything out of your *JAVA* directory before you begin the expansion and *SetUp* process. If you try to put the new version of Java on top of an old one, some of the old files will not be removed and will prevent proper operation of the updated system. If you have Java source files that you've created or downloaded, it's all right to put them back in the *JAVA\BIN* subdirectory after you've got Java up and running; meanwhile, you need to save them somewhere else. When you run the self-extracting file, it will unzip all the files for the JDK. Running *SetUp* will create whatever subdirectories are needed, and place each expanded file in its proper subdirectory. If there are still compressed files after the setup process is complete, you should not unzip them under any circumstances, as Java expects to find them and use them in their compressed form. The file *src.zip* contains the source code for Java. Normally you won't need it; if you do need to reference some source code, you can unzip this file, but it will take up a lot more space.

If you're using Windows 95/98, use your favorite editor to add

```
c:\java\bin
```

(or whatever path you're using for Java) to the *PATH* statement in your *AUTOEXEC.BAT* file. Then reboot your computer to make this statement effective.

You're now ready to find out whether the Java interpreter is working. Go to the subdirectory

```
cd java\demo\TicTacToe
```

Then run the Applet Viewer using the following statement:

```
appletviewer example1.html
```

You should see a small window appear with a crude version of TicTacToe in it. It's not very clever; you should be able to beat the computer every time. (Hint: Start in a corner and after Java makes its move, select the diagonally opposite corner. After Java's next move select a third corner and you'll have a guaranteed win on the next move.) If this window doesn't appear, you'll find a lot of troubleshooting information at the Sun homepage that will provide suggestions on how to fix any problems.

Compiling a Program

If you've come this far, there's a good chance that your Java installation is successful. Now we'll see if you can compile a Java program. First, let's consider the mechanics of how we're going to edit and compile Java programs. These instructions apply to Windows 95/98; if you are using another operating system, things will be a little different. If worst comes to worst, you can use the Windows 95 *Notepad* as an editor, but it insists on ending file names with the extension *TXT*, when you really want *JAVA*. A much better alternative is to use the free Programmer's File Editor (PFE). You'll find this on the CD-ROM or you can download the latest version from *www.windows95.com*. A somewhat fancier editor is WinEdit. This editor is shareware; if you decide to use it regularly, you need to make a payment to the author. This editor is also on the CD-ROM or you may download the latest version from *www.windowware.com*. (The version of WinEdit on the CD-ROM is not the latest one, but it is the latest that would work with my Windows 98 setup. If you try the latest version, be careful. For convenience, you should include your editor as part of your *Start* taskbar. The easiest way to do this is to double-click on the *My Computer* icon. Then select the C drive, the Windows directory, and search for your editor's running file. Select this and, holding the left mouse button down, drag its icon until it is on top of the *Start* icon. The editor icon should now appear as part of your *Start* taskbar. Select the editor and either begin typing in the listing of a Java program or use the *File* option to select an existing Java source file. When you are done, use the File option and either select *Save* if you are up grading an existing file, or *Save as* for a new file. The file name must be the same as your principal class (including case) and must end with the extension *.java*.

Listing 2.1 is a very simple Java program that you can type into your editor (or transfer from the CD-ROM) and then compile and run.

The data in the *System.out.println* statement that is within the parentheses should all be typed on the same line without any internal carriage return. We just separated it here so it would all fit on the page.

Once you've saved your Java source file, you can open a new window. Select *Programs* from the *Start* taskbar and *MSDOS Prompt* from the list of programs that comes up. (For convenience, you may want to create a shortcut to MS-DOS on your Desktop.) If the DOS window fills the entire screen, *Alt Enter* to reduce the window size. Change to the directory where your source code is located and type

```
avac Test. ava
```

where *Test* should be replaced by the name of your source code file. A Java application is a class that contains a specific method called *main()*. When the Java interpreter runs the application, it does so by running the *main()* method of this class. Your source code file may contain other classes that are accessed by *main()*. If it does, the Java compiler will produce a file having the extension *.class* for every class that you have defined in your source file. Each file consists of a set of machine-independent bytecodes that make up the compiled version of the class. Normally, you will give your source code file the same name as that of the class containing *main()*, followed by the extension *.java* as, for example, *Test.java*. Now when you are running the javac compiler you can type

```
avac Test. ava
```

```
/*

Test. ava = Simple Java Program
*/
class Test
{
    public static void main(String args[])
    {
        System.out.println("Java has successfully
            compiled and run this program.");
    }
}
```

LISTING *Simple Java Program.*
2.1

and when you run the compiled program you can type

```
ava Test
```

Once you start the Java compiler (*javac*), Java should compile for a while and then either give you a list of errors or just return the prompt. If you get errors, you can select the editor window, make any needed corrections, save the corrected file, and then return to the DOS window. Now, pressing the F3 key and Return will let you compile the corrected file. You can keep repeating this process until the file compiles without errors. At this point, you can type

```
ava Test
```

to run the program. Note that in using the Java compiler (*javac*) you must include the file extension (*.java*), but in running the compiled program with the Java interpreter (java) you don't include the file extension, which makes things a little complicated.

If you want to make things much simpler, you can go to the subdirectory that contains your *java.exe* file and add the following batch program named *javacr.bat*.

```
avac %1. ava
ava %1
```

Now you will be able to both compile and run a Java program by typing

```
avacr Test
```

and you won't need to worry about the confusing extensions or lack thereof. There is only one time when this batch file will lead you astray. Suppose you have a Java program that takes a long time to run and you decide to make some changes. However, when you insert the changes, you inadvertently put in one or more errors. The batch file will compile your program and report the errors, and since the compilation was unsuccessful, it will go ahead and run the old version of your program. You have to wait for this to finish before you can recompile and rerun.

When you run the *Test* program, the following legend will appear on the next line of the DOS window:

```
Java has successfully compiled and run this program.
```

This indicates that the program has run successfully. What have we just done? Although the class listing is quite simple, you should take another close look at it, because it is somewhat different from any other language you've ever worked with. When you type *javac Test.java*, you start the Java compiler, which compiles the program into a set of bytecodes similar to machine language instructions, but these are for a virtual computer rather than your specific computer. When you type *java Test*, you are running the compiled version of the class *Test* (from the *Test.class* file. On the run, this converts the bytecodes to the appropriate machine language for your specific type of computer. The first thing Java looks for in this class is the method *main()*. When it finds one, it then runs this method. Fortunately, the *Test* class has a *main()* method; if it didn't, running the class would probably not do anything. In the *main()* method of our *Test* class, only one thing happens: A method called *System.out.println* is run. This method is part of a class and subclass that are part of the Java language and available to every newly created class. It prints out the string in parentheses to the display DOS window.

Additional Graphics Setups

You now have Java up and running, but you may want to make some additions to increase your graphics capability. The Java 2D graphics package is included in Java 2, but the Java 2D example programs are not. You'll find them on the CD-ROM in a file called *Java2D-samples.fcs*. You can move it to whatever directory you want on your hard drive and you should then be able to compile and run the examples. Some of them run as Java applications, others as applets, and others will run in either mode. Those that run in the applet mode have the required *html* files included, so you should have no problems after you read about applets in the following chapters.

All files needed for three-dimensional work with Java are included in the file *java3D1_1-wein32opengl.jdk* on the CD-ROM. When you run this file, it will automatically put each Java 3D file in the right place in your Java installation. It includes three-dimensional examples, which are placed in the *JAVA\DEMO* directory.

Classes Used by Two or More Other Classes

You may be wondering what happens if you have two differently named Java source files, each of which contains a class with the same name, but contains different source code. For example, suppose your source code files *myfile1* and *myfile2* each contain a class called *mathematics* but *mathematics* is not the same for both files. The answer is that all classes compiled from a source code file will be updated as of the last time you run the javac compiler. Thus, if you compile *myfile1*, the classes *myfile1.class* and *mathematics.class* will be created and you will be able to run *myfile1* just fine. However, if you compile *myfile2* the classes *myfile2.class* and *mathematics.class* will be created, with the *myfile2* version of the *mathematics* class replacing the *myfile1* version. Now you will be able to run *myfile2* just fine, but *myfile1* will try to run the new version of the *Mathematics* class. Depending on the changes in *Mathematics*, *myfile1* may no longer run. The moral is, don't ever use the same class name in more than one file unless the contents of the class are the same in all files. Even then, you're going to have to set up some administrative procedures to be sure that any changes made to the class in one file are duplicated in the other file.

Actually, even if the same class is being used by two separate classes, including a copy of it as part of each source file is poor programming practice. There are a couple of other options that work a lot better. First, you can simply put the common class in a separate file. Listing 2.2 is a *Mathematics* class that does some simple mathematics within a series of *System.out.println* statements. The *Mathematics* class is set up so that when it is instantiated as an object, three

```
/*
Mathematics. ava = Class to perform some
mathematical
                    operations
*/
    public class Mathematics
    {
        static double x, y, angle;
        Mathematics(double x1, double y1, double
angle1)
        {
            x = x1;
            y = y1;
            angle = angle1;
        }
        public void writeMath()
        {
            System.out.println("x = " + x);
            System.out.println("y = " + y);
            System.out.println("x + y = " + (x+y));
            System.out.println("x - y = " + (x - y));
            System.out.println("x * y = " + (x*y));
            System.out.println("x / y = " + (x / y));
            System.out.println("cosine of " + angle +
                " degrees = " + Math.cos(angle *
            .017453292));
        }
    }
```

LISTING *Class to Display Some Mathematical Results.*
2.2

parameters are passed to the object's internal variables. The *writeMath* method then uses these variables to perform some mathematical operations. Each of the traditional mathematical operations (add, subtract, multiply, and divide) is done within a *System.out.println* statement and is concatenated with an alphanumeric string through the use of a plus sign. The last of the *System.out.println* statements shows how a trigonometric function is used in Java. The function for computing the cosine is a method of the *Math* class. As with C and C++, the argument must be in radians, which is why the angle is multiplied by a conversion factor before the cosine is found.

Listings 2.3 and 2.4 show two classes that use the same *Mathematics* class, but pass different values to it.

All three of the classes just listed need to be in the same subdirectory. You need to compile the *Mathematics* class first, then the other two classes can be compiled and run. When you run *Math1*, you should obtain a display (in the DOS window) that looks like this:

```
x = 24.3457
y = 5.81395
x + y = 30.1596
x - y = 18.5317
x * y = 141.545
x / y = 4.18746
cosine of 45 degrees = 0.707107
```

When you compile and run *Math2*, you should get a display (in the DOS window) that looks like this:

```
x = 1345.78
y = 12.471
```

```
/*
Math1. ava = Class to perform mathematical
operations using
Mathematics class
*/
class Math1
{
public static void main(String args[])
{
Mathematics m1 = new Mathematics(24.3457, 5.81395,
45.0);
m1.writeMath();
}
}
```

LISTING *Class to Do Mathematical Operations Using the Mathematics Class.*
2.3

```
/*
Math2. ava = Class to perform mathematical
operations using
Mathematics class
*/
    class Math2
    {
        public static void main(String args[])
        {
            Mathematics m1 = new
Mathematics(1345.7825, 12.47102,
30.0);
            m1.writeMath();
        }
    }
```

LISTING *Another Class to Do Mathematical Operations Using the Mathematics Class.*
2.4

```
x + y = 1358.25
x - y = 1333.31
x * y = 16783.3
x / y = 107.913
cosine of 30 degrees = 0.866025
```

Packages

The technique described previously can leave you with a lot of common classes interspersed with other classes in one directory. You might find it more convenient to have a whole set of classes that are used commonly stored in a single subdirectory by themselves. You can do this through the *package* statement. Listing 2.5 shows the class *Mathpkg*, which does exactly the same thing as the *Mathematics* class described earlier, but the listing is preceded by the statement *package Mathstuff;*. The location of the source file *Mathpkg.java* is critical. All of the classes that are to reference *Mathpkg* must be in a common directory or subdirectory. *Mathpkg.java* must be in a subdirectory of this directory having the same name as the package name (in this case, *Mathstuff*). (Note that you have to be very careful with file names, because to DOS there is no difference between uppercase and lowercase letters, but to Java there is. Thus if you have letters of the wrong case in some of your file names, you may find that everything is working fine when you are performing some operations and then suddenly things cease to work when a Java operation takes place.)

Now let's look at Listings 2.6 and 2.7. The class *Math3* is the same as *Math1*, and the class *Math4* is the same as the class *Math2*, except that classes *Math3* and *Math4* have the heading *import Mathstuff.*;*. This enables each of

```
/*
Mathpkg. ava = Class in package to perform some
mathematical operations
*/
   package Mathstuff;
   public class Mathpkg
      {
         static double x, y, angle;
         public Mathpkg(double x1, double y1, double
            angle1)
         {
            x = x1;
            y = y1;
            angle = angle1;
         }

         public void writeMath()
         {
            System.out.println("x = " + x);
            System.out.println("y = " + y);
            System.out.println("x + y = " + (x+y));
            System.out.println("x - y = " + (x -
y));
            System.out.println("x * y = " + (x*y));
            System.out.println("x / y = " + (x /
y));
            System.out.println("cosine of " + angle
               + " degrees = " + Math.cos(angle *
               .017453292));
         }
      }
```

LISTING *Class to Display Some Mathematical Results Using Package.*
2.5

these classes to import any class that is in the subdirectory *Mathstuff*. (However, this will only work if *Mathstuff* is the name of a subdirectory of the importing class.) Now, you must first go to the subdirectory *Mathstuff* and run *javac* to compile *Mathpkg*. Then return to the parent directory and compile *Math3.java* and *Math4.java*. When you run the compiled programs, you'll find that the results are the same as for running *Math1* and *Math2*, respectively.

Java Resources

We've already told you how to download the JDK and Javadoc. You should be aware, however, that there are two Sun Microsystems Java sites. The main site is at *http://java.sun.com*. The other (the one we used) is in Aspen, Colorado. It

```
/*
Math3. ava = Class to perform mathematical
operations using
Mathpkg class
*/
    import Mathstuff.*;
    class Math3
    {
        public static void main(String args[])
        {
            Mathpkg m1 = new Mathpkg(24.3457,
            5.81395, 45.0);
            m1.writeMath();
        }
    }
```

LISTING *Class to Do Mathematical Operations Using the Mathpkg Class.*
2.6

is found at *http://www.javasoft.com*. There is a wealth of material available on these Websites. The most difficult thing is navigating through them to find the material you need. The author downloaded a file of documentation for Java3D that was about 500K long and took about 17 minutes to download. When printed out, it was 537 pages long and took hours to print. A tutorial for Java Swing was about the same length. When you get to the Java home page, you'll find a category called *Developer*. When you select this category, you need to register a user name and password with Sun. You'll then be able to navigate this category and will find much useful information on Java.

Gamelan is a Website that contains a large collection of Java applets as well

```
/*
Math4. ava = Class to perform mathematical
operations using Mathpkg class
*/
    import Mathstuff.*;
    class Math4
    {
        public static void main(String args[])
        {
            Mathpkg m1 = new Mathpkg(1345.7825,
            12.47102, 30.0);
            m1.writeMath();
        }
    }
```

LISTING *Another Class to Do Mathematical Operations Using the mMathpkg Class..*
2.7

as many Java demos and various Java information, much of it oriented toward game programming. You'll find it at *http://www.gamelan.com*.

If you're interested in knowing how good a Java applet that you're considering is, you need to look at the Java Applet Rating Service (JARS). It can be found at *http://www.surinam.net/java/jars.html*.

If you need to understand the organization of the Java classes, you can find Java class hierarchy diagrams at *http://rendezvous.com/java/ hierarchy/index.html*.

If you're looking for lots of free Java GIF animation files, go to *http://member.aol.com/royalef/gifanim.htm*.

Finally, if you want an index of all sites that reference Java, you can look at *http://www.yahoo.com/Computers/Languages/Java*.

3 The Java Language

The Java language grew out of a project at Sun Microsystems that was attempting to develop a small, reliable, portable, real-time operating environment that would work effectively in heterogeneous, network-wide distributed environments. Originally, C++ was selected as the language in which this operating system would be written. C and C++ are languages that put few constraints on the programmer, leaving him or her the maximum in freedom to do all sorts of neat things. Consequently, the opportunity for subtle, hard-to-debug errors is maximized. It has been said that the C language gives the programmer the rope to hang himself and C++ fashions the noose. The problems of C++ together with the difficulty in writing a system that could be transported to a lot of different platforms caused the Sun project team to decide to develop a totally new language, which was ultimately called *Java*. In structure, Java is much like C++. If you're an experienced C++ programmer, you'll often, but not always, find that when you don't know how to do something in Java, if you write a few lines of C++ like code, it will work fine.

One of the advantages of Java's object-oriented structure is that it's easy to extend the language by adding more complex objects. Since Java 1.0, there has been a complete rewrite of the way that Java handles events (mouse movement and clicking, keyboard actions, etc.). Java has also added the Java 2D graphics drawing package, which vastly extends the primitive drawing capabilities of the first Java packages. A whole package of Java Swing components now provides complex displays that can either have the look and feel of Windows 95/98 or a special Java look and feel. Finally, there is now a complete Java 3D package for creating three-dimensional graphics. This is not a part of Java 2, but it is available and easily incorporated into Java.

The downside of all this is that Java is beginning to have so many capabilities that no one can keep up with all of them, and a whole shelf of books would be needed to provide a full description. To keep things under control, in this book we have limited ourselves to describing those capabilities needed to produce a wide range of typical graphics. In this chapter, in particular, we are only going to describe the basic capabilities of the Java language. Once you learn to use these well, we'll go on to some of the more complex graphic tools.

Java as an Object-Oriented Language

Proponents of the object-oriented approach to programming always claim that it is much more natural than the procedural approach and thus easier to learn by an untutored user. For example, instead of solving a problem by the procedural approach of saying *2 + 2 = 4*, you would send two messages to the object +, each saying *2*, and the object would return a message saying *4*. If this is really the way you naturally think, then fine, but I suspect that most people with a little formal education have been exposed enough to the procedural technique so that this new approach will seem very strange to them. One of the big advantages of C++ was that it allowed programmers to become familiar with the use of objects without having to totally abandon procedural techniques. While this has made C++ the favorite language for developing new software, C++ went too far in that it did not make it easy to have classes and applications that were easily transportable from one situation to another. In the previous chapter, we looked at some simple Java programs and saw how Java runs applications by interpreting the bytecodes that form a Java class and running the method *main()* from within that class. We also saw that the Java compiler created a separate class file for every class defined by the source code, making each class available for use by other applications.

Java as a Compiled and Interpreted Language

Most popular computer languages use a compiler, which takes the language statements written by the programmer and converts them to machine language codes that run on a particular microprocessor. The compiler may be slow, but once the program has been compiled it runs like lightning on any microprocessor and operating system for which the compiler was designed. But if you compiled a program for a PC, it won't run on a Mac; that requires a completely different compiler.

A language that uses an interpreter instead of a compiler is stored in the actual form that was written by the programmer. When you run the program, each line is converted to machine language and executed as it comes up. This is a lot slower process than running a compiled file, but such a program can be run on any machine that has an interpreter for the language. Java is both a compiled and interpreted language. The Java compiler converts the Java program written by the programmer into a series of bytecodes. These bytecodes are the machine language for a virtual computer that really doesn't exist. (It doesn't exist yet, but there is no reason why someone couldn't invent a microprocessor that uses the Java bytecodes as its machine language and thus could run compiled Java programs directly.) Currently, the bytecodes are run through a Java interpreter that converts each to machine language for the microprocessor being used and runs the resulting instruction immediately. Thus, a compiled Java program can run on any computer that has an interpreter written for it. This includes Solaris, Windows 95/98, Unix, and MacIntosh computers, among others. The Java interpreter runs a program almost as fast as a compiled program in another language runs. This, then, is one of the most significant features of Java: A compiled program can run on any one of many different platforms without modification.

Java and Applets

Java can create compiled Java files that run through the Java Interpreter. Java can also produce applets, which are small, stand-alone compiled programs that can be run with a Java utility called *appletviewer*, or with any Java-aware network browser such as Microsoft Internet Explorer or Netscape . We'll describe how to write applets in future chapters.

Java as an Improvement Over C++

One of the principal problems with the C language was that a function could only return one data item. When several parameters were passed to a function, what the function received was copies of the parameter values, so that however the function manipulated them, the new values were lost when the function ended; the originals of the parameters were unchanged. To get around this, an elaborate system of pointers was created so that pointers to actual values could be passed to and manipulated in a function. When C++ added the concept of classes and objects, there was little need of pointers, since objects consisting of many pieces of data could be passed to and from functions. However, to keep compatibility with C, the pointer scheme was preserved. Java not only eliminates pointers entirely, but it also eliminates all functions; it depends upon classes and their methods to perform all actions. This eliminates one very major source of C and C++ errors, since using an incorrect pointer in C or C++ can cause an unanticipated change in the contents of a memory location that can corrupt your data or even change the operation of your program. Java still preserves the concept of arrays, but while C and C++ just blindly count from the beginning of an array to find a specified member, Java will not allow you to go outside the defined array bounds.

Java Language Structure

We're now going to look at the basic elements of Java programming. To start with, you need to understand the way in which Java programs are structured. A Java program is constructed from building blocks called *classes*. A *class* is instantiated as an *object*. Data is sent to the object and the object then performs certain actions and possibly returns some data. If a class contains a method called *main*, this class can be run by the Java interpreter. Execution of a program begins by running the *main* method. There can also be other classes that are used by the class that contains the *main* method. They are compiled as separate

```
/*
Test. ava = Simple Java Program
*/
class Test
{
    public static void main(String args[])
    {
        System.out.println("Java has successfully
            compiled and run this program.");
    }
}
```

LISTING *Simple Java Program.*
3.1

class files during the compilation process and may then be accessed by any class while running its *main* method. Listing 3.1 is the very simple Java program that we used as an example in Chapter 2. We didn't get into the mechanics then, but we'll do so now. Note that the program begins by defining a class called *Test*. The lines that are used to define this class are enclosed in curly brackets. In Java, every block of lines that belong together is enclosed in curly brackets. I like to place the opening and closing brackets each on a separate line and to use indentation to clearly show what data code belongs within a set of brackets. The *Test* class is pretty simple, it just contains the *main* method. This method has a standard way of defining its header, being of type *public static void* and passing the parameter *String[] args*. Within the *main* method is only one line of code, a call to the method *System.out.println*, a method that is part of the Java language and available to any class. It displays on the DOS window screen the material passed to it, which in this case is a string of text. Note that the statement ends with a semicolon. This is required for each statement in Java, but is not required after the closing curly bracket of a block.

Java Data Type

When you are working with C or C++, the precision of a piece of data may vary from one computer to another. If you are working with an integer of type *int*, the precision might be 16 bits on a PC clone and 32 bits on another machine. This is not true of Java, where the size of each data type is defined absolutely, regardless of what machine is used. Table 3-1 is a list of Java data types. A Java variable is defined as follows:

```
int a;
```

Java also supports arrays. Using arrays will be described later in this chapter.

Table 3-1   Java Data Types.

Group	Type	Size	Range
	byte	8 bits	−256 to +255
Integers	short	16 bits	−32768 to 32767
	int	32 bits	−2147483648 to +2147483647
	long	64 bits	−9223372036854775808 to +9223372036854775807
Floating	float	32 bits	±3.40282347 E+38
point	double	64 bits	±1.79769313486231570 E+308
Boolean	boolean	1 bit	True or false
Character	char	16 bits	Any of 65536 unicode characters enclosed in single quotes

Strings

Java supports strings of characters of zero or more characters enclosed in double quotation marks. For example,

```
String s = "This is an example of a string";
```

In C and C++ a string is equivalent to an array of characters, but this is not true of Java, where *String* is a separate class. Consequently you cannot access a particular part of a string with an array member designation. String comparisons are different from C and C++, as will be described later.

Operators

Operators used in Java statements are like those used in C and C++ and look a lot like those used in ordinary mathematical expressions, so you shouldn't have too much trouble writing equations using variables that you have defined together with Java operators. For example,

```
int a, b, c, d, e, f;
c = a + b;
d = b - a;
```

```
e, = b / a;
f = b * a;
```

The variables must first be defined, in this case as integers *a, b, c, d, e* and *f.* The first three statements look like ordinary mathematical equations for addition, subtraction, and division, respectively. The last expression as with many other computer languages uses the operator *to represent multiplication. Since you have defined all the arguments as integers, when you perform a division, you end up with an integer; if there is a fractional part of the division result, it is truncated. (If you need the fractional part, you should have defined the arguments as floating point numbers. Then the same operators would perform floating point operations instead of integer ones.) Java always keeps track of the type of data that you are using, but if you specify mixed data types in an operation, Java rarely performs automatic casting of types as do C and C++, so that you need to do your casting explicitly. This eliminates unpleasant surprises such as loss of precision because of type conversions that you are unaware of.

There are lots of operations besides these simple mathematical ones; some of the meanings are not so obvious. These are listed in Table 3-2, together with some descriptive material. You can to refer to this table to determine from a program listing what the program is doing, or when you are writing a program and need to use some unusual actions.

Table 3-2 Java Operators and Their Definitions.

Operator	Description
[]	Brackets enclose array member designations. Example: `int a[40];` sets up an array of 40 integers, a[0] to a[39]. `b = a[34];` assigns the value of `a[34]` (the 35th member of a) to `b`.
()	Parentheses group expressions, isolate conditional expressions, surround passed parameters.

{}	Curly brackets enclose a group of statements or a class or method. Example:
	
	`if (r == 3)`
	`{`
	`    a = 3;`
	`    b = 6;`
	`}`
	
	When the condition in the *if* statement is true, both statements within the curly brackets are performed, but not otherwise.

continued

Table 3-2 Java Operators and Their Definitions. *(Continued)*

Operator	Description
.	Direct component selector for a member of an object. Example: `complex.r` where `complex` is an object and *r* is defined within the class to which the object belongs.
++	Increment.
	`b = ++a;` means that *a* is incremented before it is used in the current operations. `b = a++;` means that *a* is incremented after the other operations take place. For a = 3, the first type operation yields a value of 4 for *b*, while the second type of operation yields a 3 for *b*. After the statement is executed, *a* is 4 in either case.
—	Decrement.
	`b = —a;` means that *a* is decremented before it is used in the current operations. `b = a—;` means that *a* is decremented after the other operations take place. For a = 3, the first type of operation yields a value of 2 for *b*, while the second type of operation yields a 3 for *b*. After the statement is executed, *a* is 2 in either case.
&	`a & b` means that *a* and *b* are bitwise ANDed together.
*	`a * b` means that *a* is multiplied by *b*.
+	`+ a` means that *a* is a positive number.
	`a + b` means that *a* and *b* are added together.
-	`- a` means that *a* is a negative number.
	`a - b` means that *b* is subtracted from *a*.
~	Bitwise 1's complement.
!	Logical negation.
/	Division.
%	Remainder after a modulo arithmetic operation.
	Example. `c = a % b;` means that *a* is divided by *b* and the remainder is assigned to *c*. If *a* is 17 and *b* is 3, *c* is equal to 2.
<<	Shift left. A character or integer (in the binary form in which it is stored in memory) is shifted to the left the number of places indicated. (The sign is not affected.) Example:

```
int a = 46;
int c;
c = a << 4;
```

The integer *a* is stored as 101110. Shifted 4 places to the left gives 1011100000. The decimal result of the operation (*c*) would thus be 736. |
| >> | Shift right. A character or integer (in the binary form in which it is stored in memory) is shifted to the left the number of places indicated. (The sign is not affected.) Example:

```
int a = 46;
int c;
``` |

continued

Table 3-2   Java Operators and Their Definitions. *(Continued)*

Operator	Description
	`c = a >> 3;` The integer *a* is stored as 101110. Shifted 3 places to the left gives 101. The decimal result of the operation (*c*) would thus be 5.

`<`	Relational less than. Example:
	`if (a < b)`
	`{...}`
	means that the statements within the curly brackets are executed only if *a* is less than *b*.

`>`	Relational greater than. Example:
	`if (a > b)`
	`{...}`
	means that the statements within the curly brackets are executed only if *a* is greater than *b*.

`<=`	Relational less than or equal to. Example:
	`if (a <= b)`
	`{...}`
	means that the statements within the curly brackets are executed only if *a* is less than or equal to *b*.

`>=`	Relational greater than or equal to. Example:
	`if (a <= b)`
	`{...}`
	means that the statements within the curly brackets are executed only if *a* is greater than or equal to *b*.

`==`	Relational equality. Example:
	`if (a == b)`
	`{ ... }`
	means that the statements within the curly brackets are executed only if *a* is equal to *b*.

`!=`	Relational inequality. Example:
	`if (a != b)`
	`{ ... }`
	means that the statements within the curly brackets are executed only if *a* is not equal to *b*.

`^`	Bitwise XOR (exclusive OR). `a & b` means that *a* and *b* are bitwise exclusive ORed together.
`|`	Bitwise OR. `a & b` means that *a* and *b* are bitwise ORed together.

continued

Table 3-2   Java Operators and Their Definitions. *(Continued)*

Operator	Description
&&	Logical AND. Example (if (a == 3) && (b == 4)) means that the condition is true if both *a* is equal to 3 and *b* is equal to 4.
||	Logical OR. Example: (if (a == 3) || (b == 4)) means that the condition is true if either *a* is equal to 3 or *b* is equal to 4.
?:	Conditional operation. The question mark and color separate parts of trinary conditional statement. Example: c = a < b ? 3 : 4; means that if *a* is less than *b* then *c* is set equal to 3; otherwise *c* is set equal to 4.
=	Assignment. Example. a = b; assigns the value of *b* to *a*.
*=	The value on the left side is assigned the value of the left side multiplied by the value of the right side. Example: c *= a; is the same as c = c * A;.
/=	The value on the left side is assigned the value of the left side divided by the value of the right side. Example: c /= a; is the same as c = c / a;.
%=	The value on the left side is assigned the value of the remainder when the value of the left side is divided by the value of the right side. Example: c %= a; is the same as c = c % a;.
+=	The value on the left side is assigned the value of the left side added to by the value of the right side. Example: c += a; is the same as c = c + a;.
-=	The value on the left side is assigned the value of the right side subtracted from the value of the right side. Example: c -= a; is the same as c = c - a;.
<<=	The value on the left side is assigned the value of the left side shifted left by the number of bits specified by the right side. Example: c <<= 3; is the same as c = c << 3;.
>>=	The value on the left side is assigned the value of the left side shifted right by the number of bits specified by the right side. Example: c >>= 3; is the same as c = c >> 3;.
&=	The value on the left side is assigned the value of the left side bitwise ANDed with the value of the right side. Example: c &= a; is the same as c = c & a;.
^=	The value on the left side is assigned the value of the left side bitwise XORed (exclusive ORed) with the value of the right side. Example: c ^= a; is the same as c = c ^ a;.

continued

Table 3-2 Java Operators and Their Definitions. *(Continued)*

Operator	Description
|=	The value on the left side is assigned the value of the left side bitwise ORed with the value of the right side. Example: `c |= a;` is the same as `c = c	a;`.
,	Comma (separates elements of function argument list).
;	Semicolon (statement terminator).
:	Colon (indicates labeled statement).

Operator Precedence

As mathematical expressions get more complicated, it becomes important to know how the computer handles the precedence of operators. Look at the following fairly simple expression:

```
d = a + b / c;
```

where all three parameters are integers. Suppose that *a* is 12, *b* is 6, and *c* is 3. The value of *d* depends on what precedence Java uses to assign operators. If it does addition first and then division, we'll obtain a result of 6; if it does divisions first and then additions, we'll obtain a result of 14. Whether Java starts at the left and works toward the right, or starts at the right and works toward the left may also change the result. There's no problem using enough sets of parentheses to make your equation totally unambiguous. However, if you understand the precedence that Java assigns to operators, you can eliminate many unneeded pairs of parentheses, and thus simplify your program considerably. Table 3-3 shows the precedence for the various operators and the direction used in their evaluation. The highest precedence is 1; the lowest is 15. If you follow these rules, you will get things right and not have any unpleasant surprises. In our example, then, the answer is 14, as division (precedence 3) takes place before nonunary + (precedence 4).

Initializing Data Items

Variables having primitive data types are defined by such statements as

```
int a, b, c, d, e;
char ch, ch1, ch2, ch3;
```

float x, y, z;

Java allocates sufficient memory space for each variable and initializes it to 0. If you want to initialize a variable to a value other than 0, you can do it like this.

Table 3-3   Precedence of Java Operators.

Operators	Precedence (Order of Operation)	Direction
( ) [ ] -> .	1	Left to right
! - + - ++ — b & (unary operators) * (indirection operator) (typecast) sizeof	2	Right to left
* / %	3	Left to right
+ -	4	Left to right
<< >>	5	Left to right
< <= > >=	6	Left to right
== !=	7	Left to right
&	8	Left to right
^	9	Left to right
|	10	Left to right
&&	11	Left to right
||	12	Left to right
? : (trinary conditional operators)	13	Right to left
= *= /= %= -= &= ^= |= <<= >>=	14	Right to left
,	15	Left to right

```
int a=3, b, c=4, d=0x4345, e;
float x=3.14159F, y=2.718F, z= -.34125F;
double s=789.67456, t, v=123.12;
```

You can initialize an integer variable with a number, or with a hexadecimal number preceded by *0x* characters within single quotes. A list of variables may include some that aren't initialized at all and will thus take the default value of 0. You can initialize a *double* with a floating point number (a number including a decimal point) or a *float* with a decimal number followed by an *F*. (Java, when it sees a floating point number (a number including a decimal point) always assumes that the number is of type *double*, so the following statement

```
float w = 36.45123;
```

would give an error message. Always remember to append an *F* to the number when you want it to be of type *float*.

Using Arrays

An array in Java is an object. It is defined with a fixed size that cannot be changed while the program is running. There are two ways of defining arrays in Java, they are interchangeable; you can use whichever one you like best. A single dimensional array is defined in Java like this:

```
int[] abc = new int[12];
```

or like this:

```
int abc[] = new[12];
```

Either of these statements creates an array of integers having 12 members, numbered 0 through 11. Thus, the first member of this array would be *abc[0]*, the second member *abc[1]*, and the last *abc[11]*. Whereas in C and C++, it is up to you as the programmer to assure that you don't try to access a nonexistent member of the array (such as *abc[15]* in the preceding example, Java has built-in safeguards that will reject any attempt to access outside the array boundaries. Consider the following statement:

```
abc[dr] = 45;
```

This would compile all right in C, C++, or Java. Now suppose that when your program is running and reaches this statement, the value of *dr* is 15. Java will not allow you to do this; it will display an error message in your DOS window. If you'd been using C or C++, the program would simply replace the information at the location 15 integers down from the beginning of the array *abc* with 45. If this happens to be a memory location that contains part of your program code, who knows what may happen next? Java may also have multiple dimension arrays like this:

```
int[][] ag = new int[6][7];
```

You can also initialize a Java array with a list of numbers. For example, you could define an array like this:

```
int[] abc = {123, 234, 5, 45, 67, 27, 12, 89);
```

This would automatically create an array object *abc*, establish its size as 8 integers, and fill the 8 members with the numbers listed.

Conditional Statements

The capability to make choices between different sets of actions is crucial for sophisticated computer programs. Often, this is done by setting up a test condition, which, if true, causes the program to perform a set of actions and, if false, causes the program to perform a different set of actions. Java has three ways in which the decision-making process can take place. The first is the *if-else* statement. The second uses the punctuation marks ? and :. The third, the *switch-case* statement, is used when there are a lot of different results from the test condition, each requiring a different set of actions.

The *if-else* statement begins with the word *if* followed by a test contained within parentheses. (Note that the close parenthesis is **not** followed by a semicolon.) Following this test are one or more statements (enclosed in curly brackets) to be performed if the condition of the test is true. (If there is only a single statement, you may omit the curly brackets.) Here is an example of a simple *if* statement followed by a single action:

```
if (r > 4)
{
   System.out.println("r is larger than 4.");
   System.out.println("Change r and try again.");
}
```

This example does not make use of the *else* part of the *if-else* statement, which is optional. The *else* is used when there are statements that should be executed if the test defined by the *if* statement is false. For example,

```
if (r > 4)
{
   System.out.println("r is greater than 4.");
   r—;
}
else
{
   System.out.println
      ("r is less than or equal to 4.");
   r++;
}
```

Here, if *r* is greater than 4, the legend *r is greater than 4* is displayed and *r* is decremented; otherwise, the legend *r is less than or equal to 4* is displayed and *r* is incremented. You can nest as many *if-else* statements as necessary to make whatever decision you are interested in, but you need to make sure that you use whatever sets of curly brackets are needed so that each *else* is associated with a particular *if* statement without ambiguity.

The operator > in the preceding examples is a relational operator. It says that you test the value on the left to see if it is *greater than* the value on the right. Table 3-4 shows a list of all the relational operators that are available in Java. Note that the relational *equal to* operator is written with a double equals sign (==). If you make the mistake of writing

```
if (a = 4)
   System.out.println("a is equal to 4.");
```

then after the word *if*, a is assigned the value of 4 (since the single equals sign means assignment, not to test equality), so regardless of the value of *a* going into the *if* statement, the legend *a is equal to 4* is displayed and coming out of the code segment *a* is always 4. This is not what you intended; moral, make sure that you use the double equals sign to test for equality.

Often an *if-else* conditional code segment can be written in an alternate way that makes for compact and hopefully easier-to-read code. Consider the following code in the *if-else* form that we have just learned:

```
if (a < 4)
   d = 6;
else
   d = 3;
```

Another way to write this is

```
d = (a < 4) ? 6 : 3;
```

Java notes the conditional statement that directly follows the equals sign and applies the test. If the result is true, the value of the expression following the *?* is assigned to *d*; if the result is false, the value of the expression following the colon is assigned to *d*.

Table 3-4   Java Relational Operators.

Operator	Meaning
==	equal to
!=	not equal to
>	greater than
>=	greater than or equal to
<	less than
<=	less than or equal to

The *switch-case* statement is used when one control argument, which must be an integer or character, can take on a lot of different values, each of which determines a different action on the part of the program. Here is a simple example:

```
switch(test_number)
{
    case 1:
        a++;
        b = 4;
        break;
    case 2:
        a++;
    case 4:
    case 5:
        b = 6;
        c-;
        break;
    default:
        a = 0;
        b = 0;
        c = 0;
}
```

The keyword *switch* is followed by the name of the control variable in parentheses (in this case, *test_number*). There follows a set of cases; each *case* includes statements to be executed when *test_number* takes on that particular value. For a value of 1, *a* is incremented and *b* is set to 4. Then a *break* occurs that causes the program to leave the *switch* section of code. For a value of 2, *a* is incremented; since there is no *break* the program continues, falling through cases 4 and 5 and setting *b* to 6 and decrementing *c*. These last two actions are also performed for *case* values of 4 or 5. Then another *break* occurs, which terminates action for *test_number* of 2, 4, or 5. Finally, if *test_number* takes on any other value, the *default* case is run, which sets *a*, *b*, and *c* to 0. The *default* case is optional; if present, it must be the last case and its actions are executed for all cases other than those listed above it; if it doesn't appear, the *switch* code does nothing for cases that aren't listed.

Using Loops

Java has three powerful methods for controlling program looping: the *while* loop, the *do-while* loop, and the *for* loop. Each of these provides a method whereby a section of code can be repeated a number of times with minor changes in conditions at each iteration.

The *for* loop is the most sophisticated of the loop constructions. It can usually make your loop programming simpler and faster when you want to repeat a section of code a number of times with changes in one or more parameters. The *for* command begins with the word *for* followed by three separate sections, separated by semicolons and enclosed in parentheses. The first section initializes any parameters whose values need to be set before the loop begins. You may initialize as many parameters as you want. The initialization statements are separated by commas. The second section provides a test that determines whether the loop should continue to be iterated. This may be as complex a test as you can devise as long as it can be expressed in a single statement. The third section modifies whatever parameters are to be changed at each pass through the loop. As many parameters as desired may be modified, with each modification expression separated by commas. Here's a simple example of a *for* loop:

```
int i;

for (i=0; i<10; i++)
   System.out.println("\n" + i + "    " + i*i)
```

What we want to do is print out the values of *i* and *i2* for values of *i* from 0 through 9. Without loops, we would have to use the *System.out.println* statement 10 times. Using the *for* loop, we require only two statements for the entire operation. In the initialization section the parameter *i* is set to 0 at the beginning of the loop. In the test section, *i* is tested to see whether it is less than 10 and as long as this is so, the loop continues to iterate. When *i* becomes equal to or greater than 10, the loop terminates. Note that it is your responsibility as a programmer to make sure that *i* will eventually exceed the value of 10 so that the loop will end; if you don't do this, the loop may go on forever and the program will stall. In the modification section, *i* is incremented at each pass through the loop.

The same kinds of things that are done with the *for* loop can be done with the *while* loop. It is often a matter of taste which one to use, although when no initializations are required the *while* loop is the more natural one to use. To do the same thing as the *for* loop example given previously, we write:

```
int i;

while (i<10)
{
   System.out.println("\n" + i + "    " + i*i)
   i++;
}
```

The loop iterates 10 times. At each iteration it displays *i* and *i2* on the screen. Within the *while* loop, the program iterates (loops) for as long as the condition within the parentheses following the word *while* is true. To assure that the *while* loop works properly, two things are necessary. First, the condition within the parentheses must be true when the loop starts; otherwise, the program will never enter the loop. In the sample program, this is taken care of by the fact that *i* is initialized to 0. Second, at some point the condition must become false. If this doesn't occur, your program will remain in the loop forever. In the sample program, this is achieved by incrementing the value of *i* at every pass through the loop, so that after 10 passes, it will be equal to 10. One of the common mistakes of beginning programmers, when using a *while* loop, is to fail to change the variable that is used to satisfy the condition for exiting the loop, resulting in infinite looping. Upon encountering the *while* statement, the program makes the test defined by the set of parentheses following the statement. If the condition is true, the program executes all of the statements between the curly brackets following the condition. (If there is only one statement to be executed, you may omit the curly brackets altogether.) It then returns to the point just following the word *while* and runs the test again. As long as the condition is true, the section of code in the curly brackets is repeated. When the condition finally becomes false, the program leaves the loop and proceeds to the next statement in the code.

The *do-while* loop is very similar to the *while* loop except that the test occurs at the end of the loop instead of at the beginning. This loop is used when you want to make at least one pass through the section of code in the loop, regardless of what the conditions are when you enter the loop. The same sample code used earlier looks like this for a *do-while* loop:

```
int i;

do
{
   System.out.println("\n" + i + "    " + i*i)
   i++;
}

while (i < 10);
}
```

You'll note that this is just a bit more complicated than the previous example, but this example does exactly the same thing. Thus, you would ordinarily use the simpler form unless you had a situation where you didn't know whether *i* would be within the range of 0 through 9 when the loop was entered but you wanted to make sure the loop was run at least once.

The *Math* Class

All mathematical functions in Java that are not performed by operators are performed by methods that are members of the *Math* class. This is a virtual class that may be referenced directly and is a final class, so you can't derive from it. For example, to set a double floating point number *f* to the cosine of 1.43 radians, you would write

```
f = Math.cos(1.43);
```

Now let's look at the methods that are available in the *Math* class. Table 3-5 shows the *Math* class methods.

The *Random* Class

You've just seen that the *Math* class includes a *random* method that produces pseudo-random numbers between 0.0 and 1.0 having a flat distribution. For many applications, this is the only random number generator that you'll require. Before we go on, let's look at what a set of pseudo-random numbers is. To obtain a true set of random integers between 0 and infinity, we would have a storage bank containing every integer between 0 and infinity. From this infinite set, we would randomly select as many numbers as desired. Since our computers don't have an infinite amount of memory to store the infinite set, we need some simpler way to generate a series of numbers. A common technique, given a starting seed number, is to multiply this number by a constant *a*, add another constant *c*, and then divide by a third constant *m*. The remainder is our next random number and acts as the seed for finding another number by repeating the process. This is called the *Linear Congruential Generator*. It doesn't produce truly random numbers, since a long sequence is periodic, having a period *m*. However, if we choose *m* large enough and select our other constants with care, we can come up with a series of numbers that fulfills all well-known tests of randomness.

We have already suggested that we might want to look at random integers, which is outside the scope of our *Math* class random generator, which produces numbers in the range 0.0 to 1.0. For applications that require more than the *random* method will provide, Java has a *Random* class. To use it, we first set up an object of the *Random* class like this:

```
Random r = new Random();
```

Table 3-5   Math Class Methods.

Name	Inputs	Output	Description
sin	*angle* in radians (double)	Sine of *angle* (double)	Returns sine of *angle*
cos	*angle* in radians (double)	Cosine of *angle* (double)	Returns cosine of *angle*
tan	*angle* in radians (double)	Tangent of *angle* (double)	Returns tangent of *angle*
asin	sine of an angle (double)	*angle* in radians (double)	Given the sine of an angle, returns the angle
acos	cosine of an angle (double)	*angle* in radians (double)	Given the cosine of an angle, returns the angle
atan	tangent of an angle (double)	*angle* in radians (double)	Given the tangent of an angle, returns the angle
exp	*power* (double)	*e* to the *power* (double)	Returns *e* raised to the *power* power
log	*number* (double)	Natural log of number (double)	Returns the natural logarithm (to the base *e*) of *number*
sqrt	*number* (double)	Square root of *number* (double)	Returns the square root of *number*
pow	*number* (double) *power* (double)	*number* raised to *power* (double)	Returns *number* raised to the power *power*
ceil	*number* (double)	Smallest whole number greater than or equal to *number* (double)	Returns the smallest whole number greater than or equal to number
floor	*number* (double)	Largest whole number less than or equal to *number* (double)	Returns largest whole number less than or equal to *number*
round	*number* (double)	*number* rounded to the nearest integer (int)	Rounds a floating point number off to the nearest integer
round	*number* (double)	*number* rounded to the nearest long integer (long)	Rounds a double floating point number to the nearest long integer
rint	*number* (double)	*number* rounded to the nearest integer (double)	Rounds a double floating point number to the nearest integer and returns the result in double floating point
atan2	*x* (double) *y* (double)	Angle whose tangent is *x/y* (double)	Returns the angle (in radians) whose tangent is *x/y*
random	None	Random number (double)	Returns a pseudo-random number between 0.0 (included) and 1.0 (included) and 1.0 (excluded)
abs	*number* (int)	Absolute value of *number* (int)	Returns the absolute value of an integer
abs	*number* (long)	Absolute value of *number* (long)	Returns the absolute value of a long integer
abs	*number* (float)	Absolute value of number (float)	Returns the absolute value of a floating point number
abs	*number* (double)	absolute value of *number* (double)	Returns the absolute value of a double floating point number
min	*number#1* (int) *number #2* (int)	Minimum of *number#1* and *number#2* (int)	Returns the minimum of *number#1* and *number#2*

continued

Table 3-5 Math Class Methods. *(Continued)*

Name	Inputs	Output	Description
min	*number#1* (long) *number#2* (long)	Minimum of *number#1* and *number#2* (long)	Returns the minimum of *number#1* and *number#2*
min	*number#1* (float) *number#2* (float)	Minimum of *number#1* and *number#2* (float)	Returns the minimum of *number#1* and number#2
min	*number#1* (double) *number#2* (double)	Minimum of *number#1* and *number#2* (double)	Returns the minimum of *number#1* and *number#2*
max	*number#1* (int) *number#2* (int)	Maximum of *number#1* and *number#2* (int)	Returns the maximum of *number#1* and *number#2*
max	*number#1* (long) *number#2* (long)	Maximum *number#1* and *number#2* (long)	Returns the maximum *number#1* and *number#2*
max	*number#1* (float) *number#2* (float)	Maximum of *number#1* and *number#2* (float)	Returns the maximum of *number#1* and number#2
max	*number#1* (double) *number#2* (double)	Maximum of *number#1* and *number#2* (double)	Returns the maximum of *number#1* and *number#2*

This will seed the random generator with the current time, so that each time you run a program where *Random* is defined in this way and random numbers are used, the results will be different. You can include any integer within the parentheses in the preceding statement, in which case that integer will be used as the seed and the same sequence of random numbers will occur each time the program is run. This is very useful when you are trying to debug a program and want to make sure any output changes are the result of changes that you made and not because the random numbers were different. You can also reseed the random generator at any time by the use of the *setSeed* method like this

```
r.setSeed(345);
```

There are five methods associated with the *Random* class. The statement

```
c = r.nextInt();
```

where *c* is of type *int* will place in *c* an integer between the lowest available negative integer and the highest available positive integer. The statement

```
c = r.nextLong();
```

where *c* is of type *long* will place in *c* an integer between 0 and the highest available positive long integer. The statement

```
c = r.nextFloat();
```

where *c* is of type *float* will place in *c* a floating point number between 0.0 and 1.0 having the precision of a *float* type. The statement

```
c = r.nextDouble();
```

where *c* is of type *double* will place in *c* a floating point number between 0.0 and 1.0 having the precision of a *double* type. All of the preceding methods produce numbers having a flat distribution. The statement

```
c = r.nextGaussian();
```

where *c* is of type *double* will return *c* as a double floating point number from a Gaussian or normal distribution. This is the bell-shaped curve familiar to those who work with statistics. Its tails extend to + and − infinity, but the chances are 97.7% that the number returned will be between −3.0 and + 3.0.

Random Numbers in a Given Range

Suppose we want to randomly select a number between two limits. For example, say we want a random integer between 3 and 30. Given that *c* is of type *int*, one way to do this is

```
c = (int)(r.nextDouble()*(double)n + s);
```

where *n* is the number of values your number may assume (28 in the example) and *s* is the lower bound (3 in the example). What happens here is that working in double floating point, we are taking a random number between 0 and 1.0, multiplying it by *n* (to give a double number between 0 and 28 in the example), adding the lower bound (resulting in a number between 3 and just less than 31 in the example), and then converting to an integer (yielding an integer between 0 and 30 in the example).

4

Java Swing Components

The simple Java programs that we wrote in Chapter 3 merely displayed results in a DOS window, just as if we had been writing programs using a DOS operating system. To allow Java programs to use window-like displays and to create graphics, we need some additional classes. The original Java had a package of classes called the *Abstract Window Toolkit* (AWT), which contained a number of useful classes that allowed you to assemble various kinds of displays and operate on them. One class, *Graphics*, provided rudimentary graphics capabilities such as drawing lines, rectangles, circles, ellipses, and so forth. Java 2 includes another package of classes called the Java *Swing* components. Java calls these "lightweight" because they are totally written in the Java language. The term is somewhat of a misnomer, however, since the Swing components are more sophisticated and usually faster than their AWT counterparts. In addition, they are more independent of the underlying operating system when it comes to selecting the look and feel of the graphical displays. Java recommends that whenever a Swing class is available, you use it instead of its corresponding AWT class. If you do this, you'll avoid problems with some "heavy" operations always writing on top of "lightweight" operations whether you want them to or not. However, there can be significant differences between Swing and AWT classes, so you need to be a little careful. Java Swing components have names that begin with a capital J. They are located in a package called *javax.swing*. This chapter is going to give you an overall view of the AWT and Swing packages. In the chapters that follow, we will not try to cover every possible operation of each class. Instead, we'll show a number of typical applications, some using AWT and some Swing. By the time you become familiar with these examples, you shouldn't have any trouble creating windows, displays, or Web pages using Java.

The Abstract Window Toolkit (AWT)

Java includes a class library called the Abstract Window Toolkit (AWT) that contains a whole set of classes to be used for graphics. The classes included in this library make it simple to do a whole lot of things that you might want to do in creating display packages and graphics images, but there are a lot of things that have been left out; if you encounter one of these you may find that the operation you want is in a Java Swing class. If not, finding a suitable work-around may get a little complicated. Among other things, the AWT includes all classes necessary to create windows and arrange the components of a display within them. You'll want to provide access to this library by including the following statement at the beginning of your Java program:

```
import  ava.awt.*;
```

This statement imports into your program only those classes in the toolkit that are actually used by the program, so it is the preferred way of accessing AWT classes. You can import a single AWT class by substituting its name for the asterisk in the preceding statement, but such a class is then imported whether it is used or not, so it's still using space if you modify the program so that it's not needed. In other words, the statement with the asterisk automatically imports exactly those classes that are needed; individual class import statements may need to be modified with every program change.

Java AWT Classes

In Java terminology, we construct a display window by arranging *Components* within a *Container*. Normally, there are only two types of *Containers* that are used. The first is the *Frame*, which creates a complete window. The second is the *Panel*. The *Panel* is both a *Container* and a *Component*; several panels may be arranged inside a *Frame* and in turn, each *Panel* may contain several *Components*. Table 4-1 lists the Java AWT classes with a brief description of each. As you can see, there are quite a few of these classes. When you consider that each class may contain as many as 10 methods, you'll understand why many Java books run over a thousand pages. The trouble is that if you are trying to learn Java, the amount of information to be absorbed is tremendous. And this is just the beginning. When you add in Java Swing, Java 2D, and Java 3D, you'll at least quadruple the amount of material. To make it possible for you to grasp the essentials, in this book we give you a number of examples of using Java to produce graphics and describe how the examples were created. This will give you a firm basis for creating your own programs. If you need to use classes or methods not shown in the examples, these are all described in the Java documentation. If you properly set up your Windows 95/98 system, you can select the appropriate file that you want to read without unzipping the whole master file, and then by double-clicking the selected file, bring up your browser to display it.

Swing Components

In conjunction with Netscape Communications, IBM, and Lighthouse Design, Sun Microsystems has created a set of Graphical User Interface (GUI) classes called the *Java Swing Components* for use with Java 2. These provide a more polished look and feel than the standard AWT component set and are written totally in Java so that there is no change in the appearance of the

Table 4-1   Classes of the AWT.

Class	Description
Applet	Container for a Java applet.
BorderLayout	Container with center, north, south, east, and west cells.
Button	Creates a button, with or without a label. Selecting a button by clicking the mouse over it draws a dotted rectangle inside the button and sends an action event to the button.
Canvas	A generic component used as a background for drawing graphics figures.
CardLayout	Container with file tabs that permit selection of any one of a number of pages.
Checkbox	A small box that user can click on or off. A label is optional. Several Checkboxes can be grouped in a CheckboxGroup allowing only one to be selected at a time.
CheckboxMenuItem	A checkbox that can be included in a menu.
Choice	A drop-down list of choices from which the user can select.
Color	Permits defining colors in RGB format.
Component	One of the elements that make up a screen display.
Container	A screen window made up of various components.
Dialog	A top-level free-floating window for communicating with the user.
Dimension	An object containing width and height integers.
Event	A platform-independent class that defines user events extracted from the local graphics interface.
FileDialog	Displays a dialog window from which the user can select a file.
FlowLayout	Lines up components in a row. If there are more components than fill a row, additional rows are started.
Font	Selects a type font, size, and style.
FontMetrics	Provides information on rendering a particular type font.
Frame	A top-level window with a title and border.
Graphics	An abstract class that is the default constructor for a graphics context.
GridBagConstraints	Specifies constraints for the location of components that are laid out using the GridBagLayout class.
GridBagLayout	A flexible layout manager that aligns differently sized components horizontally and vertically.
GridLayout	Causes the container's components to be laid out in a rectangular grid composed of equally sized rectangles.
Image	Defines a graphical image.
Insets	Specifies the space that a container must leave at each of its edges.
Label	A piece of text that can be typed on a component.
List	A scrollable list of text items from which the user can select. One or multiple selections may be made at any one time.

continued

Table 4-1   Classes of the AWT. *(Continued)*

Class	Description
MediaTracker	Traces the status of media images and determines the priority with which they are to be fetched and displayed.
Menu	A pull-down component that allows the user to make a choice from a number of items.
MenuBar	Attaches a number of menus to a frame.
MenuComponent	A class containing a number of menu items.
MenuItem	One of a number of items that may be selected from a menu.
Panel	A simple container that by default uses the Flow layout.
Point	Contains the integer coordinates of a point.
Polygon	A list of points, where each successive pair of points defines a side of a polygon. (Jave 1.0 did not automatically draw a line from the last point to the first point, but later versions of Java do.)
Rectangle	Specifies an area defined by its top left coordinate, its width, and its height in integers.
Scrollbar	A slideable bar that enables the user to move quickly to the desired portion of a large area.
TextArea	A component that allows the user to enter multiple lines of text
TextComponent	The superclass for any component that allows text editing.
TextField	A component containing a single line of editable text.
Toolkit	Superclass for all implementations of the AWT.
Window	A top-level window with no borders or menubar. Its default layout is BorderLayout.

graphics when moving from one platform to another. Swing is targeted toward form-based applications, but has many further applications. The Swing package is a part of Java 2. When you write a program that is to include Swing classes, you invoke Swing by including the line

```
import   avax.swing.*;
```

In this chapter, we're only going to give you a very brief overview of Swing. As you read through the rest of the book, you'll find a lot of example programs that make use of Swing components. As you work with these examples, you'll begin to understand just how many of the Swing components work, and this knowledge should carry over if you need a more unusual Swing component that isn't described in detail in the book. Keep in mind that there are hundreds of pages of instruction material on Swing at the Sun Microsystems Java site on the Web.

Swing Classes

Table 4-2 lists the principal classes that are part of the Swing package, together with a brief description of each, and a cross-reference to the original AWT class that may be replaced by each new Swing class. In general, Swing will give you faster and more professional looking applications.

Table 4-2   Java Swing Classes.

SwingClass	Replaces AWT Class	Description
BorderFactory		Creates standard border objects, such as space around a border layout.
Box		Lightweight container that uses BoxLayout.
Box.Filler		Spaces between Box Layout components.
Box.Layout		Layout manager that allows multiple components to be in either a horizontal or vertical layout.
ButtonGroup		This class includes a group of buttons with multiple-exclusion scope.
CellRendererPane		Inserted between cell renderers and the components that use them.
DebugGraphics		Provides a number of methods to help debug graphics.
DefaultBoundedRangeModel		Generic implementation of the BoundedRangeModel.
DefaultButtonModel		Default implementation of a Button component's data model.
DefaultCellEditor		Default editor for table and cell trees.
DefaultComboBoxModel		Default model for combo boxes.
DefaultDesktopManager		An implementation of the DesktopManager.
DefaultFocusManager		Default swing focus manager implementation.
DefaultListCellRenderer		Renders an item from a list.
DefaultCellRenderer.UIResource		Implements a UIResource.
DefaultListModel		Implements java.util.Vector API and notifies the JlistDataModel listeners when an event occurs.
DefaultListSelectionModel		Default data model for list selections.
DefaultSingleSelectionModel		Implementation of SingleSelectionModel.
FocusManager		Swing focus manager.

continued

Table 4-2   Java Swing Classes. *(Continued)*

SwingClass	Replaces AWT Class	Description
GrayFilter		Converts an image into grayscale and brightens pixels.
ImageIcon		Implementation of the Icon interface that paints Icons from Images.
JApplet	Applet	Extended version of java.Applet. Provides support for interposing and painting in front of applet's children (glassPane). Supports special children managed by a LayeredPane (rootPane). Supports swing MenuBars.
JButton	Button	Implementation of a *push* button.
JCheckBox	Checkbox	Implementation of a CheckBox. This item displays its state and can be selected or deselected by the user.
JCheckBoxMenuItem	Checkbox MenuItem	A menu item that can be selected or deselected.
JColorChooser		Provides a panel of colors from which one can be selected by the user.
JComboBox	Choice	Shows a text field and drop-down list. The user can type in a value or select one from a list.
JComponent		Base class for Swing components.
JDesktopPane		A container used in creating a virtual desktop or multi-document interface.
JDialog	Dialog	Swing's main class for creating a dialog window.
JEditorPane		Text component to permit editing of its content.
JFileChooser	FialDialog	Displays a directory and allows the user to scan through it and select a particular file.
JFrame	Frame	An extension of *Frame* that provides the same additional capabilities as *JApplet*.
JInternalFrame		Lightweight object that supports many of the capabilities of a native frame.
JinternalFrame.		An iconified version of *JInternalFrame*. JDesktopIcon
JLabel	Label, Canvas	Displays a text string or an image.
JLayeredPane		Adds depth to a JFC/Swing container by allowing components to overlap.

continued

Table 4-2   Java Swing Classes. *(Continued)*

SwingClass	Replaces AWT Class	Description
JList	List	A lightweight component that permits the user to select one or more from a list of objects.
JMenu	Menu	Displays a list of *JmenuItems* from which the user may select, when the user chooses the menu from the *JmenuBar* display.
JMenuBar	MenuBar	A lightweight implementation of *MenuBar.*
JMenuItem	MenuItem	A lightweight implementation of a *MenuItem.*
JOptionPane	Dialog	Pops up a dialog box for information or to permit the user to insert a value.
JPanel	Panel, Canvas	A generic lightweight container.
JPasswordField		Allows the user to modify a line of text, where there is an indication that text exists, but not what it is.
JPopupMenu		A lightweight implementation of a small window that pops up and displays a series of choices.
JPopupMenu.Separator		Inserts a separator into a popup menu.
JProgressBar		Displays an integer within a bounded interval.
JRadioButton	Checkbox	A lightweight implementation of a radio button. It displays its state and can be selected or deselected by the user. A radio button is automatically deselected when the user selects another radio button in the group.
JRadioButtonMenuItem		Provides a menu item that is a radio button.
JRootPane		The primary component in the container hierarchy.
JScrollBar	ScrollBar	A lightweight implementation of a scrollbar.
JScrollPane	ScrollPane, ScrollBar	A container that manages a viewport that may contain scrollbars and/or row and column heading viewports.
JSeparator		Provides division between menu items to separate them into logical groupings.
JSlider	ScrollBar	Permits the user to move a slider within a bounded interval to select a value.

continued

Table 4-2 Java Swing Classes. *(Continued)*

SwingClass	Replaces AWT Class	Description
JSplitPane		Can divide two (and only two) components.
JTabbedPane		Lets the user switch from one component to another within a group by clicking on a tab.
JTable		Presents data in a two-dimensional table format.
JTextArea	TextArea	A display of multiple lines of plain text.
JTextField	TextField	Lightweight component that displays a single line of text.
JTextPane		A text pane that can be marked up with graphical attributes.
JToggleButton		Implementation of a two-state button.
JToggleButton. ToggleButtonModel		The toggle button.
JToolBar		Displays frequently used buttons or controls.
JToolBar.Separator		Specific separator for a *Toolbar*.
JToolTip	Window	Displays an explanation for a component.
JTree		Displays a set of hierarchical data as an outline.
JTree.DynamicUtilTreeNode		Can wrap vectors, hashtables, arrays, and strings and create any needed children tree nodes.
JTree.EmptySelectionModel		*TreeSelectionModel* that doesn't permit selection.
JViewPort		Opens to allow you to see underlying information.
JWindow	Window	A container that can be displayed anywhere on the user's desktop display.
KeyStroke		Contains a character code and any required special codes.
LookAndFeel		Characterizes the appearance of a component.
MenuSelectionManager		Controls the selection in menu hierarchy.
OverlayLayout		Arranges components on top of one another.
ProgressMonitor		Measures the progress of some operation.

continued

Table 4-2 Java Swing Classes. *(Continued)*

SwingClass	Replaces AWT Class	Description
ProgressMonitorInputStream		Monitors the progress of reading from an *InputStream.*
RepaintManager		Manages repaint requests, eliminating unnecessary ones.
ScrollPaneLayout		Layout manager used by *JScrollPane.*
ScrollPaneLayout.UIResource		UI Resource version of *ScrollPaneLayout.*
SizeRequirements		Computes information about size and position of components.
SwingUtilities		A collection of Swing utility methods.
Timer		Causes an action to proceed at a predetermined rate.
ToolTipManager		Manages all of a system's *ToolTips.*
UIDefaults		A table of Swing component defaults.
UIManager		Keeps track of the look and feel and its defaults.
UIManager.LookAndFeel		Provides information on an installed *LookAndFeel.*
ViewportLayout		Default layout manager for *JViewPort.*

Why Use Swing Components?

Using Swing components will make things a lot easier for you as a programmer and will also benefit your users. One overwhelming reason for using Swing is that this is the direction of the future for Java. If you are having trouble with some of the old Java AWT components (for example, the old *FileFilter* method of *FileDialog* has never worked properly), you aren't likely to see these problems corrected, since most development effort is being targeted on the corresponding new Swing classes. You'll also find that many things that required you to make complex custom programs are now handled by simply invoking the proper Swing method. Swing components have separate data and state models, so that you can share data between components. Finally, Swing has a Pluggable Look-and-Feel architecture that gives you a wide choice of look-and-feel options, including the native Java look-and-feel, the Microsoft Windows look-and-feel, or allows you to create your own look-and-feel.

As you can see, there are a lot of good reasons for using Swing components and no good reason not to. Maybe we should have limited this book to the use of Swing components, but we didn't want you to be totally without experience with the AWT methods, so you'll find some examples that make use of them. As you become experienced with Java graphics programming, it will be a good learning exercise to try to convert some of these to use Swing components.

Running a Program as an Application or as an Applet

Using the new Java Swing components, it is possible to design a program so that it can be run either as an application or as an applet. You need to designate the principal class as extending *Japplet* rather than *Frame* or *Applet*. Then there are certain statements that should not be part of the applet. These include the statement for creating a window title, the method needed to detect a window closing event and shutting down the program when it occurs, and the *setSize* statement for determining the window size. You put all of these in the *main* program. Then, when you run the program as an applet, the *main* program does not run. The appletviewer or browser takes care of titling the applet, setting its size, and closing it, so you don't need these capabilities when running as an applet, and including them in the other parts of the program will cause things not to work properly. However, they are needed when running as an application; since *main* is the controlling program in this case, they will all be implemented. Throughout this book, you'll see a number of example programs that can be run as either applications or applets, which will give you some experience on how to do this.

5 Components, Containers, and Layout Management

In Java, a *component* is a part of a display and a *container* encompasses several components. This is roughly like what some other programming systems call a *window*. If you've worked at all with Windows 95, you're already familiar with what a window looks like, but you probably never dreamed that you'd be creating your own windows within programs, since Windows programming is a rather arcane subject. Now, you can do this with Java and the programs will work not only with Windows 95 and Windows 98, but with any other operating system that has a Java compiler, regardless of the underlying hardware. This chapter will give you the basics of building graphics

Containers and Components

In Java terminology, we construct a display window by arranging *Components* within a *Container*. Normally, there are only two types of *Containers* that are used. The first is the *Frame*, which creates a complete window. The second is the *Panel*. The *Panel* is both a *Container* and a *Component*; several panels may be arranged inside a *Frame* and, in turn, each *Panel* may contain several *Components*. The AWT includes definitions for a number of component classes. These are listed in Table 4-1.

Using Frames

A *Frame* is a container that defines an entire window. The program in Listing 5.1 shows you how to use a frame. The class *Frame* is a container class, defined by Java, that creates a full-sized window of the pixel dimensions designated by the *f.setSize* statement. The program begins by importing the necessary classes from Java. It then defines a class called *Framer*, which is an extension of the Java *Frame* class. This line illustrates one of the most important characteristics of Java and of object-oriented programming languages in general: that of *inheritance*. The words *extends Frame* cause the class *Framer* to inherit all of the characteristics of the class *Frame*, which is defined in the *java.awt*. The lines under the *Framer* class in the listing add to the basic *Frame* class to create the full definition of the new class. Our next concern is whether *Framer* is going to be concerned with any events caused by user actions. In this case, the only thing that the user is going to do is click the mouse on the X in the top right corner of the window to terminate the program. If we don't provide for this, we'll never be able to terminate this program and get rid of the frame that was created. We're going to describe how events are handled in more detail in the next section. Briefly, we tell the *Framer* class to implement Window Listener, which permits it to detect when the window is to be closed. Next, two double variables, *x* and *y*, are defined for use within the *Framer* class. The class then defines a *constructor* for *Framer*. A *constructor* determines how an

```
/*
   Framer. ava
   Program to generate a sample frame
*/

import  ava.awt.*;
import  ava.util.*;
import  ava.awt.event.*;

public class Framer extends Frame implements
WindowListener
{
   double x, y;
   Framer()
   {
      super("Using a Frame");
      addWindowListener(this);
   }

   public void windowActivated(WindowEvent event)
   {
   }

   public void windowDeactivated(WindowEvent event)
   {
   }

   public void windowClosed(WindowEvent event)
   {
   }

public void windowDeiconified(WindowEvent event)
   {
   }

   public void windowIconified(WindowEvent event)
      {
   }

   public void windowOpened(WindowEvent event)
   {
   }

   public void windowClosing(WindowEvent event)
   {
      System.exit(0);
   }

   public void paint(Graphics g)
```

LISTING *Class to Illustrate Use of a Frame. (continues)*
5.1

```
   {
      x = 134.52769;
      y = 26.10845;
      g.drawString("x = " + x, 75, 40);
      g.drawString("y = " + y, 75, 60);
      g.drawString("x + y = " + (x+y), 75, 80);
      g.drawString("x - y = " + (x-y), 75, 100);
      g.drawString("x * y = " + (x*y), 75, 120);
      g.drawString("x / y = " + (x/y), 75, 140);
   }

   public static void main(String args[])
   {
      Framer f = new Framer();
      f.setSize(300,200);
      f.show();
   }
}
```

LISTING *Class to Illustrate Use of a Frame. (continued)*
5.1

object that is an instance of this class is to be initialized when it is created. Our constructor here says that the window will be created with the header *Using a Frame* and that a Window Listener will be activated. The next few lines of code define what will happen when a Window event occurs. We are really only interested in the *windowClosing* event. When it occurs, we run *System.exit(0)* to shut down. However, the technique used here requires that we define every possible Windows event function, using empty functions for all the ones that are not needed. Note again that if you don't implement a *windowClosing* event, whether you trigger on the closing *x* in the upper left-hand corner, select *file* and the *Close* or press *Alt-F4*, the window remains obstinately in place, preventing you from doing anything further. This is because our own especially created window doesn't have any way of handling these events so as to terminate the window.

Next, we want to display some data in the window. To do this, we will define a paint *method*. This method has an object of the *Graphics* class passed to it. *Graphics* is a virtual class; we cannot instantiate an object of this class directly. Yet *Graphics* is the class that contains all of the tools we need to draw primitive graphic images. To use it, we must work with it indirectly through some other class, such as *paint*. It is also important to note here that we cannot use the method *System.out.println* to print a line of data on the window we have created. If we use this method, the data will be displayed on the DOS window when we get back there. To display on the window, we need to use the *draw-*

String method of the *Graphics* class. You will note that as with the *System.out. println* method, we can use a plus sign to concatenate parts of the line to be printed out by the *drawString* class and that we can use primitive data types and perform mathematical operations on them within the parameter passed to the method. Finally, the *drawString* method contains two parameters that follow the string to be displayed. They are the *x* and *y* coordinates of the bottom left corner of the text string in pixels.

After the lines that draw the data strings in the window, we come to the *main* method that is the first thing run when Java interprets the class. This does three things. First, it sets up a new object *f* of class *Framer*. Second, it establishes the size of the window. Third, it shows the window on the display screen. A word about window size: The set*Size* method defines the window in terms of pixels, the first parameter being the window width and the second the window height. Perhaps unfortunately, these do not directly relate to the width and height of your display. So if you specify a particular window size, there are two things that determine what its actual size will be. The first is the resolution of the display mode you are using. In Windows 95 you can find this out by selecting *Settings*, *Control Panel*, and *Display* from your *Start* menu. If you specify too big a window, it may be larger than the pixel size of your display so that you won't be able to see everything at one time and will have to scroll around to see all of the contents of the display. On the other hand, if you make the window small, it may look just right on one display but be too small to see clearly on a higher-resolution display. The second factor is the screen size; a window that is too small to see clearly on a 14″ monitor may show up very well on a 17″ monitor. These are things that you have to take into consideration in setting window size. We've now completed our description of the *Framer* class. If you compile and run it, you'll see a display like Figure 5.1.

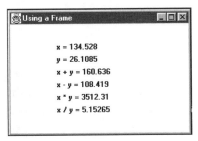

FIGURE *Result of Running Framer.class.*
5.1

Java's New Event Handling

When you set up a window to do graphics or for other purposes, you tie into an underlying set of software that allows you as the user to interact with your display. In particular, the software recognizes such events as entering text, moving the mouse, clicking mouse buttons, or pressing the *Enter* key and relates them to the context where they occur. A *java.awt.Event* object is created. The first edition of this book dealt with Java 1.0. It used a method of handling events that centered around a *HandleEvent* class. Since then, the whole technique for handling events in Java has been changed. The new method is a lot more flexible, giving you precise control over how you handle each event in a particular component. If you want your software to handle a *java.awt.event*—that is, to perform some particular action or actions in response to it—your program must have at its start the line *import.java.awt.event.*;* to provide access to the event software. In addition, you must include three sections of code in your program. These are

1. Where the class handling the event is declared, there must be code that specifies that the class implements a listener interface or extends a class that implements a listener interface. In the code listed previously, this is accomplished by the statement

```
public class Framer extends Frame implements WindowListener
```

2. There must be code that registers an instance of the event handling class as a listener upon one or more components. In the code listed previously, this is accomplished by the statement in the constructor for *Framer*

```
addWindowListener(this);
```

3. There must be code to implement an action when the listener detects an event. The code listed previously does this with the lines

```
public void windowClosing(WindowEvent event)
{
    System.exit(0);
}
```

and also with the empty functions for events that require no reaction.

As you can see, the efficiency of the preceding technique depends a lot upon the number of methods that are associated with each type of event and what you want to do with them. The *framer.java* program is not very efficient, since we only want to do something when the *windowClosing* method is activated; yet we have to provide six empty methods for the program to work. On the other hand, if you were concerned with an *ActionEvent*, which has only one method associated with it, the technique would be very efficient.

Fortunately, there are two other ways that you can handle the situation in a simpler manner. These make use of an embedded class to define the desired action. They extend an *Adapter* class that already contains empty functions for all of the associated events so that you only have to define the events that you want to use. The first method is shown in Listing 5.2.

```java
/*
Framer1.java
Program to generate a sample frame
*/

import java.awt.*;
import java.util.*;
import java.awt.event.*;

public class Framer1 extends Frame
{
    double x, y;
    Framer1()
    {
        super("Using a Frame");
        addWindowListener(new DWAdapter());
    }

class DWAdapter extends WindowAdapter
{
    public void windowClosing(WindowEvent event)
    {
        System.exit(0);
    }
}

    public void paint(Graphics g)
    {
        x = 134.52769;
        y = 26.10845;
        g.drawString("x = " + x, 75, 40);
        g.drawString("y = " + y, 75, 60);
        g.drawString("x + y = " + (x+y), 75, 80);
        g.drawString("x - y = " + (x-y), 75, 100);
        g.drawString("x * y = " + (x*y), 75, 120);
        g.drawString("x / y = " + (x/y), 75, 140);
    }

    public static void main(String args[])
    {
        Framer1 f = new Framer1();
        f.setSize(300,200);
        f.show();
    }
}
```

LISTING *Class to Illustrate Use of a Frame.*
5.2

This program differs in several ways from the preceding one. First, you are not required to characterize the *Framer1* class by *implements WindowListener*. Second, instead of activating the listener by the statement *addWindowListener(this);* we use *addWindowListener(new DWAdapter());*. Third, we now have a new class embedded within the *Framer1* class and called *DWAdapter*, which extends the *WindowAdapter* class. This class contains the same *windowClosing* function that we used in the previous program, but we do not need to define any additional empty classes since they are already defined in *WindowAdapter*.

The final technique for accomplishing the same result is shown in Listing 5.3.

```java
/*
Framer1.java
Program to generate a sample frame
*/
import java.awt.*;
import java.util.*;
import java.awt.event.*;

public class Framer2 extends Frame
{
    double x, y;
    Framer2()
    {
        super("Using a Frame");
        addWindowListener(new WindowAdapter()
        {
            public void windowClosing(WindowEvent e)
            {
                System.exit(0);
            }
        });
    }
    public void paint(Graphics g)
    {
        x = 134.52769;
        y = 26.10845;
        g.drawString("x = " + x, 75, 40);
        g.drawString("y = " + y, 75, 60);
        g.drawString("x + y = " + (x+y), 75, 80);
        g.drawString("x - y = " + (x-y), 75, 100);
        g.drawString("x * y = " + (x*y), 75, 120);
        g.drawString("x / y = " + (x/y), 75, 140);
    }
```

LISTING *Class to Illustrate Use of a Frame. (continues)*
5.3

```
public static void main(String args[])
{
    Framer2 f = new Framer2();
    f.setSize(300,200);
    f.show();
}
}
```

LISTING *Class to Illustrate Use of a Frame. (continued)*
5.3

In this case, we do not even have to name the embedded class; instead, we include it within the *addWindowListener* statement. Note that the entire function is defined before the final *);* of this statement occurs. When you're writing event code, you're free to use whichever of the three methods makes code that seems simplest and/or most understandable to you.

Table 5-1 lists the event listeners, their sources, and the methods associated with each. You can use this table to determine where you should insert listeners and which methods you should override to handle events as you would like.

Table 5-1   Event Table.

Interface	Source	Methods
ActionListener	Button, List, MenuItem,TextField	actionPerformed(ActionEvent)
ItemListener	Checkbox, CheckboxMenuItem, Choice, List	itemStateChanged(ItemEvent)
WindowListener	Dialog, Frame	windowClosing(WindowEvent) windowOpened(WindowEvent) windowIconified(WindowEvent) windowDeiconified(WindowEvent) windowClosed(WindowEvent) windowActivated(WindowEvent) windowDeactivated(WindowEvent)
ComponentListener	Dialog, Frame	componentMoved(ComponentEvent) componentHidden(ComponentEvent) componentResized(ComponentEvent) componentShown(ComponentEvent)
Adjustment Listener	Scrollbar	adjustmentValueChanged(Adjustment E vent) (You can also use the new ScrollPane class, which is simpler.

continues

Table 5-1   Event Table. *(Continued)*

Interface	Source	Methods
MouseMotionListener	Canvas, Dialog, Frame, Panel, Window	mouseDragged(MouseEvent) mouseMoved(MouseEvent)
MouseListener	Canvas, Dialog, Frame Panel, Window	mousePressed(MouseEvent) mouseReleased(MouseEvent) mouseEntered(MouseEvent) mouseExited(MouseEvent) mouseClicked(MouseEvent)
KeyListener	Component	keyPressed(KeyEvent) keyReleased(KeyEvent) keyTyped(KeyEvent)
FocusListener	Component	focusGained(FocusEvent) focusLost(FocusEvent)
ContainerListener	Container	componentAdded(ContainerEvent) componentRemoved(ContainerEvent)
TextListener	TextField	textValueChanged(TextEvent)

Before proceeding, let's look at one more example involving handling of events. The program listing for a key test program is shown in Listing 5.4.

```
/*
KeyTest.java
Keyboard Testing Program
*/

import java.awt.*;
import java.awt.event.*;

public class KeyTest extends Frame
{
    TextArea displayArea;
    TextField typingArea;
    String newline;

    KeyTest()
    {
        super("Keyboard Test");
    }

    public void init()
    {
```

LISTING *Testing Key Stroke Codes. (continues)*
5.4

```
     Button button = new Button("Clear");
     button.addActionListener(new ActionListener()
     {
        public void actionPerformed(ActionEvent e)
        {
           //Clear the text components.
           displayArea.setText("");
           typingArea.setText("");

           //Return the focus to the typing area.
           typingArea.requestFocus();
        }
     });
     displayArea = new TextArea(5, 20);
     displayArea.setEditable(false);
     typingArea = new TextField(20);
     typingArea.addKeyListener(new KeyAdapter()
     {
        public void keyPressed(KeyEvent e)
        {
           datadisplay(e);
        }
     });
     addWindowListener(new WindowAdapter()
     {
        public void windowClosing(WindowEvent
event)
        {
           System.exit(0);
        }
     });
     setLayout(new BorderLayout());
     add("Center", displayArea);
     add("South", button);
     add("North", typingArea);
     newline =
System.getProperty("line.separator");
   }

   protected void datadisplay(KeyEvent e)
   {
     String charString, keyCodeString, modString,
tmpString;
     char c = e.getKeyChar();
     int keyCode = e.getKeyCode();
     int modifiers = e.getModifiers();

     if (Character.isISOControl(c))
     {
        charString = "";
```

LISTING *Testing Key Stroke Codes. (continues)*

5.4

```
      }
      else
      {
          charString = "key character = '" + c + "'"
+ newline + " ";
      }

      keyCodeString = "key code = " + keyCode + " ("
+ KeyEvent.getKeyText(keyCode)
          + ")";

      modString = "modifiers = " + modifiers;
      tmpString = KeyEvent.getKeyModifiersText
(modifiers);
      if (tmpString.length() > 0)
      {
          modString += " (" + tmpString + ")";
      }
      else
      {
          modString += " (no modifiers)";
      }

      displayArea.append("KEY PRESSED:" + newline +
" " + charString + keyCodeString + newline + " " +
modString + newline);
    }

  public static void main (String args[])
  {
    KeyTest k = new KeyTest();
    k.init();
    k.setSize(300,200);
    k.show();
    k.typingArea.requestFocus();
                                                    }
}
```

LISTING *Testing Key Stroke Codes. (continued)*
5.4

For the moment, you can disregard the code lines that describe the creation
of the display layout and the creation of the text display and typing areas. We'll
go into more detail on such things in later sections. The first thing to note is
that after we create a *Button*, which will be used to clear the whole display window, we add an *ActionListener* to detect when the button is clicked. Within
this, we define *actionPerformed*, which sets the text in the display and typing
areas to an empty field. We then use *requestFocus* to return the cursor to the typing area. The program next defines the typing and display areas. We add

KeyListener to detect when a key is pressed. Within this, we define *keyPressed*, which runs the *datadisplay* function. Observe that this is a new object of the class *KeyAdapter*, which contains all of the empty key associated methods that we are not going to use, but which must be defined. In the similar situation just discussed where we defined *actionPerformed*, it was a new object of the class *ActionListener*. There is no *ActionAdapter* class; it's not needed since there is only one method associated with *ActionListener*. Finally, we add the *WindowListener*. You've seen this before; it closes the program when the X in the upper right corner of the window is clicked.

The *datadisplay* method gets the character, key code, and modifiers (such as the Shift key) from the key event that occurs and displays them in the display area. You can use this program to determine which information is returned for any particular key that is pressed. It also provides a good example of handling three different kinds of events.

Using Java Swing Components

So far, all of the techniques that we used for creating a frame made use of Java AWT components. Now we're going to do the same thing with Java Swing components. The program is shown in Listing 5.5. For this simple program, there isn't much difference from the previous ones we've created. First, we must add the line *import javax.swing.*; to give us access to the Swing components. Next, instead of creating a class that extends *Frame*, our class extends *Jframe*, which is the Swing counterpart. Finally, instead of the *show* method, we call *f.setVisible* with the parameter *true*. The *Jframe* display is invisible by default; calling this method with *true* makes it appear on the display. If later in your program you wanted to preserve it but not have it appear on the screen, you could call *f.setVisible* with the parameter set to *false*.

```
/*
   Framer3.java
   Program to generate a sample frame
*/

import java.awt.*;
import java.util.*;
import java.awt.event.*;
import javax.swing.*;
public class Framer3 extends JFrame
```

LISTING *Creating a Frame with Swing Components. (continues)*
5.5

```
{
    double x, y;
    Framer3()
    {
        super("Using a Frame");
        addWindowListener(new WindowAdapter()
        {
            public void windowClosing(WindowEvent e)
            {
                System.exit(0);
            }
        });
    }

    public void paint(Graphics g)
    {
        x = 134.52769;
        y = 26.10845;
        g.drawString("x = " + x, 75, 40);
        g.drawString("y = " + y, 75, 60);
        g.drawString("x + y = " + (x+y), 75, 80);
        g.drawString("x - y = " + (x-y), 75, 100);
        g.drawString("x * y = " + (x*y), 75, 120);
        g.drawString("x / y = " + (x/y), 75, 140);
    }
    public static void main(String args[])
    {
        Framer3 f = new Framer3();
        f.setSize(300, 200);
        f.setVisible(true);
    }
}
```

LISTING *Creating a Frame with Swing Components (continued).*
5.5

Applets

Up to now, we've worked with Java as if it were only an ordinary object-oriented programming language. We have been particularly impressed by its capability to create windows and by its platform independence. However, Java has an additional capability that makes it exciting for people who are working on the World Wide Web (WWW). This is the ability to create *applets*, small self-contained programs that can be downloaded from the Net and run with any Java-enabled browser, such as Netscape 2.0 or above. Chapters 12 and 25 describe how to use applets on the Net. Here, we're going to take the *Framer* class just described and show how to convert it to an applet and display the applet. Listing 5.6 defines the class *Framerap* that meets these requirements. The

```
/*
   Framerap.java
   Program to generate Framer Applet
*/

import java.awt.*;
import java.applet.*;

public class Framerap extends Applet
{
   double x, y;

   public void paint(Graphics g)
   {
      x = 134.52769;
      y = 26.10845;
      g.drawString("x = " + x, 75, 40);
      g.drawString("y = " + y, 75, 60);
      g.drawString("x + y = " + (x+y), 75, 80);
      g.drawString("x - y = " + (x-y), 75, 100);
      g.drawString("x * y = " + (x*y), 75, 120);
      g.drawString("x / y = " + (x/y), 75, 140);
   }
}
```

LISTING *Class to Set Up a Frame in an Applet.*
5.6

first thing to note is that we import the *java.applet* package that we didn't require in the previous examples. Next, instead of having *Framerap* extend *Frame*, it extends *Applet* and it doesn't include a constructor with a line to write a title, since we cannot write a title for the window when using the applet mode. Furthermore, we don't need to handle the *WindowClosing* event, since the applet viewer or browser takes care of closing down the applet. Finally, the whole *main* program is gone. This was previously used to instantiate, size, and show the frame. The *appletviewer* first reads a *.html* file that takes care of these operations. It then interprets the Java class.

The *Framerap.html program* looks like this:

```
<APPLET CODE = "Framerap.class" WIDTH=300 HEIGHT=200>
</APPLET>
```

Before you're ready to run the program, you need to use the Java compiler to compile the source code as with

```
javac Framerap.java
```

You then make sure that the resulting program (*Framerap.class* in the example), and the *.html* file (*Framerap.html* in the example) are both in your default director. Then run

```
appletviewer Framerap.html
```

and you should get the same window and contents that you had when you ran the *Framer* example. (You can't run an applet as a program, as for example, *java Framerap*, because the applet does not contain a *main* method.) You can also view *Framerap* with your network browser if you have one that is Java aware.

Programs that Run Either as an Application or as an Applet

With Java 2, you can write a program that will work either as an application or as an applet. We're going to show you an example called *FramerComb*. Once you have compiled *FramerComb*, you can run it as an application by typing *java FramerComb*. With just a simple *html* file to go with it, the program will run equally well if you call it up with your browser or by typing *appletviewer FramerComb.html*. The listing for this program is given in Listing 5.7.

```
/*
    FramerComb.java
    Program to generate Framer as a combination
applet and program
*/
import java.awt.*;
import java.applet.*;
import javax.swing.*;
import java.awt.event.*;

public class FramerComb extends JApplet
{
        double x, y;
        public void paint(Graphics g)
        {
            x = 134.52769;
            y = 26.10845;
            g.drawString("x = " + x, 75, 40);
            g.drawString("y = " + y, 75, 60);
            g.drawString("x + y = " + (x+y), 75, 80);
            g.drawString("x - y = " + (x-y), 75, 100);
            g.drawString("x * y = " + (x*y), 75, 120);
```

LISTING *Program that Runs as an Application or an Applet. (continues)*

5.7

```
            g.drawString("x / y = " + (x/y), 75, 140);
        }
   public static void main(String args[])
      {
        final FramerComb demo = new FramerComb();
        JFrame f = new JFrame();
        f.addWindowListener(new WindowAdapter()
        {
           public void windowClosing(WindowEvent e)
           {
              System.exit(0);
           }
        });
           f.getContentPane().add("Center", demo);
           f.setSize(300,200);
           f.show();
      }
   }
```

LISTING *Program that Runs as an Application or an Applet. (continued)*
5.7

Layouts

So far, we've used the *Frame* class to produce one large window with data displayed in it. Now we're going to see how to create more flexible displays that have several components arranged within a container such as a *Frame* or *Panel*. There are several standard layout arrangements that you can use, or you can create your own. I don't recommend that you create your own layout; it's very complicated and time consuming. Normally, one or more of the standard layouts can be used to produce a very satisfactory display. You can select the layout that you want to use with the method *setLayout*. You should be aware that if you do not use this statement, the default for a Java class running as an application is the Border layout, whereas the layout for a class running as an applet is the Flow layout. Thus, if you were to take a program listing that had been run as an application and which did not have a *setLayout* statement and modify it to run as an applet, your display would look entirely different.

The Border Layout

This is the default layout when running a Java class as a program. You can locate a component at one of five locations: NORTH, EAST, SOUTH, WEST, and CENTER. It doesn't matter in what order you add components to the display, the display first allocates space to the component located at NORTH, then to SOUTH, then to EAST, then to WEST, and finally to the CENTER.

You aren't likely to have any trouble with components located at NORTH or SOUTH; if you have a long line of text, it usually just fills up the line. EAST and WEST are a different story. They also keep your text on one line and make their display area wide enough to accommodate it. If your text is too long, there won't be any space left for the CENTER. You don't need to use all five locations; any that you don't use will become part of the center. In fact, one good way to define a large central display is to use the *Border* layout and specify only the CENTER location. Listing 5.8 is a sample program to demonstrate the use of the *Border* layout. The listing begins by defining the class *LayoutBorder* and then defining its constructor. The first line of the constructor uses *setTitle* to create a title for display. An alternate method that we've used before is *super*. Next, we use *setLayout* to set the display layout to the *BorderLayout* type. We then add four buttons, each with a title, at the four edges of the display. Finally, we add a label to the center, having a long line of text. We provide a window listener to detect when the window closing button is clicked and close the program as we did for the *Framer1* program. The *main* method creates an object *f* of class *LayoutBorder*, sets the window size, and finally shows the window. The result is shown in Figure 5.2.

Note that the *Border* layout was used in the Key Test program described earlier in this chapter. Now that you understand how this layout works, you can go back and look at the Key Test program with greater understanding.

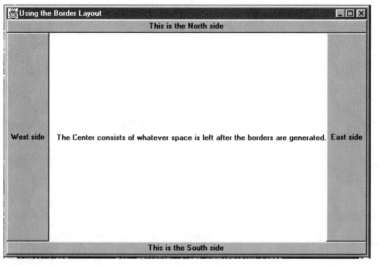

FIGURE *LayoutBorder Display.*
5.2

```
/*
LayoutBorder.java
Program to create a Border Layout
*/

import java.awt.*;
import java.awt.event.*;

public class LayoutBorder extends Frame
{
    LayoutBorder
    {
      setTitle("Using the Border Layout");
      setLayout(new BorderLayout());
      add("North",new Button("This is the North
side"));
      add("South",new Button("This is the South
side"));
      add("East", new Button("East side"));
      add("West", new Button("West side"));
      add("Center", new Label("The Center consists
of whatever space is left after the borders are
generated.",Label.CENTER));
      addWindowListener(new DWAdapter());
    }

    class DWAdapter extends WindowAdapter
    {
      public void windowClosing(WindowEvent event)
      {
        System.exit(0);
      }
    }

    public static void main(String args[])
    {
      LayoutBorder f = new LayoutBorder();
      f.setSize(600,400);
      f.show();
    }
}
```

LISTING *Demonstration Program for the Border Layout.*
5.8

The Flow Layout

The *Flow* layout is the simplest of all layouts—it just lines up components in a horizontal row. If it runs out of room, it starts another row of components. By default, the components in a *Flow* layout are centered in the container. This is what happens if you define the layout by

```
setLayout(new FlowLayout();
```

You can change this default positioning by specifying a parameter in the construct. These may be either *LEFT, RIGHT,* or *CENTER.* The layout is then defined somewhat like this:

```
setLayout(new FlowLayout(FlowLayout.RIGHT);
```

Listing 5.9 is exactly the same as Listing 5.8 except that it uses a *Flow* layout instead of a *Border* layout and the component positions are therefore not specified. Figure 5.3 shows the resulting display, which as you can see is considerably different. Remember that *FlowLayout* is the default when running an applet.

```
/*
LayoutFlow.java
Program to create a Flow Layout
*/

import java.awt.*;
import java.awt.event.*;

public class LayoutFlow extends Frame
{
    LayoutFlow()
    {
        setTitle("Using the Flow Layout");
        setLayout(new FlowLayout());
        add(new Button("This is the North side"));
        add(new Button("This is the South side"));
        add(new Button("East side"));
        add(new Button("West side"));
        add(new Label("Note that the buttons are just
lined up in a row."));
        add(new Label(" With the LayoutBorder Layout,
they would have been around the edges of the
display."));
        addWindowListener(new DWAdapter());
    }
    class DWAdapter extends WindowAdapter
    {
        public void windowClosing(WindowEvent event)
        {
            System.exit(0);
        }
    }
```

LISTING *Demonstration Program for the Flow Layout. (continues)*
5.9

```
    }

    public static void main(String args[])
    {
        LayoutFlow f = new LayoutFlow();
        f.setSize(600,400);
        f.show();
    }
}
```

LISTING *Demonstration Program for the Flow Layout. (continued)*
5.9

The Grid Layout

The *Grid* layout divides your container into a specified arrangement of equally sized rectangles. You specify this layout as follows:

```
setLayout(new GridLayout(no_of_rows, no_of_columns);
```

Thus, the expression

```
setLayout(new GridLayout(3,4);
```

would divide your container into three rows and four columns. Note carefully that in mathematical terms, this defines the space in terms of (y,x), when everything else that you come across in Java and most other programs uses the conventional form (x,y). Remember that the layout coordinates are reversed from

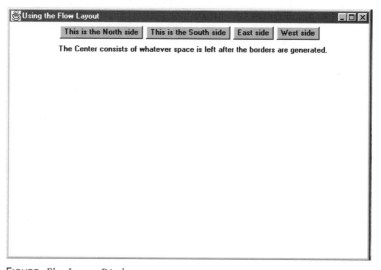

FIGURE *FlowLayout Display*
5.3

normal and you'll avoid unpleasant surprises when your display appears. However, when you start adding components to the display, the order in which they are displayed is the first cell of the first row, the second cell of the first row, the third cell of the first row, and so on. Listing 5.10 is a simple demonstration of the *Grid* layout. The program looks pretty much like those previously listed except that we have broken up the final long line of text into two halves, so that one half will appear in each of the two final grid cells. If we didn't do this, the line would be centered in a grid cell and if too long for it, the beginning and end of the line would be truncated. Note that we have used *Label.LEFT* and *Label.RIGHT* to position the two halves of the text as close as possible to the edges of the cells, but that there is still more than a single space between the two halves, as shown in Figure 5.4.

```
/*
LayoutGrid. ava
Program to create a Grid Layout
*/

import  ava.awt.*;
import  ava.awt.event.*;

public class LayoutGrid extends Frame
{
    LayoutGrid()
    {
        setTitle("Using the grid Layout");
        setLayout(new GridLayout(3,2));
        add(new Button("This is the first grid
cell."));
        add(new Button("This is the second grid
cell"));
        add(new Button("This is the third grid
cell."));
        add(new Button("This is the fourth grid
cell."));
        add(new Label("If you are going to use a long
line of text,",
            Label.RIGHT));
        add(new Label(" it may have to be broken up
into two grid cells.",
            Label.LEFT));
        addWindowListener(new DWAdapter());
    }
```

LISTING *Demonstration Program for the Grid Layout. (continues)*
5.10

```
class DWAdapter extends WindowAdapter
    {
        public void windowClosing(WindowEvent
event)
        {
            System.exit(0);
        }
    }
    public static void main(String args[])
    {
        LayoutGrid f = new LayoutGrid();
        f.setSize(600,400);
        f.show();
    }
}
```

LISTING *Demonstration Program for the Grid Layout. (continued)*
5.10

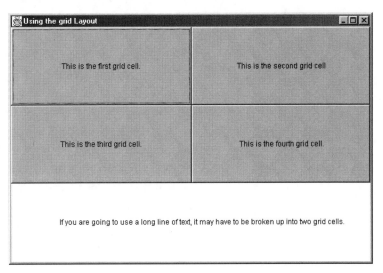

FIGURE *GridLayout Display.*
5.4

The *Grid Bag* Layout

The *Grid Bag* layout is the most flexible and also the most complicated of the layout types. Unlike the *Grid* layout, you don't specify the number of rows and columns; instead, you create a set of specifications for each component and then Java puts them together for you. To create a *Grid Bag* layout, you first need to set up an object of class *GridBagLayout* to be the layout manager for the container and then set up an object of class *GridBagConstraints* to specify the position and size of the component that is to be added to the container. The parameters for the *GridBagConstraints* object are as follows:

gridx
Determines the column position in which the upper left-hand corner of the component is to be placed. Instead of a number, you can set *gridx* equal to *GridBagConstraints.RELATIVE* and let Java take care of the horizontal positioning for you.

gridy
Determines the row position in which the upper left-hand corner of the component is to be placed. Instead of a number, you can set *gridy* equal to *GridBagConstraints.RELATIVE* and let Java take care of the vertical positioning for you.

gridwidth
Determines how many horizontal grid cells the component will occupy.

gridheight
Determines how many vertical grid cells the component will occupy.

weightx
Determines the percentage of unused horizontal space that will be assigned to the cell for this component. (The sum for all components should be 100 percent. If it isn't, Java will adjust things, but it may be hard for you to determine how.)

weighty
Determines the percentage of unused vertical space that will be assigned to the cell for this component. (The sum for all components should be 100 percent. If it isn't, Java will adjust things, but it may be hard for you to determine how.)

fill
If you let *fill* equal *GridBagConstraints.BOTH* (the default value), a component will take up the entire grid cell allotted to it. If you let it equal *GridBagConstraints.HORIZONTAL* or *GridBagConstraints.VERTICAL*, the component will occupy the entire cell width or height respectively, but only fill as much of the cell as it actually requires in the other direction. If you let it equal *GridBagConstraints.NONE*, the component will only fill as much of the space as it actually needs in both directions. (The cell size remains the same, so if you're using a component such as *Label* you won't notice any difference. For a component such as a button, however, although any text and its location remain the same, the button boundary and its background shading will change in dimensions.)

anchor   If you've specified fill so as to cause a component to use the entire cell area, *anchor* determines where the component will be located within the cell. You can set *anchor* equal to *GridBagconstraints.CENTER*, *GridBagConstraints.NORTH*, *GridBagConstraints.NORTHEAST*, *GridBagConstraints.EAST*, etc.

Listing 5.11 is a demonstration of a simple *Grid Bag* layout. We begin as usual by defining the primary object as the window title. Next, the object *layout_object* of class *GridBagLayout* and *constraint_object* of class *GridBag-Constraints* are instantiated. We then set the layout to be of type *layout_object*. We then define each of the components that are to make up the display. Next, we define the constraints that are to control the size and placing of the first component in the display. Since the *weighty* value is set to 20, only 20 percent of the unused y space will be assigned to this component. The *gridx* and *gridy* values of 0,0 say that the first component will be at the top left of the display.

```
/*
LayoutGridBag. ava
Using the Grid Bag Layout
*/

import  ava.awt.*;
import  ava.awt.event.*;

public class LayoutGridBag extends Frame
{
    public LayoutGridBag()
    {  setTitle("Using the Grid Bag Layout");
       GridBagLayout layout_ob ect = new
GridBagLayout();
          GridBagConstraints constraint_ob ect = new
GridBagConstraints();
       setLayout(layout_ob ect);
       Button button1 = new Button("This is the first
grid cell");
       Button button2 = new Button("This is the
second grid cell");
       Button button3 = new Button("This is the third
grid cell");
       Button button4 = new Button("This is the
fourth grid cell");
```

LISTING *GridBag Layout Program. (continues)*
5.11

```
       Label label1 = new Label("If we are going to
have a long line, it needs two cells",Label.CENTER);
       constraint_ob ect.weightx = 100;
       constraint_ob ect.weighty = 20;
       constraint_ob ect.fill =
GridBagConstraints.BOTH;
       constraint_ob ect.gridx = 0;
       constraint_ob ect.gridy = 0;
       constraint_ob ect.gridwidth = 1;
       constraint_ob ect.gridheight = 1;
         layout_ob ect.setConstraints(button1,
constraint_ob ect);
       add(button1);
       constraint_ob ect.gridx = 1;
         layout_ob ect.setConstraints(button2,
constraint_ob ect);
       add(button2);
       constraint_ob ect.weighty = 40;
       constraint_ob ect.gridx = 0;
       constraint_ob ect.gridy = 1;
         layout_ob ect.setConstraints(button3,
constraint_ob ect);
       add(button3);
       constraint_ob ect.gridx = 1;
         layout_ob ect.setConstraints(button4,
constraint_ob ect);
       add(button4);
       constraint_ob ect.gridx = 0;
       constraint_ob ect.gridy = 2;
       constraint_ob ect.gridwidth = 2;
         layout_ob ect.setConstraints(label1,
constraint_ob ect);
       add(label1);
       addWindowListener(new DWAdapter());

}

   class DWAdapter extends WindowAdapter
   {
     public void windowClosing(WindowEvent event)
     {
         System.exit(0);
     }
   }

   public static void main(String[] args)
   {  Frame f = new LayoutGridBag();
      f.setSize(500,400);
      f.show();
   }
```

LISTING *GridBag Layout Program. (continued)*
5.11

The *gridwidth* and *gridheight* values of 1 say that this component will occupy only one cell in both x and y dimensions. Next, we set the constraints for the first component with the *setConstraints* method, passing as parameters the name of the component object and the name of the *GridBagConstraints* object. Finally, we add the component to the display. The only constraint parameter that we have to change for the second component is *gridx*, which is set to 1 to place this component to the right of the first component. Then the *setConstraints* method is run to set up the new values and the second component is added to the display. For the third component, we set *weighty* to 40 to increase its share of unused y space. The values of *gridx* and *gridy* are set to 0 and 1, respectively, to place this component below the first component. Then the *setConstraints* method is run to set up the new values and the third component is added to the display. The only constraint parameter that we have to change for the fourth component is *gridx*, which is set to 1 to place this component to the right of the third component. For the fifth component, we change the values of *gridx* and *gridy* to 0 and 2, respectively, to place this component below the third components. We then set *gridwidth* to 2 so that this component will occupy two horizontal cells. Finally, the *setConstraints* method is run to set up the new values and the fifth component is added to the display. The remainder of the program is like the previous ones we've described. Figure 5.5 shows the resulting display.

FIGURE *GridBagLayout Display.*
5.5

The *Card* Layout

If you've seen Windows layouts that have a set of file card tabs at the top, any one of which you can select for viewing, then you understand the theory behind Java's *Card* layout. The Java *Card* layout is not as professionally done as the Windows one, but it does allow you to select from one of a number of *Panel* containers, which are stacked up in memory so that you can select any one to be instantly viewed. Listing 5.12 is a demonstration program for the *Card* layout. Typically, the program begins by defining the *LayoutCard* class and setting up a constructor for it. The constructor starts by setting the title for the window. It then sets up *tabs*, a container of class *Panel*. Within this Panel we add a set of buttons: seven for cards of each color, two for going to the next adjacent card front or back, and two for going to the first or last card. This Panel is then added at the north of a *Border* layout. Next, a new object called *cards* of class *Panel* is defined and set to have the *CardLayout*. Next, for each card, a new object of class *contents* is created. If you'll look further down in the program, you'll see that the *contents* class is an extension of the *Panel* class, having a string parameter passed to it. Each card causes a panel with different text and font characteristics. An object of this class adds in the center of the Panel the text created in the *contents* class. Now, to go back, we create an object called *pink* that passes the string *Pink*. We then set the background color to pink (you'll learn more about setting colors in the next chapter) and then add this Panel to the *Card* layout. This is repeated for six more colors. Finally, the whole *Card* layout is added to the center of the *Border* layout. The program also includes the typical embedded class to handle the *WindowClosing* event produced by clicking the X at the right-hand top corner of the display and directing it to shut down the program. It also has an *action* method that detects when the mouse is clicked on one of the buttons and selects the proper member of the *Card* layout to be moved to the front and become the one that is displayed. The result is that you can select one of the buttons and the proper card will be displayed on a background of the selected color. This is not just a complex way of changing colors. You can put on each page of the *CardLayout* a completely different set of text.

```
/*
LayoutCard. ava
Program to Demonstrate Use of Card Layout
*/
```

LISTING *Demonstration Program for the Card Layout.(continues)*
5.12

```
import   ava.awt.*;
import   ava.awt.event.*;

public class LayoutCard extends Frame implements
ActionListener
{
    public LayoutCard()
    {
        Button button1, button2, button3, button4,
            button5, button6, button7, button8,
            button9, button10, button11;
        setTitle("Using Card Layout");
        addWindowListener(new DWAdapter());
        tabs = new Panel();
        button1 = new Button("<<");
        button1.addActionListener(this);
        tabs.add(button1);
        button2 = new Button("<");
        button2.addActionListener(this);
        tabs.add(button2);
        button3 = new Button("Pink");
        button3.addActionListener(this);
        tabs.add(button3);
        button4 = new Button("Magenta");
        button4.addActionListener(this);
        tabs.add(button4);
        button5 = new Button("Cyan");
        button5.addActionListener(this);
        tabs.add(button5);
        button6 = new Button("Yellow");
        button6.addActionListener(this);
        tabs.add(button6);
        button7 = new Button("Green");
        button7.addActionListener(this);
        tabs.add(button7);
        button8 = new Button("Blue");
        button8.addActionListener(this);
        tabs.add(button8);
        button9 = new Button("Red");
        button9.addActionListener(this);
        tabs.add(button9);
        button10 = new Button(">>");
        button10.addActionListener(this);
        tabs.add(button10);
        button11 = new Button(">");
        button11.addActionListener(this);
        tabs.add(button11);
        add("North", tabs);
        cards = new Panel();
```

LISTING *Demonstration Program for the Card Layout.(continues)*
5.12

```
        layout = new CardLayout();
        cards.setLayout(layout);
        contents pink = new contents("Pink");
        pink.setBackground(Color.pink);
        cards.add("Pink", pink);
        contents magenta = new contents("Magenta");
        magenta.setBackground(Color.magenta);
        cards.add("Magenta", magenta);
        contents cyan = new contents("Cyan");
        cyan.setBackground(Color.cyan);
        cards.add("Cyan", cyan);
        contents yellow = new contents("Yellow");
        yellow.setBackground(Color.yellow);
        cards.add("Yellow", yellow);
        contents green = new contents("Green");
        green.setBackground(Color.green);
        cards.add("Green", green);
        contents blue = new contents("Blue");
        blue.setBackground(Color.blue);
        blue.setForeground(Color.white);
        cards.add("Blue", blue);
        contents red = new contents("Red");
        red.setBackground(Color.red);
        cards.add("Red", red);
        add("Center", cards);
    }
    public void actionPerformed( ava.awt.
        event.ActionEvent evt)
    {
        if (evt.getActionCommand().equals("<<"))
layout.first(cards);
        else if
(evt.getActionCommand().equals("<"))
layout.previous(cards);
        else if
(evt.getActionCommand().equals(">"))
layout.next(cards);
        else if
(evt.getActionCommand().equals(">>"))
layout.last(cards);
        else layout.show(cards,
evt.getActionCommand());
    }
    class DWAdapter extends WindowAdapter
    {
        public void windowClosing(WindowEvent event)
        {
            System.exit(0);
        }
```

LISTING *Demonstration Program for the Card Layout.(continues)*
5.12

```java
   }

   public static void main(String[] args)
   {
      Frame f = new LayoutCard();
      f.setSize(600, 200);
      f.show();
   }

      private Panel cards;
      private Panel tabs;
      private CardLayout layout;
   }

   class contents extends Panel
   {
      contents(String name)
      {
         if (name.equals ("Pink"))
         {
            Font ft = new Font("TimesRoman",
Font.PLAIN, 14);
            setFont(ft);
            add ("Center", new Label("This is the
first card of a series in the cards layout."));
            add ("Center", new Label("It is printed
in Times Roman 14 point on a pink background."));
         }
         if (name.equals ("Magenta"))
         {
            Font ft = new Font("TimesRoman",
Font.BOLD, 16);
            setFont(ft);
            add ("Center", new Label("For the second
card, we have changed the type face to Times Roman
Bold 16 point."));
            add ("Center", new Label("We are using a
magenta background and a completely different set of
text."));
         }
         if (name.equals ("Cyan"))
         {
            Font ft = new Font("Helvetica",
Font.PLAIN, 14);
            setFont(ft);
            add ("Center", new Label("As you can
see, the contents of each card can be completely
different from the others."));
```

LISTING *Demonstration Program for the Card Layout.(continues)*
5.12

```
                add ("Center", new Label("This page, for
example, uses 14 point Helvetica type on a cyan
background."));
                add ("Center", new Label("This is the
third card."));
            }
            if (name.equals ("Yellow"))
            {
                Font ft = new Font("Helvetica",
Font.BOLD, 18);
                setFont(ft);
                add ("Center", new Label("Now we have
come to the fourth card,"));
                add ("Center", new Label("which is
printed on a yellow background."));
                add ("Center", new Label("It uses 18
point Helvetica Bold type."));
            }
            if (name.equals ("Green"))
            {
                Font ft = new Font("Courier",
Font.PLAIN, 12);
                setFont(ft);
                add ("Center", new Label("We are
printing card five in 12 point Courier on a Green
Background"));
                add ("Center", new Label("You can put
any kind of display on a card and have it appear
when called."));
            }
            if (name.equals ("Blue"))
            {
                Font ft = new Font("Courier",
Font.BOLD, 14);
                setFont(ft);
                setForeground(Color.white);
                add ("Center", new Label("Card six is
in 14 point Courier on a Blue background."));
                add ("Center", new Label("Maybe blue
isn't a very good background color,"));
                add ("Center", new Label("but you can
have it if you want it."));
            }
            if (name.equals ("Red"))
            {
                Font ft = new Font("Helvetica",
Font.ITALIC, 12);
                setFont(ft);
```

LISTING *Demonstration Program for the Card Layout.(continues)*

5.12

```
                    add ("Center", new Label("By now
you're probably getting sick of seeing different
cards."));
                    add ("Center", new Label("This one is
in 12 point Helvetica Italics on a red
background."));
            }
        }
    }
```

LISTING *Demonstration Program for the Card Layout.(continued)*
5.12

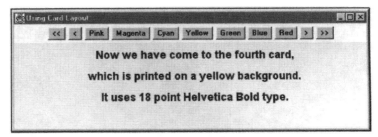

FIGURE *CardLayout Display*
5.6

The *Box* Layout

All of the layout tools we have described so far are members of the Java AWT, although each has its counterpart in the new Java Swing components. The *Box* layout is new; it is available only as a Swing component. It provides a very simple means of doing some layouts that might otherwise require quite complicated use of the *GridLayout* or *GridBagLayout*. Listing 5.13 is a simple program to demonstrate this layout. The program begins by opening a new Swing frame, giving it a title, and then including a Listener to detect when a window closing is requested and shut down the program at that point. Otherwise, a new component of type *JPanel* is created. The next line defines this panel to have the *BoxLayout*. The term *BoxLayout.Y_AXIS* determines that this box will consist of a top-to-bottom layout. Four new labels are then defined and added to the box. An empty border is then created around the box. The last three statements assemble this box within the viewing frame and make it visible to the user. (You'll note that this is done a little differently than the way we display frames in the AWT.)

```
/* BoxLayout2. ava
Program to Demonstrate the Box Layout
*/

import   avax.swing.*;
import   ava.awt.*;
import   ava.awt.event.*;

public class BoxLayout2 extends JDialog
{
    public static void main(String[] args)
    {
        JFrame f = new JFrame("Vertical Box Layout
Demo");
        f.addWindowListener(new WindowAdapter()
        {
            public void windowClosing(WindowEvent e)
            {
                System.exit(0);
            }
        });
        JPanel listPane = new JPanel();
        listPane.setLayout(new BoxLayout(listPane,
BoxLayout.Y_AXIS));
        JLabel label1 = new JLabel("This is the first
label ");
        listPane.add(label1);
        JLabel label2 = new JLabel("Label 2" );
        listPane.add(label2);
        JLabel label3 = new JLabel("This is the the
third label ");
        listPane.add(label3);
        JLabel label4 = new JLabel("This is the the
fourth and last of these labels");

listPane.setBorder(BorderFactory.createEmptyBorder(1
0,10,10,10));
        f.setContentPane(listPane);
            listPane.add(label4); f.pack();
        f.setVisible(true);
    }
}
```

LISTING *Demonstration Program for the Box Layout.*
5.13

Figure 5.7 shows the display resulting from running this program. To change from having the components listed vertically to having them listed in a line from left to right, all you have to do is change the line *BoxLayout.Y_AXIS* to *BoxLayout . X_AXIS*. The program will then produce a display that looks like

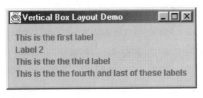

FIGURE *Vertical BoxLayout Display.*
5.7

Figure 5.8. There are several other features for controlling the *Box* layout that are not shown in the program. By using the line

```
container.add(Box.createRigidArea(new Dimension(0,5)));
```

you can add empty space between two components, the first coordinate representing the width and the second the height for this empty space. By using the line

```
container.Box.createHorizontalGlue());
```

you can cause all of the extra space in a horizontal line to appear between the two components between which you insert this statement. Normally, a top-to-bottom box tries to make all of its components the same width as the widest component; if the widest component is wider than the container, it makes all of the components as wide as the container.

Alternately, you can specify the size of a component, using such statements as

```
comp.setMinimumSize(new Dimension, 100, 35);
comp.setPreferredSize(new Dimension, 100, 35);
comp.setMaximumSize(new Dimension, 100, 35);
```

Another way that you can control the size and spacing of a box is to include the line

```
container.add(new Box.Filler(minSize, prefSize,
maxSize);
```

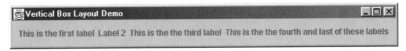

FIGURE *Horizontal BoxLayout Display.*
5.8

between the *add* statements for two components. The *minSize*, *prefsize*, and *maxSize* variables are of type *dimension* and define the width and height of the box for the minimum, preferred, and maximum sizes.

Finally, if you have different-sized components, you can control their alignment using such statements as

```
comp.setAlignmentX(Component.CENTER_ALIGNMENT);
comp.setAlignmentY(Component.TOP_ALIGNMENT);
```

The X alignment choices are *LEFT_ALIGNMENT, CENTER_ALIGNMENT*, and *RIGHT_ALIGNMENT*. The Y alignment choices are *TOP_ALIGNMENT, CENTER_ALIGNMENT*, and *BOTTOM_ALIGNMENT*. If you don't specify a particular alignment, the default alignments for various Swing components are as shown in Table 5-2.

Table 5-2   Default Alignment for Swing Components.

Swing Component	Default X Alignment	Default Y Alignment
Buttons, menu items menu items	LEFT_ALIGNMENT	TOP_ALIGNMENT
Labels	LEFT_ALIGNMENT	CENTER_ALIGNMENT
Toolbars	CENTER_ALIGNMENT	TOP_ALIGNMENT
All other Swing components	CENTER_ALIGNMENT	CENTER_ALIGNMENT

6 Checkboxes, Lists, Menus, and Scrolling

Often you're going to want to have buttons on your display so that by clicking on them with your mouse you can direct the program to take certain desired actions. This chapter describes various such buttons that are provided by Java. As with many Java classes and methods, many of these were available in the AWT. However, improved versions are a part of the Swing components of Java 2. Whenever you can, it's a good idea to use these. This is particularly true of *Menus* and *MenuBars*. If you use the original version of these, they will always be on top of other components of the display, whether that is what you want or not. Furthermore, these classes only work with the *Frame* container, not with *Applet*. So if you want a menu on an applet, you must use the Swing version. The following sections describe how to use a number of these classes. If you don't find exactly what you want, there may still be a Java Swing class that will do the job for you. We've only described the most useful ones.

Checkboxes

Checkboxes come in two forms. The first form is a set of square checkboxes. By clicking the mouse on any square box, you place a check in the box and initiate an event that you can use to take any action you want. You can check as many of the boxes in a set as you desire. If you click on a box that already contains a check, the check will go away. A second form of button interaction uses a set of round buttons. You can only select one of these by clicking it with a mouse. This will enter a small filled-in circle within the circle representing the selected button and will remove the filled-in circle from any button that was previously checked. If you click the box containing the filled-in circle again, nothing will happen. However, if you click another box, the filled circle will disappear from its original location and reappear in the box most recently clicked. In other words, with the first form of checkbox, as many items as desired may be selected simultaneously; but with this second technique, only one item can be selected at a time. You can group together checkboxes to accomplish this second technique, but the preferred way is to use Radio Buttons, which are supported by Java Swing. Listing 6.1 is a demonstration program showing how to use checkboxes. We're going to use the checkboxes to choose the font and style of a couple lines of type. When we select the font, it can be only one of *Helvetica*, *TimesRoman*, or *Courier*. Consequently, we want to use the second form of checkboxes for this selection. For type style, we want no boxes checked for plain, the *Bold* box for boldface, the *Italic* box for Italic, or both boxes if we want both boldface and italic. Consequently, for this selection we use the first form of checkboxes, where we can have no boxes, one, or two boxes checked.

```
/*
CkBox.java
Demonstrates use of Check Boxes
*/

import java.applet.*;
import java.awt.*;
import java.awt.event.*;
import javax.swing.*;

public class CkBox extends JApplet implements
ItemListener
{
    String s = "Helvetica";
    int m = 0, oldM = 0;
    Choice font = new Choice();

    TextCanvas canvas;
    private Checkbox bold;
    private Checkbox italic;
    private Checkbox helv;
    private Checkbox trom;
    private Checkbox cour;

    public void init()
    {
      Panel p = new Panel();
      Panel p1 = new Panel();
      Panel p2 = new Panel();
      CheckboxGroup g = new CheckboxGroup();
      p.setLayout(new GridLayout(1,2));
      p1.setLayout(new GridLayout(2,1));
      p2.setLayout(new GridLayout(3,1));
      p1.add(bold = new Checkbox("Bold"));
      p1.add(italic = new Checkbox("Italic"));
      p2.add(helv = new Checkbox("Helvetica", g,
true));

      p2.add(trom = new Checkbox("TimesRoman", g,
false));
      p2.add(cour = new Checkbox("Courier", g,
false));

      p.add(p1);
      p.add(p2);
      getContentPane().add("South", p);
      bold.addItemListener(this);
      italic.addItemListener(this);
      helv.addItemListener(this);
```

LISTING *Demonstrating the Use of Checkboxes.(continues)*
6.1

```java
      trom.addItemListener(this);
      cour.addItemListener(this);
      getContentPane().add("Center", canvas = new
TextCanvas());
   }

   public void itemStateChanged(ItemEvent e)
   {
      String w;
      int i;

      w = (String)e.getItem();
      if (w.equals("Bold"))
      {
         if (e.getStateChange() == 1)
            m += Font.BOLD;
         else
            m -= Font.BOLD;
      }
      else if (w.equals("Italic"))
      {
         if (e.getStateChange() == 1)
            m += Font.ITALIC;
         else
            m -= Font.ITALIC;
      }
      else
         s = w;
      canvas.setFont(m,s);
}

   public static void main(String argv[])
   {
      JFrame f = new JFrame("Test of Check Boxes");
      final CkBox demo = new CkBox();
      f.getContentPane().add(demo);
      f.addWindowListener(new WindowAdapter()
      {
         public void windowClosing(WindowEvent e)
         {
            System.exit(0);
         }
      });
      f.pack();
      f.setSize(new Dimension(300, 200));
      demo.init();
      f.pack();
      f.setVisible(true);
   }
```

LISTING *Demonstrating the Use of Checkboxes. (continues)*
6.1

```
}

class TextCanvas extends Canvas
{
   public TextCanvas()
   {
   }

   public Dimension getPreferredSize()
   {
      return new Dimension(300, 200);
   }

   public void update(Graphics g)
   {
      paint(g);
   }

      public void setFont(int m, String s)
      {
         setFont(new Font(s, m, 12));
         repaint();
      }

      public void paint(Graphics g)
      {
         g.drawString
            ("The type style of this sample of text
can be", 0, 50);
         g.drawString
            ("changed using the check boxes below.",
0, 66);
      }
}
```

LISTING *Demonstrating the Use of Checkboxes.(continued)*

6.1

We've written this program so that it can be run either as an application or as an applet. To do this, we set up the principal class *CkBox* to extend the class *Applet* rather than *Frame*. In addition, we put the lines that define the application title and window size in the *main* routine. The software for handling a window closing event (a window listener and code to end the program when the window closing event occurs) is put here. We need these things for running an application. However, when running as an applet, no title is allowed (since the browser or applet viewer provides one automatically), no window size can be specified (since the size is specified in the *html* file that calls the applet), and now window closing software is needed (since the applet is automatically closed when the user clicks on the X in the top right corner of the applet). The *main* program is only run when the program is run as an application; it is ignored when the program is run as an applet. Now note how we're building the general layout of the window, which takes place in the *init* method of class *CkBox*. We're going to have three panels; *p, p1,* and *p2.* The first panel, *p,* has a grid layout consisting of two cells arranged side by side. In the first cell, we put panel *p1,* which has a grid layout consisting of two vertical cells that contain the two style checkboxes *Bold* and *Italic.* In the second cell, we put panel *p2,* which has a grid layout consisting of three vertical cells that contain the three font checkboxes *Helvetica, TimesRoman,* and *Courier.* All of this panel *p* is placed at the *South* (bottom) location of the window, while the object *text* (of class *TextCanvas*), which contains the sample text, is located in the center of the window. Previously, we did this with a simple *add* statement. Using Java Swing components we must use *getContentPane().add* instead. Note carefully how each checkbox is defined. The boxes for *Bold* and *Italic* are defined by setting up new objects of the class *Checkbox.* Each is passed a parameter which is the name associated with the box. This results in ordinary square checkboxes, any number of which may be selected simultaneously. The boxes for *Helvetica, TimesRoman,* and *Courier* are defined in a similar manner except that they are passed two additional parameters: *g,* and *true* or *false.* The *g* is an object of class *CheckBoxGroup* that has been defined just before the checkbox definitions. This determines that all checkboxes that are passed the *g* parameter form a group of round checkboxes, of which only one may be selected at a time. The selected box when the display first comes up is the one that is passed the parameter *true.* (You may wonder what will happen if you pass the *true* parameter to more than one of these checkboxes, inasmuch as only one is supposed to be selected at any time. The answer is that only the first box that has the true parameter passed to it will come up as selected.)

Before we see how to use the checkboxes for selection, let's look at the *TextCanvas* class, which places the sample text at the center of the window. This class includes the *setFont* method, which overrides the *setFont* method that is a part of the *Canvas* class. It is passed an integer that defines the type style and a string containing the font name. It calls *setFont* (which is the original *setFont* method), which requires that it be passed three parameters: the font name string, the type style integer, and the type size in points, which in our case we always make 12 points. Then our new *setFont* method calls *repaint* so that whenever it is called to change the type characteristics, the center display is repainted with the new characteristics. Finally, we have the *paint* method, which simply uses the *drawString* method of the *Graphics* class to display the desired text in the selected location.

Let's return to the *init* method. For each of the checkboxes, we add a listener with a statement of the form

```
bold.addItemListener(this);
```

The text is then added to the display, which terminates the *init* part of the program.

The *itemStateChanged* method is called each time one of the listeners detects that the state of one of the checkboxes has been changed. First we use the *getItem* method to place a string containing the selected checkbox's name in the parameter *w*. If this string is *Bold* or *Italic* the method first checks whether the checkbox was activated or deactivated (using the method *e.getStateChange*) and then properly changes the parameter *m*, which is an integer that designates the style of the text. If the event that occurred had a type face name instead of a style name, we set the string *s* (which is the current type face name) equal to *w* (the type face named by the event). We then call the *setFont* method to convert the text display style and type face. Note that if the event was a style one, *s* (and consequently the type face) remains unchanged, whereas if the event was a type face one, *m* (and consequently the type style) remains unchanged. Figure 6.1 is a picture of a typical run of this program.

In using this program, the first thing we need to do is type

```
javac CkBox.java
```

to compile the program. You can then type

```
java CkBox
```

to run the program as an application. To run the program as an applet, you need the program *CkBox.html*, which is listed in Listing 6.2. You can either

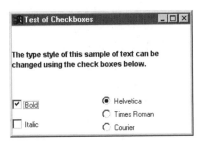

FIGURE *The CkBox Display.*
6.1

```
<APPLET CODE = "CkBox.class" WIDTH=300 HEIGHT=200>
</APPLET>
```

LISTING *HTML Program for Running the CkBox Applet.*
6.2

type *appletviewer* followed by the name of this *html* program to view the applet, or you can use your browser to run the *html* program.,

Using Radio Buttons

Listing 6.3 shows how the program for checkboxes can be modified to use radio buttons to select the type face rather than using checkboxes. Sun recommends using radio buttons in such a situation, but you can see that it's actually a little more complicated than using checkboxes. The resulting display is shown in Figure 6.2.

```
/*
RadioButtons.java
Demonstrates use of Check Boxes
*/

import java.applet.*;
import java.awt.*;
import java.awt.event.*;
import javax.swing.*;

public class RadioButtons extends JApplet implements
ItemListener
{
    String s = "Helvetica";
    int m = 0;

    TextCanvas canvas;
    private Checkbox bold;
    private Checkbox italic;
    private JRadioButton helv;
    private JRadioButton trom;
    private JRadioButton cour;

    public void init()
    {
        JPanel p = new JPanel();
```

LISTING *Changing Text with Radio Buttons. (continues)*
6.3

```
        JPanel p1 = new JPanel();
        JPanel p2 = new JPanel();
        ButtonGroup g = new ButtonGroup();
        g.add(helv);
        g.add(trom);
        g.add(cour);
        p.setLayout(new GridLayout(1,2));
        p1.setLayout(new GridLayout(2,1));
        p2.setLayout(new GridLayout(3,1));
        p1.add(bold = new Checkbox("Bold"));
        p1.add(italic = new Checkbox("Italic"));
        p2.add(helv = new JRadioButton("Helvetica"));
        helv.setSelected(true);
        helv.setActionCommand("Helvetica");
        p2.add(trom = new JRadioButton("TimesRoman"));
        trom.setActionCommand("TimesRoman");
        p2.add(cour = new JRadioButton("Courier"));
        cour.setActionCommand("Courier");
        p.add(p1);
        p.add(p2);
        getContentPane().add("South", p);
        bold.addItemListener(this);
        italic.addItemListener(this);
        RadioListener myListener = new
RadioListener();
        helv.addActionListener(myListener);
        trom.addActionListener(myListener);
        cour.addActionListener(myListener);
        getContentPane().add("Center", canvas = new
TextCanvas());
    }

    public void itemStateChanged(ItemEvent e)
    {
        String w;
        int i;

        w = (String)e.getItem();
        if (w.equals("Bold"))
        {
            if (e.getStateChange() == 1)
                m += Font.BOLD;
            else
                m -= Font.BOLD;
        }
        else if (w.equals("Italic"))
        {
            if (e.getStateChange() == 1)
                m += Font.ITALIC;
```

LISTING *Changing Text with Radio Buttons. (continues)*
6.3

```
            else
                m -= Font.ITALIC;
        }
        else
            s = w;

        canvas.setFont(m,s);
    }

    class RadioListener implements ActionListener
    {
        public void actionPerformed(ActionEvent e)
        {
            s = e.getActionCommand();
            canvas.setFont(m,s);
        }
    }

    public static void main(String argv[])
    {
        JFrame f = new JFrame("Check Boxes and Radio
Buttons");
        final RadioButtons demo = new RadioButtons();
        f.getContentPane().add(demo);
        f.addWindowListener(new WindowAdapter()
        {
            public void windowClosing(WindowEvent e)
            {
                System.exit(0);
            }
        });
        demo.init();
        f.pack();
        f.setVisible(true);
    }
}
class TextCanvas extends Canvas
{
    public TextCanvas()
    {
    }

    public Dimension getPreferredSize()
    {
        return new Dimension(300, 200);
    }

    public void update(Graphics g)
    {
```

LISTING *Changing Text with Radio Buttons. (continues)*
6.3

```
      paint(g);
   }

   public void setFont(int m, String s)
   {
      setFont(new Font(s, m, 12));
      repaint();
   }

   public void paint(Graphics g)
   {
      g.drawString
         ("The type style of this sample of text can
be ", 0, 50);
      g.drawString
         ("changed using the check boxes below.", 0,
66);
   }
}
```

LISTING *Changing Text with Radio Buttons. (continued)*
6.3

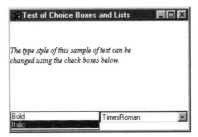

FIGURE *Changing Text with Radio Buttons.*
6.2

Using Icons with Checkboxes

The Java Swing version of the checkbox allows you to define a checkbox to have an associated text label and/or icon. As a demonstration of this, we have a program that shows four small pictures of a kitchen along the left side of a window, with the rest of the window displaying a large version of one of these views. By clicking your mouse on any one of the four small views, you can cause a large version of its picture to appear in the rest of the window. This is an ideal way to allow someone to select an item from your Web page for a closer look. The resulting picture is shown in Plate 1. The program listing is given in Listing 6.4.

```java
import java.awt.*;
import java.awt.event.*;
import javax.swing.*;

public class KitchenViews extends JPanel
{
    JCheckBox k1Button;
    JCheckBox k2Button;
    JCheckBox k3Button;
    JCheckBox k4Button;
    StringBuffer choices;
    JLabel pictureLabel;

    public KitchenViews()
    {
        ImageIcon thumbnail = null;
        ImageIcon tmpIcon = new
ImageIcon("Bgkit164.gif");
        thumbnail = new ImageIcon(
            tmpIcon.getImage().getScaledInstance(130, -
1, Image.SCALE_DEFAULT));
        k1Button = new JCheckBox(thumbnail);
        k2Button = new JCheckBox(new
ImageIcon("kit2.gif"));
        k3Button = new JCheckBox(new
ImageIcon("kit3.gif"));
        k4Button = new JCheckBox(new
ImageIcon("kit4.gif"));
        CheckBoxListener myListener = new
CheckBoxListener();
        k1Button.addItemListener(myListener);
        k2Button.addItemListener(myListener);
        k3Button.addItemListener(myListener);
        k4Button.addItemListener(myListener);
        pictureLabel = new JLabel(new
ImageIcon("Bgkit164.gif"));
        JPanel checkPanel = new JPanel();
        checkPanel.setLayout(new GridLayout(0, 1));
        checkPanel.add(k1Button);
        checkPanel.add(k2Button);
        checkPanel.add(k3Button);
        checkPanel.add(k4Button);
        setLayout(new BorderLayout());
        add(checkPanel, BorderLayout.WEST);
        add(pictureLabel, BorderLayout.CENTER);

setBorder(BorderFactory.createEmptyBorder(20,20,20,2
0));
    }
```

LISTING *Checkboxes with Icons. (continues)*
6.4

```
class CheckBoxListener implements ItemListener
{
   public void itemStateChanged(ItemEvent e)
   {
       int index = 0;
       Object source = e.getItemSelectable();

       if (source == k1Button)
           pictureLabel.setIcon(new
ImageIcon("Bgkit164.gif"));
       else if (source == k2Button)
           pictureLabel.setIcon(new
ImageIcon("Bgkit264.gif"));
       else if (source == k3Button)
           pictureLabel.setIcon(new
ImageIcon("Bgkit364.gif"));
       else if (source == k4Button)
           pictureLabel.setIcon(new
ImageIcon("Bgkit464.gif"));
   }
}
public static void main(String s[])
{
   JFrame frame = new Jframe(
       "Kitchen Views - Click Icon for Large
View");
   frame.addWindowListener(new WindowAdapter() {
       public void windowClosing(WindowEvent e)
       {
           System.exit(0);}
       });
   frame.setContentPane(new KitchenViews());
   frame.pack();
   frame.setVisible(true);
}
}
```

LISTING *Checkboxes with Icons. (continued)*
6.4

In order for this program to work, you have to have some *gif* image files in the same directory as the compiled version of the program. For this program, the four kitchen views are in the files *BgKit164.gif, BgKit264.gif,* and *BgKit364.gif.* These files contain the full-sized kitchen pictures. There are two ways to construct the smaller icon pictures. We have used a photo processing program to make new, smaller pictures of the four kitchen views, and have stored them in the files *kit1.gif, kit2.gif, kit3.gif,* and *kit4.gif.* You can either use these directly for the icon views or you can use the original large picture files and scale them down to make the icons. We've done both, so you can see how each technique works. The program begins with the *KitchenViews* class, which extends *Jpanel*. First, the *tmpIcon* and *thumbnail* image objects are defined. We load the first large kitchen view image from the file into *tmpIcon*. Then we create the thumbnail image by scaling down the image in *tmpIcon* using the method *getScaledInstance*. The first parameter sent to this method is the width of the new image in pixels. For the second parameter, you can use –1 to instruct the method to make the height change proportional to that of the width. Alternately, you can specify a number of pixels for the scaled height, but depending on how you set this, the resulting picture may be distorted. The third parameter determines the scaling algorithm that will be used. There are several available; we've chosen to use the default version, which is preferable for most applications. Next, you will see that the program sets up a checkbox using the *thumbnail* image as the first checkbox icon. For the remaining three checkboxes, we have used the small view files directly to create the checkbox icons. This requires that you store additional image files, but permits the program to operate faster.

We then add a listener for each checkbox. A new label is then created that contains the first full-sized picture as *pictureLabel*. We next create a Check-BoxListener and add to it listeners for each of the four checkboxes. We then create a panel called *CheckPanel* and add each of the four checkboxes to it. This is then placed at the west side of a BorderLayout and *pictureLabel* is used to fill the center of the display. Finally, a border is created around the display window.

When one of the checkbox icons is clicked, the appropriate listener implements the *itemStateChanged* method. This method first uses the *getItemSelectable* method to determine which icon was clicked and stores this information into *source*. It then creates the appropriate large image for the icon clicked.

Choice Boxes and Lists

We are now going to look at some other ways to make selections: *Choices* and *Lists*. The *List* class enables you to create a list of items. You pass two parameters. The first parameter is the number of items in the list. The second parameter, if *true*, allows you to select as many items as you want from the list; if *false,* you can select only one list item, all others are automatically deselected. When you select an item, by clicking with the mouse, it changes to a distinctive set of colors to indicate selection. The *Choice* class normally only shows a selected item. Clicking on an arrow at the right of this item enables you to bring up a sublist containing all items available. When you click on one of them, the sublist goes away, leaving the selected item on display. Listing 6.5 is a program that demonstrates how these two classes are used. We generate text with the

```
/*
   ChoiceBox.java
   Demonstrates use of Choice Boxes
 */

import java.applet.*;
import java.awt.*;
import java.awt.event.*;
import javax.swing.*;

public class ChoiceBox extends JApplet implements
ItemListener
{
   String s = "Helvetica";
   int m = 0;
   Choice font = new Choice();
   List style = new List(2,true);
   TextCanvas canvas;

   public void init()
   {
      getContentPane().setLayout(new
BorderLayout());
      Panel p = new Panel();
      Panel p1 = new Panel();
      Panel p2 = new Panel();
      p.setLayout(new GridLayout(1,2));
      style.add("Bold");
      style.add("Italic");
      font.add("Helvetica");
      font.add("TimesRoman");
      font.add("Courier");
      p1.add(style);
      p2.add(font);
      p.add(p1);
      p.add(p2);
      style.addItemListener(this);
      font.addItemListener(this);
      getContentPane().add("South", p);
      getContentPane().add("Center", canvas =
new TextCanvas());
   }

   public void itemStateChanged(ItemEvent e)
   {
      String [] w;
      int i;

      if (e.getSource().equals (style))
```

LISTING *Demonstrating Choice and List Classes. (continues)*
6.5

```
        {
            m = 0;
            w = style.getSelectedItems();
            for (i=0; i<w.length; i++)
            {
                if (w[i].equals("Bold"))
                    m += Font.BOLD;
                if (w[i].equals("Italic"))
                    m += Font.ITALIC;
            }
        }
            if (e.getSource().equals (font))
                s = (String)e.getItem();
            canvas.setFont(m,s);
    }

   public static void main(String argv[])
   {
      JFrame f = new JFrame("Test of Choice Boxes");
      final ChoiceBox demo = new ChoiceBox();
      f.getContentPane().add(demo);
      f.addWindowListener(new WindowAdapter()
      {
          public void windowClosing
(WindowEvent e)
          {
              System.exit(0);
          }
      });
      f.pack();
      f.setSize(new Dimension(300, 200));
      demo.init();
        f.pack();
      f.setVisible(true);
   }
}

class TextCanvas extends Canvas
{
    public TextCanvas()
    {
    }

   public Dimension getPreferredSize()
   {
      return new Dimension(300, 200);
   }

   public void update(Graphics g)
```

LISTING *Demonstrating Choice and List Classes. (continues)*
6.5

```
   {
      paint(g);
   }

   public void setFont(int m, String s)
   {
      setFont(new Font(s, m, 12));
      repaint();
   }

   public void paint(Graphics g)
   {
      g.drawString
         ("The type style of this sample of text can
be ", 0, 50);
      g.drawString
         ("changed using the check boxes below.", 0,
66);
   }
}
```

LISTING *Demonstrating Choice and List Classes. (continued)*
6.5

class *TextCanvas1*, which is the same as the *TextCanvas* class we used in the previous program. (If you were sure that both of these programs would always be available in the same directory, you could use a common *TextCanvas* class for both of them and it would only need to be listed in the first program to be compiled.) Our *ChoiceBox* class has two panels, *p1* and *p2*, each of which has a single grid cell. The first contains an object *style* of class *List*. This contains two items, *Bold* and *Italic*. Either or both can be selected. The panel *p2* contains an object *font* of class *Choice*. The two are combined side by side in the panel *p*. As with the previous program, this panel is displayed at the bottom of the window and the sample text is displayed in the center of the window. Possible selections are added to the *style* and *font* objects by using the *addItem* method and passing it, as a parameter, a string containing the text to be displayed for this item.

We detect the events caused by clicking the mouse on the list or choice items through the use of an *addItemListener* statement for each type. Whenever an item is selected by clicking the mouse button, the *itemStateChanged* method is called. This method first checks whether a list type item (*style*) or a choice box item (*font*) was selected. If a list event was detected, the method gets the names of all the selected items and puts them in an array of strings, *w*. begins by using the method *getSelectedItems* to return an array of strings that contains the names of the selected items. We then scan through this array with a *for* loop. If

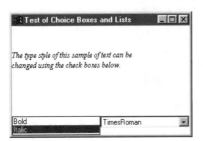

FIGURE *ChoiceBox Display.*
6.3

a string having the name *Bold* is found, we add *FontBOLD* to the type style parameter *m*; if a string having the name *Italic* is found, we add *FontITALIC* to *m*. At the end of this method, we use *m* to reset the type style. If a choice item was selected, the method gets the name of the selected item and puts it in the string *s*, which is used to select the type font. Finally, regardless of the type of event selected, the *canvas.setFont* method is called to apply the new choices to the displayed text, Figure 6.3 shows the result of using this demonstration program.

Using Menus

We can also make use of menus in our selection process. The menu line appears at the top of the display. When you click the mouse on a menu item, either an action may take place or a submenu may appear that allows you to make another selection. Listing 6.6 is a demonstration program for using menus. This program makes use of the original AWT Menu class. This class only works with the *Frame* container, not with *Applet*. Consequently, the demonstration program can only be run as an application, not as an applet. Also, if you use this Menu class in conjunction with Java Swing components, the menu will always appear on top of other components, regardless of whether that is what you want or not.

```
/*
   MenuUse1. ava
   Program to demonstrate use of Menus
*/

import  ava.awt.*;
import  ava.awt.event.*;
```

LISTING *Program to Demonstrate Use of Menus. (continues)*
6.6

```
public class MenuUse1 extends Frame
{
    String s = "Helvetica";
    String type;
    int st;

    public MenuUse1()
    {
        setTitle("Using Menus");
        addWindowListener(new DWAdapter());
        MenuBar mbar = new MenuBar();
        Menu mf = new Menu("Font");
        mf.add(new MenuItem("Helvetica"));
        mf.add(new MenuItem("TimesRoman"));
        mf.add(new MenuItem("Courier"));
        mf.addSeparator();
        mf.add(new MenuItem("Quit"));
        mbar.add(mf);

        Menu ms = new Menu("Style");
        ms.add(new MenuItem("Plain"));
        ms.add(new MenuItem("Bold"));
        ms.add(new MenuItem("Italic"));
        ms.add(new MenuItem("BoldItalic"));
        mbar.add(ms);

        Menu mc = new Menu("Color");
        mc.add(new MenuItem("Black"));
        mc.add(new MenuItem("Blue"));
        mc.add(new MenuItem("Cyan"));
        mc.add(new MenuItem("Red"));
        mbar.add(mc);

        Menu mh = new Menu("Help");
        mh.add(new MenuItem("Index"));
        mh.add(new MenuItem("About"));
        mbar.add(mh);

        ActionListener mte = new ActionListener()
        {
            public void actionPerformed
( ava.awt.event.ActionEvent mte)
            {
                s = (String)mte.getActionCommand();
                if(s == "Quit")
                    System.exit(0);
                else
                    text.setFont(st, s);
            }
```

LISTING *Program to Demonstrate Use of Menus. (continues)*

6.6

```
        };

    ActionListener mse = new ActionListener()
    {
        public void actionPerformed
( ava.awt.event.ActionEvent mse)
        {
            type = (String)mse.getActionCommand();
            if (type ==  "Plain")
               text.setFont(st=0,s);
            if (type == "Bold")
               text.setFont(st=1,s);
            if (type == "Italic")
               text.setFont(st=2,s);
            if (type =="BoldItalic")
               text.setFont(st=3,s);
    }
    };

    ActionListener mce = new ActionListener()
    {
        public void actionPerformed
( ava.awt.event.ActionEvent mce)
        {
            type = (String)mce.getActionCommand();
            if (type == "Black")
               text.color = Color.black;
            if (type =="Cyan")
               text.color = Color.cyan;
            if (type == "Blue")
               text.color = Color.blue;
            if (type == "Red")
               text.color = Color.red;
             text.repaint();
        }
    };

    ActionListener mhe = new ActionListener()
    {
        public void actionPerformed
( ava.awt.event.ActionEvent mhe)
        {
            type = (String)mhe.getActionCommand();

            if (type =="About")
            {
               About about = new About();
               about.show();
            }
```

LISTING *Program to Demonstrate Use of Menus. (continues)*
6.6

```
            }
        };

        mf.addActionListener(mte);
        ms.addActionListener(mse);
        mc.addActionListener(mce);
        mh.addActionListener(mhe);
        setMenuBar(mbar);
        text = new TextCanvas2();
        add("Center", text);
    }

    class DWAdapter extends WindowAdapter
    {
        public void windowClosing(WindowEvent event)
        {
            System.exit(0);
        }
    }

    public static void main(String[] args)
    {
        Frame f = new MenuUse1();
        f.setSize(300, 200);
        f.show();
    }
    private TextCanvas2 text;
}

class About extends Frame
{
    About()
    {
        setTitle("About Program");
        setLayout(new GridLayout(3,1));
        add(new Label
            ("This program designed by",Label.CENTER));
        add(new Label("Roger T. Stevens",
Label.CENTER));
        add(new Label("October 22,
1998",Label.CENTER));
        setSize(200,80);

        class WAdapter extends WindowAdapter
        {
            public void windowClosing(WindowEvent
event)
            {
                dispose();
```

LISTING *Program to Demonstrate Use of Menus. (continues)*
6.6

```
            }
        };

        addWindowListener(new WAdapter());
    }
}

class TextCanvas2 extends Canvas
{
    Color color = new Color(0);

     public TextCanvas2()
    {
        setFont(Font.PLAIN, "Helvetica");
    }

    public void setFont(int m, String s)
    {
        setFont(new Font(s, m, 12));
        repaint();
    }

    public void paint(Graphics g)
    {
        g.setColor(color);
        g.drawString
            ("The type style, font, and color of this
sample of text ", 0, 50);
        g.drawString
            ("can be changed using the various menus.",
0, 66);
    }
```

LISTING *Program to Demonstrate Use of Menus. (continued)*
6.6

We start creating a menu by creating an object *mbar* of class *MenuBar*. This will be the set of menu items along the top of the screen. Next, we define an object *mf* of class *Menu*, passing the title *Font*. A little later, we'll add *mf* to *mbar*, where it will become the first item on the menubar. First, however, we define some new menu items and add them to *mf*. They form the first submenu, which is called up when you trigger the *Font* menu item. These are *Helvetica, TimesRoman,* and *Courier*. We add a separator to this menu and then add the item *Quit*. We repeat this process for a menu *ms* called *Style*, which contains the menu items *Plain, Bold, Italic,* and *BoldItalic*. After this is added to *mbar*, we do the same thing for a menu *mc* called *Color*, which contains the menu items *Black, Blue, Cyan,* and *Red*, and for the menu *mh*, called *Help*, which contains the menu items *Index* and *About*. object. Note that the method *add.Separator* adds a line that separates previous menu items from the ones that follow.

We detect the events caused by clicking the mouse on the list or choice items through the use of an *addActionListener* statement for each type. Each type of event is handled by an embedded *ActionListener* class through an *actionPerformed* method. This method for *Style* begins by using the method *getActionCommand* to return a string that contains the name of the selected item. If the string has the name *Plain* , we set the parameter *st* to 0. If the string has the name *Bold* , we set the parameter *st* to 1. If the string has the name *Italic*, we set the parameter *st* to 2. If the string has the name *BoldItalic*, we set the parameter *st* to 3. At the end of this method, we use *st* to reset the type style. The corresponding method for *Font* simply gets the name of the list item and uses it to reset the type font. The corresponding method for *Color* gets the name of the menu item and uses a series of *if* statements to set the text color to the proper color value. It then repaints the text to reset the type font. The corresponding method for *Help* enables us to select *Index* (which is not implemented to do anything) or *About*, which sets up a new window of program information. When all of the menubar items have been added to *mbar*, we set up the menu with the method *setMenuBar*. Looking at the items, you can see that we have a *Font* menu item whose submenu allows us to choose *Helvetica*, *TimesRoman*, or *Courier* type fonts, or to select *Quit*, which provides an alternative method for quitting the program. We have a *Style* menu item whose submenu allows us to select *Plain, Bold, Italic*, or *BoldItalic* type styles. We have a *Color* menu item whose submenu allows us to select type colors of black, blue, cyan, or red. We have the *Help* menu that allows us to select *Index* or *About*.

When we select one of the main menubar items, the display of the submenu is handled automatically. When we select any submenu item, an *action* event is initiated. For the submenu item *About* under *Help*, we set up a new window (of class *Canvas*), set its title and layout, add three cells of text of the *Label* class, size this window (it is smaller than the main window), and call *show* to display it. This window will now appear on the display when we select the submenu item *About*. Since we don't paint or repaint this window, we can make it disappear by triggering anywhere on the main window. Figure 6.4 shows an example of running the *MenuUse1* program.

Scrolling

If you are going to create text or graphics that are larger than the limits of your display window, you need to provide a scrolling capability that allows you to control what part of your data is within the display limits. The program listed

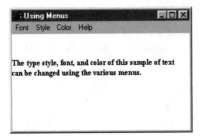

FIGURE *Menu Demonstration Program.*
6.4

in Listing 6.7 shows how this is done. We are going to create data that extends beyond the limits of the 300 × 200 pixels window in which we display it. This actual viewing window size is defined in the *main* method by calling *sc.set-Size();*. The sample program uses the *paint* method to create a block of text in the *TextCanvas* class. Each *g.drawString* call in this *paint* method specifies the

```
/*
   Scroller. ava
   Program to demonstrate scrolling.
*/

import   ava.awt.*;
import   ava.util.*;
import   ava.awt.event.*;

public class Scroller extends Frame
{
   Scroller()
   {
      super("Scroller Demonstration");
      canvas can = new canvas();
      ScrollPane sp = new ScrollPane();
      sp.add(can);
      add(sp);
      addWindowListener(new DWAdapter());
   }

   class DWAdapter extends WindowAdapter
   {
      public void windowClosing(WindowEvent event)
      {
         System.exit(0);
```

LISTING *Program to Show How Scrolling Is Used. (continues)*
6.7

```
        }

    }

    public static void main(String args[])
    {

        Scroller sc = new Scroller();
        sc.setSize(300,200);
        sc.show();
    }
}

class canvas extends Canvas
{
    Dimension preferredSize = new Dimension(600,400);

    public Dimension getPreferredSize()
    {
        return preferredSize;
    }

    public void paint(Graphics g)
    {
        g.drawString("This is a block of text that is
too big to fit in the window as we have sized
it",0,10);
        g.drawString("so we have to scroll if we are
interested in reading all of it, Even then",0,26);
        g.drawString("we can't see all of the text at
once. We scroll back and forth and back and
forth",0,42);
        g.drawString("to read complete lines. Finally,
we reach the bottom of the window but we haven't
read all the text yet ",0,58);
        g.drawString("so we scroll down a little and
then some more partial lines will then become
visible to us.",0,74);
        g.drawString("This is a block of text that is
too big to fit in the window as we have sized
it",0,90);
        g.drawString("so we have to scroll if we are
interested in reading all of it, Even then",0,106);
        g.drawString("we can't see all of the text at
once. We scroll back and forth and back and
forth",0,122);
        g.drawString("to read complete lines. Finally,
we reach the bottom of the window but we haven't
read all the text yet ",0,138);
```

LISTING *Program to Show How Scrolling Is Used. (continues)*
6.7

```
            g.drawString("so we scroll down a little and
    then some more partial lines will then become
    visible to us.",0,154);
            g.drawString("This is a block of text that is
    too big to fit in the window as we have sized
    it",0,170);
            g.drawString("so we have to scroll if we are
    interested in reading all of it, Even then",0,186);
            g.drawString("we can't see all of the text at
    once. We scroll back and forth and back and
    forth",0,202);
            g.drawString("to read complete lines. Finally,
    we reach the bottom of the window but we haven't
    read all the text yet ",0,218);
            g.drawString("so we scroll down a little and
    then some more partial lines will then become
    visible to us.",0,234);
            g.drawString("This is a block of text that is
    too big to fit in the window as we have sized
    it",0,250);
            g.drawString("so we have to scroll if we are
    interested in reading all of it, Even then",0,266);
            g.drawString("we can't see all of the text at
    once. We scroll back and forth and back and
    forth",0,282);
            g.drawString("to read complete lines. Finally,
    we reach the bottom of the window but we haven't
    read all the text yet ",0,298);
            g.drawString("so we scroll down a little and
    then some more partial lines will then become
    visible to us.",0,314);
        }
    }
```

LISTING *Program to Show How Scrolling Is Used. (continued)*
6.7

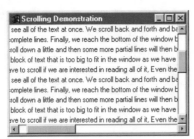

FIGURE *Demonstrating Scrolling*
6.5

coordinates of the beginning point for the string in absolute coordinates that begin with (0,0) at the top left of the display window. These coordinates need not be within the actual window size of 300 × 200 pixels. Early versions of Java required that you create scrollbars and a lot of software to cause mouse movements of the scrollbars to change the relative position of the display. The latest versions of Java have a *ScrollPane* class that takes care of all these operations for you. We create a *Scroller* class that is an extension of *Frame* and add to it our canvas and scroll pane. The actual scrolling procedures are then taken care of automatically. Figure 6.5 shows a typical view in running this program.

7

Colors

W hen you used the *System.out.println* command to display data in Chapter 2, the resulting display was the standard white characters on a black background. Once you get into creating a display window with containers and components as described in Chapter 5 and want to produce some graphics displays, you're going to need some capability for color display. The Java 2D API provides support for producing high-quality color output that meets the needs of highly advanced color applications as well as simple color graphics applications. Usually, you'll be able to do everything that you want to with the default Java color settings. In this chapter, we're going to give an overall description of how Java handles color and then provide a more detailed description of how you can use Java's color handling ability to your best advantage.

How Java Defines Colors

Java 2D manages colors through three key color management classes: *Color-Space, Color,* and *ColorModel.* A color space is so-called because a particular color is defined by three coordinates, thus corresponding to the three coordinates that define a point in three-dimensional space. Java 2D supports two color *spac*es, the CIEXYZ color space and the sRGB color space. The former is an internationally defined device-independent color space. It is capable of very precise color definition, but the complexity of the color transforms needed to translate colors to the device-dependent color spaces such as those for monitors or color printers is burdensome. Furthermore, the only way in which you can be sure that the color relationships are exactly maintained is to attach a profile of the input color space to a transmitted image and compare it with the output. This substantially increases the size of the file being transmitted.

The sRGB color space, while not completely device independent, is based on a calibrated colorimetric and is well suited to use with color monitors and printers. This color space is quite similar to the way in which colors have been defined in the color television industry for years. It has been defined as a standard through the efforts of Hewlett-Packard and Microsoft. A *ColorSpace* object defines a system for measuring colors using three or more separate numerical values. Each *ColorSpace* object must be capable of converting a color in its system to the sRGB color space (through the *toRGB* method) or converting the color from the sRGB color space to that of the defined *ColorSpace* object (through the *fromRGB* method.). The *ColorSpace* class also has the methods *toCIEXYZ* and *fromCIEXYZ* to permit conversions to and from the *CIEXYZ* color space. Java also has an implementation of the *ColorSpace* class called *ICC_ColorSpace,* which supports the device-independent color space defined by the International Color Consortium. Java uses the sRGB color space by default. Most program developers will find that this default color space will meet all of their requirements; unless you have some very unique color requirements, you can ignore all of the above and just work with the default setup.

Using the default color space, the Java *Color* class defines a color in terms of its red, green, and blue components. There are three ways of doing this. The one most familiar to those who have worked with a PC SVGA or VGA is the constructor:

```
public Color(int r, int g, int b);
```

Each of these integers must be in the range 0 to 255. The integer *r* is the red component, *g* is the green component, and *b* is the blue component. For example, a light blue would be defined as:

```
public Color(84, 84, 255);
```

You'll remember that Java integers are 32 bits long, whereas we only need 8 bits of each integer to define each color component. Thus this constructor is very wasteful of memory. This technique is capable of defining 16,777,216 shades of color. Normally, the human eye cannot display this many shades of color, so a picture whose colors are digitally defined by this method does not suffer any degradation. However, we are talking here about how Java stores color information. When the Java interpreter transfers color data to your particular computer, the number of colors actually displayed may be a lot different. In particular, if you are using Windows 95/98, you will have chosen a particular display mode to be used by Windows. If you don't know what setting you are using, click the Windows 95/98 *Start* button. Then select *Settings* and *Control Panel*. Double-click on the *Display* icon and from the resulting display choose the *Settings* tab. You'll see an item labeled *Color Palette* that will tell you what your current color setting is. If you have a *Color Palette* setting that is capable of 32K color or more, any Java color display should work just fine. If your *Color Palette* setting is 16 colors or 256 colors, you are going to lose a lot when you try to display Java colors. If you want more shades of color than are available with your current setting, you can choose any other setting that is supported by your monitor and SVGA or VGA card. Remember that it is this setting that will determine how many shades of color are displayed on your screen. The Java interpreter will automatically modify its color information to conform with the number of colors supported by your color setting.

Another way of defining a color is shown by this constructor:

```
public Color(int rgb);
```

In this case, the integer *rgb* contains all three color components. You'll remember that a Java integer is 32 bits long. The red component (in the range from 0 to 255) is in bits 16 to 23 of the *rgb* integer, the green component in bits 8 to 15, and the blue component in bits 0 to 7. For example, the light blue color defined above, when written in binary would be 0101010001010100 11111111, which in ordinary integer form is 2,774,271.
A third way of defining a color is shown by this constructor:

```
public Color(float r, float g, float b);
```

In this case, each of the color components is in the range 0.0 to 1.0. (Remember that when you insert a decimal number into a statement it is taken as being of type *double*. To make it compatible with this version of *Color* you need to follow it with an *F*.

The Java Predefined Colors

We've seen that you can define a color in three different ways. For example, if you're using the *Graphics* object defined like this:

```
public void paint(Graphics g){...}
```

you can specify the color in which a figure is to be drawn by

```
g.setColor(Color(45,9,234);
```

However, Java also has 13 predefined standard colors. You can set one of them by using its name, like this:

```
g.setColor(Color.orange);
```

Table 7-1 shows the standard colors and their corresponding red, green, and blue components. (In other words, if you use the three numbers given for a standard color to set the color, you will get exactly the same color that you would by using the color name in the *setColor* statement.) You'll be able to use these preset colors for many of your applications, thereby simplifying the coding.

Table 7-1   Java Standard Colors.

Color Name	Red Component	Green Component	Blue Component
white	255	255	255
lightGray	192	192	192
gray	128	128	128
darkGray	64	64	64
black	0	0	0
red	255	0	0
pink	255	175	175
orange	255	200	0
yellow	255	255	0
green	0	255	0
magenta	255	0	255
cyan	0	255	255
blue	0	0	255

16-Color PC Displays

If you're familiar with the 16-color displays that once were all you could get from the early PCs, you'll note that there are some substantial differences between the Java colors and the PC colors. You might have occasion to create a display that uses these early colors. Table 7-2 shows the red, green, and blue components that make up the 16-color PC display colors. If you want to create a display that is made up of these colors, you need to include the following code in your *paint* method:

```
Color[] color = new Color[16];
color[0] = Color.black;
color[1] = new Color(0, 0, 168);
color[2] = new Color(0, 168, 0);
color[3] = new Color(0, 168, 168);
color[4] = new Color(168, 0, 0);
color[5] = new Color(168, 0, 168);
color[6] = new Color(168, 84, 0);
color[7] = new Color(168, 168, 168);
color[8] = new Color(84, 84, 84);
color[9] = new Color(84, 84, 255);
color[10] = new Color(84, 255, 84);
color[11] = new Color(84, 255, 255);
color[12] = new Color(255, 84, 84);
```

Table 7-2 Colors Used in DOS 16-Color Display.

Color	Number	Red Component	Green Component	Blue Component
Black	0	0	0	0
Blue	1	0	0	168
Green	2	0	168	0
Cyan	3	0	168	168
Red	4	168	0	0
Magenta	5	168	0	168
Brown	6	168	84	0
Light Gray	7	168	168	168
Dark Gray	8	84	84	84
Light Blue	9	84	84	255
Light Green	10	84	255	84
Light Cyan	11	84	255	255
Light Red	12	255	84	84
Light Magenta	13	255	84	255
Yellow	14	255	255	84
White	15	255	255	255

```
color[13] = new Color(255, 84, 255);
color[14] = new Color(255, 255, 84);
color[15] = Color.white;
```

You can now write a statement like:

```
g.setColor(color[6]);
```

to set up one of the 16 early PC colors.

256 Color VGA Displays

If you need to duplicate the 256 default colors used by SVGAs and VGAs in their 256-color modes, you can set up a *color* array just like that of the preceding paragraph except that the array has 256 members. You can find the proper components in any early book that describes the VGA in detail.

Setting Colors

There are three ways in which you can set up colors in Java. If you are working within a Component Object, you can use the expression *setBackground()*; to set the background color of the component. Similarly, you can use the expression *setForeground()* to set up the color in which any characters that you write in the component will appear. If you're using the *Graphics* class to draw some complex figures, you can use the expression *setColor()*. Using this expression repeatedly allows you to control the color of each thing that you draw with the *Graphics* class; if almost everything will be of the same color, you're better off using *setForeground()* in the Component before you begin drawing. Finally, if you're creating a Java *Image*, you build an array in which each pixel is represented by an integer that expresses its color and then the entire array is transformed into an *Image* object.

Color Gradients

Java 2D has a class called *GradientPaint*, that makes it possible to fill a *Shape* with a linear color gradient pattern. The class is passed parameters consisting of the x and y coordinates of a point P1 and its color C1 and the x and y coordinates of a point P2 and its color C2. The color of a Point on the line connecting P1 and P2 is proportionally changed from C1 and C2. To find the color of point P that is not on the connecting line, draw a line from P perpendicular to the connecting line and then color P the same as the color of point of intersection. A final optional parameter, if specified as *true* causes the colors to cycle back and forth between C1 and C2. If this parameter is *false*, all points before P1 are of the color C1 and all the points after P2 are of the color C2. Listing 7.1 shows a program that causes the colors to move back and forth, accentuating a headline. This might be suitable for an advertising page on the Web.

```java
/* GradBurst1.java
      Program to Generate Animated Gradient Burst
*/

import java.awt.*;
import java.awt.font.*;
import java.awt.event.*;
import java.awt.geom.Rectangle2D;
import javax.swing.*;

public class GradBurst1 extends JApplet implements
Runnable
{
   private Thread thread;
   float m1=.35f, m2=.65f, sgn=1.0f;
```

LISTING *Animated Gradient Burst Program. (continues)*
7.1

```java
public void GradBurst1()
{
}

public void start()
{
   thread = new Thread(this);
   thread.setPriority(Thread.MIN_PRIORITY);
   thread.start();
}

public synchronized void stop()
{
   thread = null;
}

public void run()
{
   Thread me = Thread.currentThread();
   while (thread == me)
   {
      repaint();

      m1 += sgn * .01;
      m2 -= sgn * .01;
      if ((m1 >= 1.0) || (m2 >= 1.0))
         sgn = -sgn;
      try
      {
         thread.sleep(5);
      }
      catch (InterruptedException e)
      {
         break;
      }
   }
   thread = null;
}

public void init()
{
   Demo demo = new Demo();
   getContentPane().add(demo);
}
public class Demo extends JPanel
{
   public Color innerColor, outerColor;

   public Demo()
```

LISTING *Animated Gradient Burst Program. (continues)*
7.1

```
    {
        setBackground(Color.white);

    }
        public void drawDemo(int w, int h, float
m1, float
            m2, Graphics2D g2)
    {
        float[] tlx = {0.0f, w, 0.0f, w};
        float[] tly = {0.0f, 0.0f, h, h};
        float[] limx = {m1*w, m2*w, m1*w,m2*w};
        float[] limy = {m1*h,m1*h,m2*h,m2*h};

        for (int i=0; i<4; i++)
        {
            Rectangle2D rect1 = new
                Rectangle2D.Float(tlx[i]/2, tly[i]/2,
w/2, h/2);

                GradientPaint gp =
            new GradientPaint(tlx[i],
tly[i],Color.orange,limx[i],limy[i],Color.red);
            g2.setPaint(gp);
            g2.fill(rect1);
        }

    g2.setColor(Color.black);
    Font ft = new Font("Helvetica", Font.BOLD,
36);
    setFont(ft);
    TextLayout tl = new TextLayout(
        "Latest Bargains!", ft,
g2.getFontRenderContext());
        tl.draw(g2, (int) (w/2-
tl.getBounds().getWidth()/2),
        (int) (h/2+tl.getBounds().getHeight()/2));
    }

    public void paint(Graphics g)
    {
        Graphics2D g2 = (Graphics2D) g;
        Dimension d = getSize();
        g2.setBackground(getBackground());
        g2.clearRect(0, 0, d.width, d.height);
        drawDemo(d.width, d.height, m1, m2, g2);
    }
}

public static void main(String argv[])
{
```

LISTING *Animated Gradient Burst Program. (continues)*
7.1

```
        final GradBurst1 demo = new GradBurst1();
        demo.init();
        JFrame f = new JFrame("Moving Color
Gradient");
        f.addWindowListener(new WindowAdapter() {
            public void windowClosing(WindowEvent e)
{System.exit(0);}
        });
        f.getContentPane().add("Center", demo);
        f.pack();
        f.setSize(new Dimension(400,300));
        f.show();
        demo.start();
    }
}
```

LISTING *Animated Gradient Burst Program. (continued)*

7.1

The heart of this program is the *drawDemo* method. This method contains a *for* loop that iterates four times, each time drawing a rectangle that is one quarter of the large rectangle that makes up the final display. The *tlx* and *tly* arrays define the top left corner of each of the rectangles and also the first point for each iteration of the *GradientPaint* method, which is associated with the color orange; the *w/2* and *h/2* are the width and height, respectively, of each rectangle. The *limx* and *limy* arrays define the second point for *GradientPaint*, which is associated with the color red. The final two statements in the *for* loop set up the *gp* object and fill each rectangle with the gradient colors. Note that the height and width of the large rectangle are passed to the *drawDemo* method as parameters, as are the variables *m1* and *m2*, which control the location of the second gradient point. The remainder of the *drawDemo* method creates the color and font for the text "Latest Bargains!" and paints it on the center of the screen. Next, we have the method *paint*, which creates a Java 2D graphics object *g2* and then sets the display size. Next, it resets the background, clears the rectangle, and then calls the *drawDemo* method.

The *main* program is about the same as those we've described for previous programs. The main differences are that it first initializes the program by setting up a new *demo* class and adding it to the display, and at its end calls *demo.start()*, which causes the thread to start running. The thread is defined under class *GradBurst1*, together with its *start, stop,* and *run* methods. The *start* method just gets the thread started, with minimum priority.

The *run* method is what is used to cause the color to cycle back and forth. The color begins with the center of the display red and the outskirts orange.

FIGURE *Animated Gradient Display.*
7.1

Each time the thread is run (which happens repeatedly as long as the program is running) the whole display is repainted. The parameters *m1* and *m2* are then changed, which moves the points P1 and P2, causing a change in the relative locations of red and orange the next time the display is repainted. The thread then sleeps awhile until it runs again. The two parameters of the gradient continue to change until either *m1* reaches 1 (display all red) or *m2* reaches 1 (display all orange), at which point the sign of the variable *sgn* is reversed, causing the changes in the two parameters to start moving in the opposite direction. The rate at which the display changes color is determined by the amount by which each of the two parameters is changed at each cycle of the thread and the amount of time during which the thread method sleeps before running again. Figure 7.1 is a static snapshot of the *GradBurst1* program, but you really need to run the application to enjoy the color change. This is not true animation, but it gives a motion effect to the display page. Similar techniques can be used to provide the appearance of all kinds of motions for Web pages.

8 Displaying Text in a Graphics Window

J ava enables you to interact with the font information in your computer system so as to be able to display or print text without having to resort to pixel-by-pixel representation of each character. In this chapter, we're first going to look at the text capabilities that were part of the original Java re lease. These were centered on a *drawString* method that enabled one to draw a character string on the screen, but required that the x and y coordinates of the string starting position be specified. Later in the chapter, we'll describe some improvements that are part of Java 2. These include ways that a long string of text can be broken up into lines that match the size of the window being displayed. Finally, Java Swing components include some additional, sophisticated ways of handling these items.

Drawing a Line of Characters

The basic tool used in drawing strings of characters to a graphics window is the method:

```
drawString(String s, int x, int y);
```

The parameter *s* is the name of a string of characters defined elsewhere, or you may place the string itself (enclosed in double quotes) in place of *s*. The integers *x* and *y* are the location of the top left corner of the string in pixels, measured from the top left corner of the graphics window. You may wonder how long a string you can draw using this technique. The answer is about as long as you want, but there is no wrap-around at the end of the display window. If your string is too long, it all gets written, but you will never see the part of it that's off the edge of the window. Of course, if you're using Windows 95/98, you can trigger the small rectangle at the upper left of your screen to display a full-screen window, which may be large enough to display the full string. Alternately, you can use the cursor to extend the screen width on the right-hand side and to reposition the screen as necessary and may in that way be able to see the end of the string.

A Text Program

Listing 8.1 shows a program that demonstrates how to use different type fonts and styles in a display and how to properly position text. You'll note that the general structure of the program (for example, the way it creates a *Frame* object and a *paint* method) is the same as the program listed in Chapter 4. The display window generated by this program is shown in Figure 8.1.

```
/*
   Text.java
   Program to Display Text in A Graphics Window
*/

import java.awt.*;
import java.awt.event.*;

public class Text extends Frame
{
private Font HelB18 = new Font("Helvetica",
     Font.BOLD, 18);
   private Font HelBIt18 = new Font("Helvetica",
     Font.BOLD + Font.ITALIC, 18);
   private Font Hel12 = new Font("Helvetica",
     Font.PLAIN, 12);;
   private Font TRB14 = new Font("TimesRoman",
     Font.BOLD, 14);;
   private Font TR12 = new Font("TimesRoman",
     Font.PLAIN, 12);;
   private Font TRIt12 = new Font("TimesRoman",
      Font.ITALIC, 12);;
   private Font Co12 = new Font("Courier",
     Font.PLAIN, 12);;
   private FontMetrics HelB18m;
   private FontMetrics HelBIt18m;
   private FontMetrics Hel12m;
   private FontMetrics TRB14m;
   private FontMetrics TR12m;
   private FontMetrics TRIt12m;
   private FontMetrics Co12m;
   private boolean setFonts = false;

   Text()
   {
       super("Using Text in a Graphics Window");
       addWindowListener(new DWAdapter());
   }

   class DWAdapter extends WindowAdapter
   {
          public void windowClosing(WindowEvent
 event)
          {
              System.exit(0);
          }
   }

   public void paint(Graphics g)
```

LISTING *Program to Display Text in a Graphics Window. (continues)*
8.1

```
    {
        if (!setFonts)
        {
            HelB18m = g.getFontMetrics(HelB18);
            HelBIt18m = g.getFontMetrics(HelBIt18);
            Hel12m = g.getFontMetrics(Hel12);
            TRB14m = g.getFontMetrics(TRB14);
            TR12m = g.getFontMetrics(TR12);
            TRIt12m = g.getFontMetrics(TRIt12);
            Co12m = g.getFontMetrics(Co12);
            setFonts = true;
        }
        String s1 = "A ";
        String s2 = "Helvetica Bold ";
        String s3 = "Headline";
        String s4 =
         "We can have plain text under the
headline.";
        String s5 = "A Smaller Headline in Times
Roman";
        String s6 = "We can use ";
        String s7 = "Times Roman ";
        String s8 = "for text also.";
        String s9 = "This is a sample of Courier.";
        int width1 = HelB18m.stringWidth(s1);
        int width2 = HelBIt18m.stringWidth(s2);
        int width3 = HelB18m.stringWidth(s3);
        int width4 = Hel12m.stringWidth(s4);
        int width5 = TRB14m.stringWidth(s5);
        int width6 = TR12m.stringWidth(s6);
        int width7 = TRIt12m.stringWidth(s7);
        int width8 = TR12m.stringWidth(s8);
        int width9 = Co12m.stringWidth(s9);
        Dimension dim = getSize();
        Insets inner = getInsets();
        int x, y, s_width;

        g.drawString("This long string of text is
designed to show what happens when the length of a
line exceeds the space in the window available to
display it.", 0, 50);
        s_width = dim.width - inner.right -
inner.left;
        x = (s_width - width1 - width2 - width3) /
2;
        g.setFont(HelB18);
        g.drawString(s1, x, 80);
        x += width1;
        g.setFont(HelBIt18);
```

LISTING *Program to Display Text in a Graphics Window. (continues)*
8.1

```
            g.drawString(s2, x, 80);
            x += width2;
            g.setFont(HelB18);
            g.drawString(s3, x, 80);
            x = (s_width - width4) /2;
            g.setFont(Hel12);
            g.drawString(s4, x, 100);
            x = (s_width - width5) /2;
            g.setFont(TRB14);
            g.drawString(s5, x, 130);
            x = (s_width - width6 - width7 - width8) /
     2;
            g.setFont(TR12);
            g.drawString(s6, x, 150);
            x += width6;
            g.setFont(TRIt12);
            g.drawString(s7, x, 150);
            x += width7;
            g.setFont(TR12);
            g.drawString(s8, x, 150);
            x = (s_width - width9) / 2;
            g.setFont(Co12);
            g.drawString(s9, x, 170);
        }

    public static void main(String args[])
    {
        Text f = new Text();
        f.setSize(600, 400);
        f.show();
    }
 }
```

LISTING *Program to Display Text in a Graphics Window. (continued)*
8.1

Selecting a Font   The long string of text created in the listing by the first use of the *drawString* method uses the default font setting. What you see in the display is what you get as far as font, style, and type size if you do not specify any font in particular. If you want other than the default font, you can specify just about any font you wish. If you're programming only for your own computer installation, there is no problem; just select a font name corresponding to one that is installed in your system and you can set up the program to faithfully display text in that font. If you're programming for an unknown system, such as if you're writing an applet for use on the Net, the font you specify may not be available, in which case the system selects one of its available fonts which it thinks is the best match for the font name that you have specified. The result may be quite

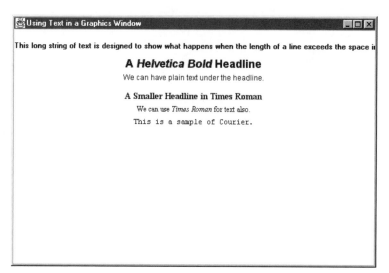

different from what you expect. If you stick to such standard fonts as *Helvetica*, *Times Roman*, or *Courier*, they are likely to be understood by almost any system and you will avoid unpleasant surprises.

Now, let's see how we specify a font. First, in the class you are using to create your window, normally by extending the *Frame* class (*Text*, in this case), you need to define an object of class *Font* for each font you need. We've defined seven of these in the listing and classified each one as *private*, so it can be accessed only by methods of the *Text* class. Each is initialized when it is defined. However, when we initialize the metrics for each of these fonts. we need to use a method of the *Graphics* class. This can conveniently be done in the *paint* method, but we need to bear in mind that *paint* can run many times, while we only need to perform the initialization once. Consequently, we define a boolean parameter *setFonts* in the *Text* class definition and initialize it as *false*. Each time *paint* runs, we use an *if* statement to determine the state of *setFonts*. The first time, it is false, so we initialize all of the font metrics and then change *setFonts* to *true*, so that on any future passes through *paint* the font metric initialization is skipped.

A new object of class *Font* is initialized with three parameters. The first is the name of the font in double quotation marks ("Helvetica", "TimesRoman", and so forth). Note that if the font name contains two or more words, in this parameter the words are not separated by spaces. The second parameter is the type style. Acceptable entries are *Font.PLAIN, Font.BOLD, Font.ITALIC*, and *Font.BOLD + Font.ITALIC*. The third parameter is the size of the font in points. A point is a printer's measure of type size, where 72 points equal 1 inch. Thus, 12-point type is 1/6 of an inch high. Normal type size for books is from 10 to 12 points, with 12-point type giving a page that can be comfortably read by most people. If you try displaying and then printing the text generated by Listing 8.1, you'll see that while the 12-point size is great for reading a printed page, you usually need something larger on a display screen.

Now that we have an initialized object of class *Font* for each combination of font name, style, and size that we want, we can use the *Graphics* class method *setFont*, with the proper *Font* object passed to it, to set up for displaying text with that font, style, and size. From the time *setFont* is called, every call to the *drawString* method uses these type characteristics until another *setFont* call is encountered. Note that the *x* parameter in *drawString* may take on negative values; if it does, the string starts at the left-hand edge of the window.

Text Positioning

Some computer languages make text writing easy by automatically wrapping a line of text around to the next display line when the end of a window is reached and by storing the location of the end of a section of text that is written so that the next call to write text can start writing where the previous one left off. Java does not do either of these things. The Java *drawString* method specifies a precise location for the beginning of the string and this must be determined for each call to *drawString*. If we're going to write several consecutive text strings in Java, we need to know the exact width of each string. Since the width of each character in each font may be different, obtaining this width is not a trivial task. The first thing to note is that if we are concerned with string widths, we cannot insert the string directly into the *drawString* method. Instead, we must define the string separately and pass only its name to *drawString*. Next, to get string widths, we need to make use of the class *FontMetrics*. In fact, we need an object of the *FontMetrics* class for every font that we have defined. In the listing, you'll see that at the beginning we have defined a *private* object of Class *FontMetrics* for each font, its name being the same as the corresponding font name followed by an *m*. Based upon what you've seen of Java thus far, you might think that we would now initialize each *FontMetrics* object by using *new* and specifying a font name—things don't work that way in this particular situation. Instead, we set the *FontMetrics* object equal to the return from the *Graphics* class method *getFontMetrics*, which has the font object passed to it. You can see this happening in the listing at the beginning of the *paint* method, just below where we've initialized the fonts. The code is included in the *if* statement so that it only is run the first time *paint* is called.

Next, you'll see that we have defined nine strings (*s1* through *s9*) that we're going to use to create our text display. Below this, we've defined *width1* through *width9*, each of which uses the appropriate *FontMetrics* object and the method *stringWidth* (with the string as the passed parameter) to return and store the width of the associated string. Next, we define *dim* of class *Dimension* and set it equal to the return from *size* which is a method of *Component*, the parent class of *Frame*. This now contains the width and height of the display window. We also define *inner* of class *Insets* and set it equal to the return from *insets*, which is another method of *Component*. It returns the amount of space used for borders, titles, and so forth. at the *top, bottom, left,* and *right* of the window.

Before drawing any strings with fonts, we set up a value for *s_width*. This is the space available within the window for drawing and is equal to the width of the window (*dim.width*) less the space already used on the left and right (*inner.left* and *inner.right*). We are next about to draw a line of text that consists of three strings. We want this text to be centered horizontally in the display window. To find the starting position, we subtract the length of the three strings from the available width and divide by 2. We then set the font and draw the first string. We now change the starting position by moving right by the length of the first string and then change the font and draw the second string. We then change the starting position again by moving right by the length of the second string and then change the font and draw the third string. A similar procedure is used for drawing the other strings. Incidently, *FontMetrics* has a *getHeight* method that determines the standard height of your font, and a *getLeading* method that determines the standard leading (inter-line spacing) of your font. You can use these in planning the *y* values to pass to the *drawString* method if you so desire.

Word Wrap with Java 2

Word wrap is a feature of word processors that allows you to keep typing continuously without having to insert a carriage return at the end of each line. The software automatically determines when the end of a line is reached and causes the text to advance to the beginning of the next line. When applied to text in a window, we need to be aware that the size of the window can be changed by the user so that not only must the software determine the line endings for the original display, but it must also reposition the text each time the window size is changed. Listing 8.2 is a program that demonstrates how this is done.

```
/*
   ManyLines. ava
   Program to display many lines of text
*/

import  ava.awt.*;
import  ava.util.*;
import  ava.awt.event.*;
import  avax.swing.*;
import  ava.awt.font.*;
import  ava.text.*;

public class ManyLines extends Frame
{
    private LineBreakMeasurer lineMeasurer;
    private int paragraphStart;
    private int paragraphEnd;

    ManyLines()
    {
       super("Displaying Many Lines of Text");
       addWindowListener(new DWAdapter());
    }

    class DWAdapter extends WindowAdapter
    {
       public void windowClosing(WindowEvent event)
       {
          System.exit(0);
       }
    }

    public void paint(Graphics g)
    {
       Graphics2D graphics2D = (Graphics2D) g;
       AttributedString ats = new
AttributedString("This is the beginning of a sample
of text that is to be used in testing the display
action of this program. Hopefully a paragraph will
be printed out with the proper font, type size,
style and suitable line breaks. Java does not yet
support line  ustification, but is otherwise capable
of properly positioning type for a good printed
paragraph.");
```

LISTING *Program to Demonstrate Word Wrap. (continues)*
8.2

```
        Font theFont = new Font("TimesRoman",
Font.BOLD, 18);
        ats.addAttribute(TextAttribute.FONT, theFont,
20, 100);
        AttributedCharacterIterator paragraph =
        ats.getIterator();

    FontRenderContext frc =
        graphics2D.getFontRenderContext();
    paragraphStart = paragraph.getBeginIndex();
    paragraphEnd = paragraph.getEndIndex();
    lineMeasurer = new LineBreakMeasurer(paragraph,
frc);
    Dimension size = getSize();
    float formatWidth = (float) size.width- 20;
    float drawPosY = 30;
    float drawPosX = 10;
    lineMeasurer.setPosition(paragraphStart);
    while (lineMeasurer.getPosition() < paragraphEnd)
    {
        TextLayout layout =
            lineMeasurer.nextLayout(formatWidth);
        drawPosY += layout.getAscent();
        layout.draw(graphics2D, drawPosX, drawPosY);
        drawPosY += layout.getDescent() +
            layout.getLeading();
    }
    }
    public static void main(String args[])
    {
        ManyLines f = new ManyLines();
        f.setSize(300,200);
        f.show();
    }
}
```

LISTING *Program to Demonstrate Word Wrap. (continued)*
8.2

The *ManyLines* class and the *main* program are very similar to those in other program examples we have shown. All that is new is included in the *paint* method. First, we set up an object *graphics2D* of class *Graphics2D*. Next, we set up an object *ats* of the class *AttributedString*, which is initialized to contain the entire string of text that we want to display. In the listing printed in this chapter, the text string is distributed over several lines, but this is only because the book page isn't wide enough to contain it all; when writing or copying the program all the text should be in a single continuous line. We then define a new *Font* class object called *theFont*. We then add this as an attribute to *ats*. The first parameter passed to this attribute adding method is *TextAttribute.FONT*, which tells the method that we are assigning it font information. The second parameter is *theFont*, which passes it the description of this font. The third parameter is a number that represents the number of the first character in the string that is to be written with these font characteristics. The fourth parameter is the number in the string of the last character that is to be written with these fon characteristics. We now create an object *paragraph* of class *AttributedCharacterIterator*. We need the text to be in this class's format to use with the methods that determine when line breaks occur. We then create an object *frc* of class *FontRenderContent* and fill it with the information that is needed about the font to calculate line breaks.

Now we are ready to calculate the actual line lengths. First we set up objects *paragraphStart* and *paragraphEnd* and fill them with data on the beginning and end of the text. We then set up the object *lineMeasurer* of class *LineBreakMeasurer*, which is the critical object in determining where line breaks occur. We now set up the object *size* of class *Dimension*, get the size of the window, and place it in this object. The parameter *drawPosY* determines the vertical position where we begin to write text. If you set it to 0, we start at the very top of the window and our first line of text may be partially covered by the title. Consequently, in this program we set it at 30, to be sure the first line is visible. Similarly, each line of text will begin at the horizontal position determined by *drawPosX*. When set to 0, this will cause each line to begin at the very left-hand edge of the window, which might cause the first character of each line to be partially obscured by the window border. We've thus set it to 10 to move the beginning of each line a little to the right. The next parameter to be defined, *formatWidth*, if set to the width of the window would cause a line the exact width of the window to be drawn. Since we've already displaced each line a bit from the left window edge, such a width would cause us to lose characters at the right window edge. Thus we make this smaller than the window width by 20 pixels so there'll be a little room at each side.

We now set *lineMeasurer* at the beginning of the text and enter a *while* loop. At each iteration through the loop, *lineMeasurer* gets the position in the *AttributedCharacterIterator* paragraph that moves forward one line length of text for the current window from the current position of *lineMeasurer*. This text is then put in the object *layout*, which is of class *TextLayout*. The method *layout.draw* then causes this text to be displayed on the screen. The parameter *drawPosY* is then moved down by the height of the type font plus the leading (extra space between lines). The *while* loop keeps doing this to produce additional lines of text until the value of *lineMeasurer* becomes greater than the end of the text string (*para-*

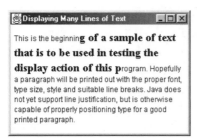

FIGURE   *Displaying Many Lines with Java 2D.*
8.2

graphEnd), at which point the loop terminates. Figure 8.2 shows the resulting display. Now let's see what happens when the user uses the mouse click-and-drag capabilities to expand the width of the window. The result is shown in Figure 8.3. You'll note that the program automatically rewrites the text in the new window, with the line lengths changed to properly fit the new window width.

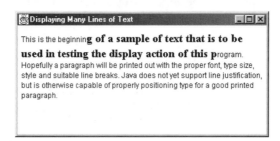

FIGURE   *Displaying Many Lines with Java 2D After the User Has Stretched the*
8.3   *Window.*

Building a Swing Text Menubar

In Chapter 6, we learned how to create a menubar and a series of menus using the original Java AWT methods. However, that menubar wouldn't work with the Applet class. Java Swing has a set of menubar and menu components that will work with the Applet class as well as with the Frame class. In addition, it has some advanced components for working with text that permit text handling to be much simplified. Listing 8.3 is a program to create a menubar and operate on text with these new components.

The constructor for *MenuUser* begins by creating a *DefaultStyledDocument* object called *lpd* and a *JtextPane* object called *textPane*. It then sets up the document and establishes its margins. The size of the text pane is then set up. Finally, the object *contentPane* of class *Jpanel* is set up to contain the window for display. The remainder of this constructor is used to create the menubar. A method is called to create each menu and then the menu is added to the menubar.

```
/*
   MenuUser. ava
   Program to Manipulate Text Characteristics with a
Menu Bar
*/

import   ava.awt.*;
import   ava.awt.event.*;
import   avax.swing.*;
import   avax.swing.text.*;
import   avax.swing.event.*;

public class MenuUser extends JApplet
{
   JTextPane textPane;
   DefaultStyledDocument lpd;

   public MenuUser ()
   {
      lpd = new DefaultStyledDocument();
      textPane = new JTextPane();
      textPane.setDocument(lpd);
      textPane.setMargin(new Insets(5,5,5,5));
      textPane.setPreferredSize(new Dimension(300,
150));
      JPanel contentPane = new JPanel(new
BorderLayout());
      contentPane.add(textPane,
BorderLayout.CENTER);
      setContentPane(contentPane);
      JMenuBar mb = new JMenuBar();
      JMenu styleMenu = createStyleMenu();
      mb.add(styleMenu);
      JMenu fontMenu = createFontMenu();
      mb.add(fontMenu);
      JMenu sizeMenu = createSizeMenu();
      mb.add(sizeMenu);
      JMenu colorMenu = createColorMenu();
      mb.add(colorMenu);
      setJMenuBar(mb);
      initDocument();
   }

   protected JMenu createStyleMenu()
   {
      JMenu menu = new JMenu("Style");
      Action action = new
StyledEditorKit.BoldAction();
      action.putValue(Action.NAME, "Bold");
```

LISTING *Using a Swing Menubar to Work with Text. (continues)*
8.3

```
        menu.add(action);
        action = new StyledEditorKit.ItalicAction();
        action.putValue(Action.NAME, "Italic");
        menu.add(action);
        action = new
StyledEditorKit.UnderlineAction();
        action.putValue(Action.NAME, "Underline");
        menu.add(action);

        return menu;
    }

    protected JMenu createFontMenu()
    {
        JMenu menu = new JMenu("Font");
        menu.add(new
StyledEditorKit.FontFamilyAction("Serif",
            "Serif"));
        menu.add(new
StyledEditorKit.FontFamilyAction("SansSerif",
"SansSerif"));return menu;
    }

    protected JMenu createSizeMenu()
    {
        JMenu menu = new JMenu("Size");
        menu.add(new
StyledEditorKit.FontSizeAction("12", 12));
        menu.add(new
StyledEditorKit.FontSizeAction("14", 14));
        menu.add(new
StyledEditorKit.FontSizeAction("18", 18));

        return menu;
    }

    protected JMenu createColorMenu()
    {
        JMenu menu = new JMenu("Color");
        menu.add(new
StyledEditorKit.ForegroundAction("Black",
            Color.black));
        menu.add(new
StyledEditorKit.ForegroundAction("Blue",
            Color.blue));
        menu.add(new
StyledEditorKit.ForegroundAction("Cyan",
            Color.cyan));
```

LISTING *Using a Swing Menubar to Work with Text. (continues)*
8.3

```
      menu.add(new
StyledEditorKit.ForegroundAction("Red",
        Color.red));

      return menu;
  }

  protected void initDocument()
  {
     String initString =
        "The font, style, color, and size of this
type can be changed using the menus at the top of
this display.";
     Style def = textPane.addStyle("default",
     textPane.getLogicalStyle());
     StyleConstants.setFontSize(def, 16);
     StyleConstants.setFontFamily(def,
"SansSerif");
     try
     {
        lpd.insertString(lpd.getLength(),
initString,
           textPane.getStyle("default"));

     }
     catch (BadLocationException ble)
     {
        System.err.println("Couldn't insert initial
text.");
     }
  }

  public static void main(String[] args)
  {
     JFrame frame = new JFrame("Using Menus");
     final MenuUser demo = new MenuUser();
     frame.getContentPane().add(demo);
     frame.addWindowListener(new WindowAdapter()
     {
        public void windowClosing(WindowEvent e)
        {
           System.exit(0);
        }
     });
     frame.pack();
     frame.setVisible(true);
  }
}
```

LISTING *Using a Swing Menubar to Work with Text. (continued)*

8.3

Now let's look at a typical menu creation method. The method *createStyle-Menu* begins by setting up a new menu and giving it the title "Style". Next, we define an object *action* of class *Action* to be the *StyledEditorKit.BoldAction*. Following this, we call the *action.PutValue* method, passing it the parameters *Action.NAME* and *Bold*. This *action* object is then added to the menu. These predetermined text control objects handle the necessary changing if the type style to bold when the "Bold" menu item is selected without our having to write a specific program to do this. Similar statements are then set up for the menu items "Italic" and "Underline". Similar methods are also used to make up the type family name menu, the type size menu, and the color menu.

The *initDocument* method sets up the initial characteristics for the type and copies the string to *textPane* with the proper characteristics. If the text couldn't be properly initialized. The *main* program names the display, points it to the window, and handles the window closing action.

Figure 8.4 shows the display that results from running this program. To control the characteristics of the displayed text, the user clicks the mouse at the beginning of the portion of text that is to be changed and then holds the mouse button down while dragging to the end of the section of text to be changed. That portion of the text will now appear shaded. Then the user clicks on a menu and then on a menu item within that menu. The shaded portion of text will be changed as requested. The predefined methods will take care of changing and repainting without any further action by the programmer. Sometimes, particularly with certain font family designations, the program will not compile properly and clicking on a style menu subitem will also change the color. If this occurs, recompiling the program will usually clear up the problem.

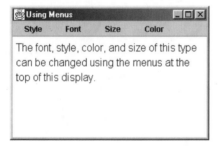

FIGURE *Swing Menubar Display.*
8.4

PLATE **1** *Check Boxes with Icons.*

PLATE **2** *Sample Display of JPG File.*

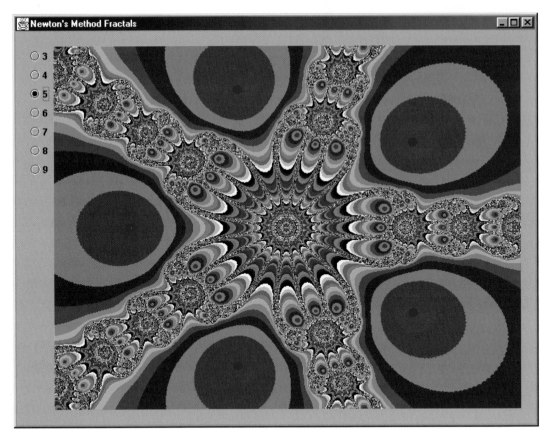

PLATE Fifth Order Newton's Method Fractal.
3

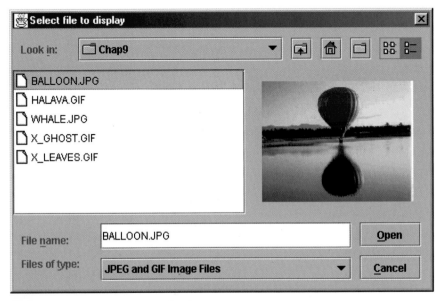

PLATE Displaying a GIF or JPG File—Directory.
4

PLATE *Displaying a GIF or JPG File—Image Display.*

5

PLATE *Displaying a BMP File.*

6

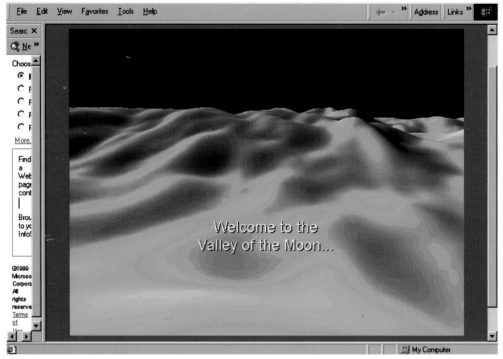

PLATE *Displaying a Voxel Landscape Image.*

7

PLATE *Displaying an Image with Lake Reflection.*

8

Applet Viewer: Page.class   _ □ ×

Applet

A Graphics Tip
By Roger T. Stevens

Have you ever been told that if you convert a JPEG graphics file to another format for editing and
then convert it back to JPEG again and repeat this several times, the accumulated loses of the JPEG
conversions will leave your picture unuseable? This is simply not true. True, the first JPEG
conversion causes some loss of detail, but succeeding conversions cause no additional losses because
the algorithm attempts to remove the very same detail that was already removed by the first conversion.
That detail is already gone. Nothing else is removed. To demonstrate this, I took a BMP graphics file
and converted it to JPEG. The resulting picture is shown below on the left. I then converted this file
back to BMP format and then converted back to JPEG again and repeated this process 20 times. The
JPEG picture is shown below on the right. As you can see, there is no discernible difference in quality
after 20 JPEG conversions.

Applet started.

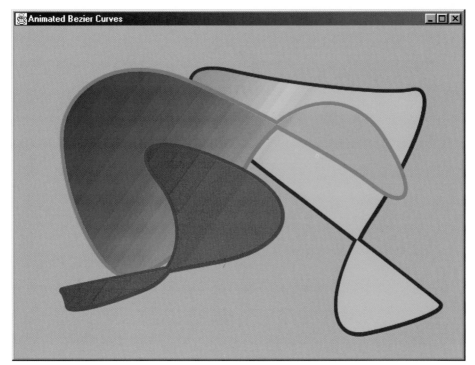

PLATE **11** *Animated Bezier Curves.*

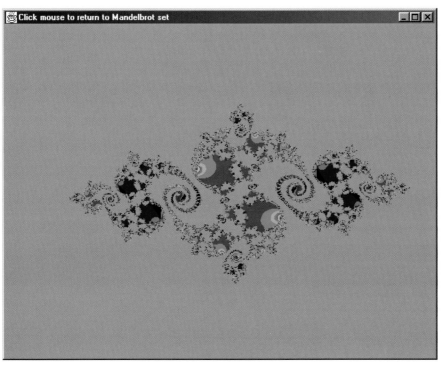

PLATE **12** *A Julia Set Image.*

Golden Gate | Rocks | Rose

PLATE
13
Running Two Threads Simultaneously.

PLATE
14
Animated Ellipses.

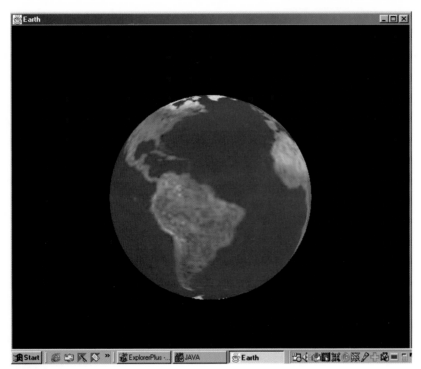

PLATE
15
Three Dimensional Sphere with Texture.

PLATE
16
Three Dimensional Shapes.

CHAPTER

9 Working with Images

J AVA has the capability to create and display image files without the programmer having to create a lot of specialized code. With simple Java commands, you can read, decode, and display graphics files in the *GIF* and *JPG* formats, the two formats most often used to store graphics images for the Internet. Java handles these files in a fast and efficient manner. In addition, you can create your own image files and display them immediately if this is more effective than displaying ready stored graphics files. The following sections show you how to use this capability.

The Graphics Interchange Format *(GIF)*

Graphics Interchange Format and *GIF* are trademarks of CompuServe, Incorporated, an H&R Block Company. If you're interested in the details of this format, you can download the latest specification for the *.GIF* format from CompuServe or from many local bulletin boards. It is in the file GIF89A.ARC. *GIF* files use Lempel-Ziv–Welch (LZW) compression, a highly effective method for compressing many kinds of graphics data. The *GIF* technique reads the screen pixel by pixel rather than on a memory plane oriented basis, a technique that works well with 256 color modes. *GIF* files are only capable of handling 256 different colors, which limits their capability to reproduce full color photographs. However, many photographs and graphics images have a limited number of colors; you'll be surprised at what good images you can produce using the *GIF* format. *GIF* encoding is somewhat slow, speed of encoding having been sacrificed for small file size. The *LZW* technique uses a table of character strings, together with a code assigned to each. Instead of storing each character string, only the codes are stored. The table is generated as the data is scanned, the strings being those encountered in the actual data. For decompression, the table can be regenerated from the stored compressed data and used to recreate the original file, so the table need not be saved. If the table gets filled, it is simply discarded and a new table begun for the succeeding data.

Originally, anyone could use the *.GIF* format to create and decode highly compressed files. As the format became popular, however, CompuServe began to feel that they should be trying to obtain sum remuneration for its use. Ironically, the *LPZ* compression used in *.GIF* was patented by Unisys. A long legal battle ensued, which was finally won by Unisys, and now anyone who wants to write a program for encoding or decoding using the *LZW* technique must pay Unisys a royalty. But luckily for the ordinary user, such software is already incorporated in Java (a responsibility assumed by Sun Microsystems), so that your use of Java to operate upon *GIF* programs does not make you responsible for any payments.

JPEG File Exchange Format

The Joint Photographic Experts Group (JPEG) is an international standards organization that was originally set up to produce a set of industry standards for the transmission of digital graphics and image data. *JPEG* provides a compression technique that works with grayscale or color continuous-tone images such as photographs with colors represented by 6 to 24 bits. It doesn't work well with line drawings. Most of the files that you'll find using the *JPEG* format have the extension *.JPG* so you'll often find this file format called the *JPG* format. It differs from other graphics formats in several important ways. First, it is not a single algorithm, but is a collection of compression methods that are combined to produce the final graphics file. *JPG* files use a variety of ways to compress photographic data. The technique begins by transforming the image to the most effective color space. It then downsamples chrominance components, averaging groups of pixels to reduce resolution for chrominance components to which the eye is less sensitive. A Discrete Cosine Transformation is then applied to each 8×8 pixel block, and a *quantization coefficient* is applied to each block to reduce high frequency information. Finally, Huffman encoding is applied to remove redundant data. The result is a good representation of a full color photograph using up to 24 bits per pixel of original color information. The only drawbacks are that the process can use a lot of computer time and that the process is lousy; that is, some picture information is lost during the compression process and never can be recovered. If you are creating a new graphic that is limited to a particularly sized storage space, the additional resolution that you can get from using the *JPEG* format provides an increase in quality that more than offsets any effects caused by losses in the compression technique. Finally, the *JPEG* technique allows the user to specify a quality factor when compressing an image, usually on a scale of 1 to 100. The smaller the number, the higher the compression and the poorer the decompressed image quality. For optimum results a little cut-and-try is necessary. A good place to begin is with a setting of 75; if the resulting image quality is unacceptable, you should increase the quality factor; if it is okay, you may want to decrease the quality factor to see if you can get more compression with an image that is still acceptable.

For color pictures, the first step in *JPG* encoding is to transform the color space of the image. The most widely used color system is RGB (Red-Green-Blue). These three colors, when added together in the proper proportions, can represent any color of an image. Another color system is CMY (Cyan-Magenta-Yellow). This is a subtractive color system used by printers and in producing color slides or prints on layers of emulsions. Each color layer subtracts some proportion of its color from white light. When all subtractions are complete, we have a pixel having the color of the remaining light. Another color system is HSV (Hue-Saturation-Value). In this system, H specifies the actual color, S specifies the amount of white in a hue, and V specifies the brightness of the color. All of the color systems spread their visual information evenly across the three parameters so that if you wish to compress by removing some information, you have to operate equally on each of the three components. On the other hand, with the YCbCr color system, the luminance component (Y) contains the high frequency gray-scale information to which the eye is most sensitive, while the two chrominance components (Cb and Cr) contain high-frequency color information to which the eye is much less sensitive. Consequently, much of the Cb and Cr information can be discarded in compressing without the eye seeing much difference. The first step in *JPG* compression of color images is therefore to convert the image, if it is in one of the first three color representations, into a YCbCr color space.

Next, the *JPG* compression system downsamples the chrominance components (Cb and Cr) by combining them into 2 × 2 pixel blocks and storing only the average Cb and Cr value of each block. The result is a 50% decrease in required data storage volume with almost no effect on the perceived quality of the image by the eye.

The next step in *JPG* compression is to divide the each color component of the image into blocks of 8 × 8 pixels and process each block by applying a Discrete Cosine Transform (DCT). This converts each block from a spatial representation to a representation in the frequency domain. The output is a set of 64 frequency coefficients. This is the most complex and time-consuming step in the *JPG* compression process. The frequency data is then divided by a *quantization factor* (which is determined by the quality factor discussed earlier) and each result is rounded off to an integer. The result is that many of the higher-frequency components are rounded off to zero (the lower the quality factor, the more zeroes are produced). Next, the DC coefficient at (0,0) is changed from an absolute value to a value relative to the previous block. Since color changes from one block to the next are apt to be small, this results in a much smaller number to store. The 64 frequencies are then scanned in a zig-zag fashion to reorder them with the DC component first and the remaining components in order of ascending frequency. Finally, the block is encoded by run-length-encoding the zeroes and then Huffman encoding the resulting data. To convert a *JPG* graphics file back to data suitable for display, all of the processes just discussed need to be reversed.

A Simple *JPEG* File Viewing Program

Listing 9.1 shows a very simple program for displaying a *JPEG* graphics file. It consists of only a *main* program for the class *FrameDemo*. The program begins by opening a new frame, *frame*, and giving it a title. We then add our usual *WindowListener* to take care of shutting down the program. Then, a new label is created. The parameters passed to *label* are the title, an icon to be added to the label, and the label position. Fortunately, the label doesn't care what size the *JPEG* file that is called by *NewIcon* is; it simply creates an image of the size specified by the *JPEG* file. In this case, our *JPEG* file is large enough to fill the entire window. We then set the position for the text part of the label and then display the label text and picture. Note that you must have the correct name of the *JPEG* file and that this file must be in the same subdirectory as your *FrameDemo.java*. If you have a *GIF* file instead of a *JPEG* file, the program will work equally well, as long as you have the proper file name inserted into the program. Plate 2 shows the result of running this program.

```
import  ava.awt.*;
import  ava.awt.event.*;
import  avax.swing.*;

public class FrameDemo {

    public static void main(String s[])
    {
      JFrame frame = new JFrame("A Basic Frame");
      frame.addWindowListener(new WindowAdapter()
      {
         public void windowClosing(WindowEvent e)
         {
            System.exit(0);
         }
      });
      JLabel label = new JLabel("Portrait of a
Puppy",
           new ImageIcon("Vandy. pg"), JLabel.CENTER);
      label.setVerticalTextPosition(JLabel.TOP);

label.setHorizontalTextPosition(JLabel.CENTER);
      frame.getContentPane().add(label,
BorderLayout.CENTER);
      frame.pack();
      frame.setVisible(true);
    }
}
```

LISTING *Simple Program for Displaying a JPEG File.*
9.1

Creating Your Own Image File

We've just gone through the process of converting a compressed graphics image file in the *JPEG* format into a Java image and then displaying that image, all with a few very simple lines of code. But what if we want to generate our own image from scratch? The actual format and display is almost as simple as the previous program. You collect your picture in an array of integers representing pixel colors, then convert them to a Java image, and then use the *ImageIcon* method to get them into displayable form. The mechanics of computing every point on the display are a lot more complicated than producing the display itself. We're now going to show you a complete program that demonstrates these techniques.

We all know that a line is a figure of one dimension. But what if we draw a line that goes round and round in a convoluted path until it completely fills a plane? According to Euclidian geometry, this is still a figure in one dimension, but intuitively we feel that in filling a plane it must be two dimensional. For such figures, where Euclidian dimensionality seems to fail us, mathematicians can assign a dimension called the *Hausdorff-Besicovitch* dimension that appears to more nearly represent the characteristics of the figure. Figures that have a *Hausdorff-Besicovitch* dimension greater than their Euclidian dimension were called *Fractals* by Benoit Mandlebrot. When plotted, fractals tend to have an interesting and complex shape and color pattern that makes them ideal for demonstrating graphics display capabilities. An interesting fractal can be created from Newton's method for solving polynomial equations that do not have a closed form solution. The following paragraphs describe the mathematics by which this fractal is created. If you're not interested in this level of detail, just skip down to where the program listing begins.

Suppose we have a generalized equation

$$f(z) = 0 \qquad\qquad\qquad (Eq. 9\text{-}1)$$

where *z* may be a complex number. Newton found that a root of this equation may be found by first guessing that the root has the value z_0 and then iteratively computing the expression:

$$Z_{n+1} = Z_n - \frac{f(Z_n)}{f'(Z_n)}. \qquad\qquad (Eq. 9\text{-}2)$$

The expression $f'(z)$ is the derivative of $f(z)$. For the first iteration of Equation 9-2, $z_n = z_0$. Each iteration of the equation approaches closer to the actual value of the root until ultimately, the actual value of the root is reached and the derivative becomes zero. (It is easy to get a very close approximation of the root value with not too many iterations, but if you want the exact value of an irrational root, an infinite number of iterations may be required.) We are going to apply this technique to equations from $z^3 - 1 = 0$ to $z^9 - 1 = 0$ where

$z = x - iy$ (Eq. 9-4)

Our fractal is created by taking every point within a selected area and using it as our starting guess for applying Newton's method. A couple of things should be evident. First, if we make a lucky guess and get the root right the first time, no more iterations are necessary. For choices that aren't so lucky, various numbers of iterations are needed before some prespecified accuracy is achieved. Second, when the original equation has a number of roots, Newton's method only guarantees to find the value of one root; it doesn't specify which root it will be. If your first guess is very near one root, it is likely that the process will converge to that root; guesses that are midway between two roots may converge to either of the two roots; we have to use the process to see which one is obtained. The fractal is created by coloring each point in the selected area with a color that represents the number of iterations required to obtain the root to a prespecified accuracy. Listing 9.2 is a program to draw Newton fractals.

```
import  ava.awt.*;
import  ava.awt.event.*;
import  avax.swing.*;
import  ava.awt.image.*;

public class Newton7 extends JPanel
{
    static JFrame frame;
    int type;
    Image image;
    JLabel picture;
    int  index, row, col, xres=640, yres=480;
    int pixels[] = new int[xres*(yres+1)];

    public Newton7()
    {
        JRadioButton three = new JRadioButton("3");
        three.setActionCommand("3");
        three.setSelected(true);
        JRadioButton four = new JRadioButton("4");
        four.setActionCommand("4");
        JRadioButton five = new JRadioButton("5");
        five.setActionCommand("5");
```

LISTING *Program to Draw Newton Fractals.*
9.2

```
        JRadioButton six = new JRadioButton("6");
        six.setActionCommand("6");
        JRadioButton seven = new JRadioButton("7");
        seven.setActionCommand("7");
        JRadioButton eight = new JRadioButton("8");
        eight.setActionCommand("8");
        JRadioButton nine = new JRadioButton("9");
        nine.setActionCommand("9");

        ButtonGroup group = new ButtonGroup();
        group.add(three);
        group.add(four);
        group.add(five);
        group.add(six);
        group.add(seven);
        group.add(eight);
        group.add(nine);

        RadioListener myListener = new
RadioListener();
        three.addActionListener(myListener);
        four.addActionListener(myListener);
        five.addActionListener(myListener);
        six.addActionListener(myListener);
        seven.addActionListener(myListener);
        eight.addActionListener(myListener);
        nine.addActionListener(myListener);
        picture = new JLabel();
        picture.setPreferredSize(new Dimension(640,
480));
        fractalMaker(3);
        JPanel radioPanel = new JPanel();
        radioPanel.setLayout(new BoxLayout(radioPanel,
BoxLayout.Y_AXIS));
        radioPanel.add(three);
        radioPanel.add(four);
        radioPanel.add(five);
        radioPanel.add(six);
        radioPanel.add(seven);
        radioPanel.add(eight);
        radioPanel.add(nine);

        setLayout(new BorderLayout());
        add(radioPanel, BorderLayout.WEST);
        add(picture, BorderLayout.CENTER);
        setBorder(BorderFactory.createEmptyBorder
(20,20,20,20));
    }
```

LISTING *Program to Draw Newton Fractals. (continues)*
9.2

```
   public void fractalMaker(int type)
   {
     double left, right, top, bottom;
     double deltaP, deltaQ, x, x2, x3, x4, x5, x6,
x7, x8,
         y, y2, y3, y4, y5, y6, y7, y8, ss2, ss4,w,
v,
         square_sum, denom,prev_x, prev_y, temp;
     Color[] color = new Color[16];
     color[0] = Color.black;
     color[1] = new Color(0, 0, 168);
     color[2] = new Color(0, 168, 0);
     color[3] = new Color(0, 168, 168);
     color[4] = new Color(168, 0, 0);
     color[5] = new Color(168, 0, 168);
     color[6] = new Color(168, 84, 0);
     color[7] = new Color(168, 168, 168);
     color[8] = new Color(84, 84, 84);
     color[9] = new Color(84, 84, 255);
     color[10] = new Color(84, 255, 84);
     color[11] = new Color(84, 255, 255);
     color[12] = new Color(255, 84, 84);
     color[13] = new Color(255, 84, 255);
     color[14] = new Color(255, 255, 84);
     color[15] = Color.white;
     left = -1.5;
     right = 1.5;
     top = 1.25;
     bottom = -1.25;
     deltaP = (right - left)/xres;
     deltaQ = (top - bottom)/yres;
     for(col=0; col<xres; col++)
     {
         for (row=0; row<yres; row++)
         {
            x = left + col*deltaP;
            y = top - row*deltaQ;
            prev_x = prev_y = 42;
            index = 0;
            switch (type)
            {
               case 3:
                  while(((Math.abs(prev_x - x) >
1E-10)
                     || (Math.abs(prev_y - y)
                        > 1E-10)) && index < 512)
                  {
                        prev_x = x;
                        prev_y = y;
```

LISTING *Program to Draw Newton Fractals. (continues)*
9.2

```
                            x2 = x*x;
                            y2 = y*y;
                            denom = 3.0*((x2 - y2)*(x2 -
y2)

                               + 4.0*x2*y2);
                            if (denom == 0.0)
                               denom = 0.00000001;
                            temp = .6666667*x + (x2 -
y2)/denom;

                            y = .6666667*y -
2.0*x*y/denom;

                            x = temp;
                            index++;
                        }
                        pixels[row*xres + col] =
color[index%16].getRGB();
                        break;

                    case 4:
                    while(((Math.abs(prev_x - x) >
1E-10)
                            || (Math.abs(prev_y - y)
                               > 1E-10)) && index < 512)
                    {
                        prev_x = x;
                        prev_y = y;
                            w = x*x*x - 3.0*x*y*y;
                            v = 3.0*x*x*y - y*y*y;
                            denom = 4.0 * (w*w + v*v);
                            if (denom == 0.0)
                               denom = 0.00000001;
                            temp = .75*x - w/denom;
                            y = .75*y + v/denom;
                            x = temp;
                            index++;
                        }
                        pixels[row*xres + col] =
color[index%16].getRGB();
                        break;

                    case 5:
                    while(((Math.abs(prev_x - x) >
1E-10)
                            || (Math.abs(prev_y - y)
                               > 1E-10)) && index < 512)
                    {
                        prev_x = x;
                        prev_y = y;
```

LISTING *Program to Draw Newton Fractals. (continues)*
9.2

```
                              w = x*x*x*x - 6.0*x*x*y*y +
y*y*y*y;
                              v = 4.0*x*x*x*y -
4.0*x*y*y*y;
                              denom = 5.0 *(w*w + v*v);
                              if (denom == 0.0)
                                 denom = 0.00000001;
                              temp = .8*x - w/denom;
                              y = .8*y + v/denom;
                              x = temp;
                                 index++;
                              }
                              pixels[row*xres + col] =
color[index%16].getRGB();
                              break;

                       case 6:
                              while(((Math.abs(prev_x - x)
> 1E-10)
                                  || (Math.abs(prev_y - y)
                                    > 1E-10)) && index <
512)
                              {
                                 prev_x = x;
                                 prev_y = y;
                                 w = x*x*x*x*x*x -
10.0*x*x*x*y*y +
                                    5.0*x*y*y*y*y;
                                 v = 5.0*x*x*x*x*x*y -
10.0*x*x*y*y*y + y*y*y*y*y;
                                 denom = 6.0 *(w*w + v*v);
                                 if (denom == 0.0)
                                    denom = 0.00000001;
                                 temp = .8333333*x -
w/denom;
                                 y = .8333333*y + v/denom;
                                 x = temp;
                                 index++;
                              }
                              pixels[row*xres + col] =
color[index%16].getRGB();
                              break;

                       case 7:
                              while(((Math.abs(prev_x - x)
> 1E-10)
                                  || (Math.abs(prev_y - y)
                                    > 1E-10)) && index <
512)
```

LISTING *Program to Draw Newton Fractals. (continues)*
9.2

```
                                {
                                    prev_x = x;
                                    prev_y = y;
                                    w = x*x*x*x*x*x
-15.0*x*x*x*x*y*y

                                        + 15.0*x*x*y*y*y*y -
y*y*y*y*y*y;

                                    v = 6.0*x*x*x*x*x*y -
                                        20.0*x*x*x*y*y*y +
6.0*x*y*y*y*y*y;

                                    denom = 7.0 *(w*w + v*v);
                                    if (denom == 0.0)
                                        denom = 0.00000001;
                                    temp = .85714285*x -
w/denom;

                                    y = .85714285*y +
v/denom;

                                    x = temp;
                                    index++;
                                }
                                pixels[row*xres + col] =
color[index%16].getRGB();
                                break;

                        case 8:
                                while(((Math.abs(prev_x - x)
> 1E-10)

                                    || (Math.abs(prev_y - y)
                                        > 1E-10)) && index <
512)
                                    {
                                        prev_x = x;
                                        prev_y = y;
                                        w = x*x*x*x*x*x*x*x
-21.0*x*x*x*x*x*x*y*y + 35.0*x*x*x*x*y*y*y*y -
7.0*x*x*y*y*y*y*y*y;
                                        v = 7.0*x*x*x*x*x*x*x*y -
35.0*x*x*x*x*x*y*y*y + 21.0*x*x*y*y*y*y*y*y -
y*y*y*y*y*y*y*y;
                                        denom = 8.0 *(w*w + v*v);
                                        if (denom == 0.0)
                                            denom = 0.00000001;
                                        temp = .875*x - w/denom;
                                        y = .875*y + v/denom;
                                        x = temp;
                                        index++;
                                    }
                                pixels[row*xres + col] =
color[index%16].getRGB();
```

LISTING *Program to Draw Newton Fractals. (continues)*
9.2

```
                                break;

                        case 9:
                        while(((Math.abs(prev_x - x)
> 1E-10)

                            || (Math.abs(prev_y - y)
                                > 1E-10)) && index <
512)
                            {
                                prev_x = x;
                                prev_y = y;
                                x2 = x*x;
                                y2 = y*y;
                                x3 = x*x2;
                                x4 = x2*x2;
                                x5 = x4*x;
                                x6 = x4*x2;
                                x7 = x6*x;
                                x8 = x7*x;
                                y3 = y*y2;
                                y4 = y2*y2;
                                y5 = y4*y;
                                y6 = y4*y2;
                                y7 = y6*y;
                                y8 = y7*y;
                                square_sum = x2 + y2;
                                ss2 = square_sum *
square_sum;
                                ss4 = ss2 * ss2;
                                denom = 9.0*ss4 * ss4;
                                if (denom == 0)
                                    denom = 0.0000001;
                                temp = 0.88888888*y -
(8.0*x7*y -
                                    56.0*x5*y3 +
56.0*x3*y5 - 8.0*x*y7)/denom;
                                x = 0.88888888*x + (x8 -
                                    28.0*x6*y2 +
70.0*x4*y4 -
                                    28.0*x2*y6 +
y8)/denom;
                                y = temp;
                                index++;
                            }
                            pixels[row*xres + col] =
color[index%16].getRGB();
                            break;
                    }
                }
```

LISTING *Program to Draw Newton Fractals. (continues)*
9.2

```
        }
        image = createImage(new
MemoryImageSource(xres, yres,
            pixels, 0, xres));
        ImageIcon bp = new ImageIcon(image);
        picture.setIcon(bp);
    }

  class RadioListener implements ActionListener
  {
    public void actionPerformed(ActionEvent e)
    {
        type =
Integer.parseInt(e.getActionCommand());
        fractalMaker(type);
    }
  }

  public static void main(String s[])
  {
    frame = new JFrame("Newton's Method
Fractals");
    frame.addWindowListener(new WindowAdapter()
    {
        public void windowClosing(WindowEvent e)
        {
            System.exit(0);
        }
    });

        frame.getContentPane().add(new Newton7(),
BorderLayout.CENTER);
        frame.pack();
        frame.setVisible(true);
    }
}
```

LISTING *Program to Draw Newton Fractals. (continued)*
9.2

First, we've created a window by defining the class *Newton7* as an extension of *JPanel.* The program then creates a group of seven numbered radio buttons. We set these up with their titles and listeners and put them at the west side of a new *BorderLayout.* At the center of this layout we put a new *Jlabel* called *Picture.* This is set to a preferred size of 640 by 480 pixels. We'll fill it with something later.

Now let's look at the class *RadioListener,* which implements *ActionListener.*

This class contains the method *actionPerformed*. Each time a radio button is clicked, this method gets an integer corresponding to the number of the button clicked. It then calls the method *fractalMaker*, which performs the mathematics for generating the fractal display. This method starts by defining the 16 EGA colors. We then set some limits and then enter a pair of nested *for* loops that iterate once for each pixel of the entire display. At each iteration, we enter a *switch* statement. Each case of this statement contains the mathematics for one of the Newton's method fractals. Each has a *while* loop that iterates until the initial values of x and y are changing insignificantly. It assumes this means we have zeroed in on a root and exits the loop. If this condition hasn't been reached after 512 iterations, it gives up and exits anyway. At each iteration, the loop uses the previous values of x and y with Newton's method to compute new x and y values. Since the computation might break down if a zero denominator tried to make us divide by zero, we've included code in the loop that sets the denominator to a very small value if its actual value is zero. Once we are out of the loop, we use the number of iterations to select one of the 16 colors by using modulo arithmetic. We put this color in an integer and store it in the *pixels* array, which is large enough to hold all the pixels that make up the display. We could draw each point of the pixel array to create the display, but it's much faster to convert this array to an image and then use *ImageIcon* to display the image as we did in the previous program. Finally, in the *main* program, we create a new frame and add a title to it and a *WindowListener* to detect when we click to close the program. This is associated with the embedded method *windowClosing,* which actually closes the program when the event is detected. We also get the contents of the *Border* layout and display it. The resulting picture, for a fifth order Newton's method fractal, is shown in breathtaking beauty and detail in Plate 3.

A Java Program for Viewing *GIF* and *JPG* Files

We've already seen that Java makes it simple and fast to decode and display a *GIF* or *JPEG* graphics file, even though writing the software to read and decode these files would be a substantial task if we had to do it from scratch. Let's extend the complexity of our program some more by enabling it to display a directory of *GIF* and *JPEG* files from which we can select one for display. Listing 9.3 shows how one might have written a part of such a program using the *AWT.*

```
/*
      ViewPic.java
      GIF and JPG Image Viewer
*/
import java.awt.*;
import java.io.
class Extension implements FilenameFilter
{
      public Extension()
      {
      }

      public boolean accept(File dir, String name)
      {
         if (name.endsWith("gif") ||
            name.endsWith("jpg"))
               return true;
         return false;
      }
}

public class ViewPic extends Frame
{
      FileDialog d = new FileDialog(this,
         "Select File for Display",
         FileDialog.LOAD);
         Image display_image;
         String s;
         Extension e = new Extension();
      ViewPic()
      {
         d.setDirectory(".");
         d.setFilenameFilter(e);
         d.show();
         s = d.getFile();
         t = d.getDirectory();
         setTitle("Picture Viewer - " + s);
         s = new String(t + s);
            display_image =
Toolkit.getDefaultToolkit().getImage(s);
         resize(640,480);
         show();
      }
   }
}
```

LISTING *Part of a Program to View GIF and JPG Images.*
9.3

The *FileDialog* Class

The *FileDialog* class displays a window with a list of files in the current directory. You have the capability to change the drive, directory, or subdirectory. When a new one of any of these is selected, a new list of files appears in the window. At any time you can select one of the files from the list and choose *Open* to pass this file to your program. As long as the *FileDialog* class is operative, it suspends the operation of the rest of your program. If you want to limit the directory to just *GIF* and *JPEG* files, rather than showing all files, you need a filter to do this. Our program defines the class *Extension*, which implements the class *FileFilter* and under it defines the method *Accept* to do this. Unfortunately, this part of Java has never worked properly with Windows from the beginning.

Using the Java Swing *fileChooser* Class

As we've already noted, Java 1.2 includes a whole suite of advanced methods that are included in files labeled *javax.swing*. One of these is *java.swing.fileChooser*, which displays a list of selected files from a directory. In other words, it does what *FileDialog* and its associated filter method are supposed to do. We're going to use this to create a program for displaying *GIF* and *JPG* files. This program is listed in Listing 9.4.

```
/*
   ViewPic.java
   GIF and JPG Image Viewer
*/

import javax.swing.*;
import javax.swing.filechooser.*;
import java.awt.*;
import java.io.File;
import java.awt.event.*;
import java.beans.*;
import java.util.Hashtable;
import java.util.Enumeration;

public class ViewPic extends JPanel
{
    static JFrame frame;
    Picture picture = new Picture();
    String pictureName;
    Image displayImage;
    SelectFileFilter jpgFilter, gifFilter,
bothFilter;
    FilePreviewer previewer;
```

LISTING *Program to View GIF and JPG Images Using Java Swing Components.*
9.4 *(continues)*

```
JFileChooser chooser = new JFileChooser();

public ViewPic()
{
fileDisplay();
}

public void fileDisplay()
{
    jpgFilter = new SelectFileFilter(new String[]
        {"jpg"}, "JPEG Compressed Image Files");
    gifFilter = new SelectFileFilter(new String[]
        {"gif"}, "GIF Image Files");
    bothFilter = new SelectFileFilter(new String[]
        {"jpg", "gif"},
        "JPEG and GIF Image Files");
    previewer = new FilePreviewer(chooser);
    chooser.setDialogTitle
        ("Select file to display");
    chooser.setAccessory(previewer);
    chooser.resetChoosableFileFilters();
    chooser.addChoosableFileFilter(jpgFilter);
    chooser.addChoosableFileFilter(gifFilter);
    chooser.addChoosableFileFilter(bothFilter);

    chooser.cancelSelection();
    chooser.repaint();
    int retval = chooser.showDialog(frame, null);
    if (retval == 1)
        System.exit(0);
    if(retval == JFileChooser.APPROVE_OPTION)
    {
        File theFile = chooser.getSelectedFile();
        if(theFile != null)
        {
            pictureName = chooser.getSelectedFile
                ().getAbsolutePath();
            displayImage= Toolkit.getDefaultToolkit
                ().getImage(pictureName)
            .getScaledInstance(-1, 600,
            Image.SCALE_DEFAULT);
            picture.setTitle("Viewing File " +
                pictureName);
            picture.setSize(800,600);
            picture.show();
        }
    }
}

class Picture extends Frame
```

LISTING *Program to View GIF and JPG Images Using Java Swing Components.*
9.4 *(continues)*

```
   {
      Picture()
      {
         addWindowListener(new WindowAdapter()
         {
            public void windowClosing(WindowEvent e)
               {
                  dispose();
                  fileDisplay();
               }
         });
      }

      public void paint(Graphics g)
      {
         g.drawImage(displayImage, 0, 0, this);
      }
   }
}

class FilePreviewer extends JComponent implements
   PropertyChangeListener
{
   ImageIcon thumbnail = null;
   File f = null;
      public FilePreviewer(JFileChooser fc)
   {
      setPreferredSize(new Dimension(100, 50));
      fc.addPropertyChangeListener(this);
   }

   public void loadImage()
   {
      if(f != null)
      {
         ImageIcon tmpIcon = new
            ImageIcon(f.getPath());
         thumbnail = new ImageIcon(
            tmpIcon.getImage().getScaledInstance
               (90, -1, Image.SCALE_DEFAULT));
      }
   }

   public void propertyChange
      (PropertyChangeEvent e)
   {
      String prop = e.getPropertyName();
      if(prop == JfileChooser.
SELECTED_FILE_CHANGED_PROPERTY)
         {
            f = (File) e.getNewValue();
```

LISTING *Program to View GIF and JPG Images Using Java Swing Components.*
9.4 *(continues)*

```
            loadImage();
            repaint();
        }
    }

    public void paint(Graphics g)
    {
        if(thumbnail == null)
        {
            loadImage();
        }
        if(thumbnail != null)
        {
            int x = getWidth()/2 -
                thumbnail.getIconWidth()/2;
            int y = getHeight()/2 -
                thumbnail.getIconHeight()/2;
            if(y < 0)
            {
                y = 0;
            }
            if(x < 5)
            {
                x = 5;
            }
            thumbnail.paintIcon(this, g, x, y);
        }
    }
}

    public static void main(String s[])
    {
        ViewPic panel = new ViewPic();
    }
}

class SelectFileFilter extends FileFilter
{
    private Hashtable filters = null;
    private String description = null;
    private boolean useExtensionsInDescription =
true;

    public SelectFileFilter(String[] filters, String
        description)
    {
        this.filters = new Hashtable(filters.length);
        for (int i = 0; i < filters.length; i++)
        {
            addExtension(filters[i]);
```

LISTING *Program to View GIF and JPG Images Using Java Swing Components.*
9.4 *(continues)*

```
      }
      setDescription(description);
   }

   public boolean accept(File f)
   {
      if(f != null)
      {
         if(f.isDirectory())
         {
            return true;
         }
         if(filters.get(getExtension(f)) != null)
         {
            return true;
         };
      }
      return false;
   }

   public String getExtension(File f)
   {
      if(f != null)
      {
         String filename = f.getName();
         int i = filename.lastIndexOf('.');
         if(i>0 && i<filename.length()-1)
         {
            return filename.substring(i+1)
               .toLowerCase();
         };
      }
      return null;
   }

   public void addExtension(String extension)
   {
      filters.put(extension.toLowerCase(), this);
   }

   public String getDescription()
   {
      return description;
   }

   public void setDescription(String description)
   {
      this.description = description;
   }
}
```

LISTING *Program to View GIF and JPG Images Using Java Swing Components.*
9.4 *(continued)*

Working with Images

Let's skip for a moment to how we draw an image. We're going to do this in a class called *Picture*, which is an extension of *frame*. The constructor for this class includes a window listener and the embedded class for processing a window closing event. It also has a *paint* method, which draws an image contained in an object *display_image*, which is of class *Image*. The drawing is done with a statement like:

```
drawImage(Image display_image, int x, int y,
    ImageObserver observer);
```

The parameter *display_image* is the *Image* object that contains the data for the image you want to display. The *x* and *y* values are the coordinates of the top left-hand corner of the display. The *observer* is the object to notify when the image is loaded. This last parameter is needed because the *drawImage* method may start before all of the data in *display_image* has been loaded. The program then needs to know that it must keep returning to *drawImage* to draw more of the display until all of the data has been received and converted to a picture. You'll note that we use *this* for the observer in the *drawImage* call in our *paint* method. This assures that the *ViewPic* constructor (where we construct the image) is the source from which we get information on how much of the image has been completed.

We've already seen that coding and decoding *GIF* and *JPG* files is a pretty complicated business. If we had to write the method to decode these files and then convert them into data of the *Image* format, we'd have a very large job on our hands. Fortunately, Java has already done this for us. A method called *getImage* is a part of the object *getDefaultToolkit()*, which is part of the object *Toolkit*. We pass this the name of a *GIF* or *JPG* file and it returns an *Image* object containing all of the picture data in the proper format. In our viewing program this is done with the following line:

```
display_image =
    Toolkit.getDefaultToolkit().getImage(s);
```

where *s* is a string containing the name of the desired picture file.

The *GIF* and *JPG* Picture Viewing Program

Now its time to take a look at the overall program structure. We have a class *ViewPic*, which is an extension of *JPanel*. The constructor for this class calls the *fileDisplay* method, which controls file selection and display. This method first sets up an object *chooser* of the *JFileChooser* class. We then set up filters for *JPG*, *GIF*, and both types of images. These will control the files shown in the file choosing display. Next is the definition of *previewer*, which will be used to create a thumbnail image of the selected file. We then select the title for this display and activate the previewer. Next, we, cancel any previously made file name selection, and then reset the file name filters and add the three we have defined earlier. The method then repaints the file selecting display. After this, the program pauses until the user has selected a file. A box at the bottom of the display allows you to choose which types of files you want displayed. By default, all files in the selected directory are displayed. Instead, you may choose *JPG* files, *GIF* files, or both *JPG* and *GIF* files. In addition to the selected files, all subdirectory names will be displayed. You can select a subdirectory and get a new display by double-clicking a subdirectory name. Note that unlike Windows 95, if you select a subdirectory name and click the open box, you will not get a display of the subdirectory contents. Instead, you are most likely to terminate the program.

Selecting the List of Files to Be Displayed

At the bottom of the file selection display, as shown in Plate 4, there is a box labeled *Files of type:*, which by default contains the legend *All Files (*.*)*. This default condition for the display results in all files in the currently selected directory being displayed in the file listing that appears above it. We would like to have the options of showing all *GIF* files, all *JPG* files, or all files of both these types in the listing. If you're using the program, you'll see that by clicking the arrow at the right of the just described box, a menu is displayed that allows you to select one of these three choices or return to the default condition. Upon your selection, the file list is changed accordingly. To achieve this, at the beginning of the *fileDisplay* method, we define three filter conditions: *jpgFilter*, *gifFilter*, and *bothFilter*. Each definition includes one or more file extensions and a title. Farther down in the method, we reset the *ChoosableFileFilter* and then add each of the three choices. When the user selects one of the three file filter conditions from the file selection display, the *SelectFileFilter* class is used to perform the filtering. The *SelectFileFilter* constructor sets up a hash table item for each of the file extensions passed to it as the first item of the filter condition definition. Then it calls *SetDescription*, which uses the second item of the filter condition definition as the title in the box *Files of type:*.

The method *accept* in the *SelectFileFilter* class is called once for each file or subdirectory in the directory selected for the file selection display. It returns *true* if the file or subdirectory name is to be displayed, and *false* if it is not to be displayed. The method begins by checking if the name is that of a subdirectory. If it is, then the method returns *true*. Otherwise, the method gets the extension (if any) of the file name by calling the method *getExtension*. It then calls the hashtable *get* method, passing the file extension as a parameter. If the file extension is the same as one of the ones in the hashtable, the *accept* method returns *true*; otherwise, it returns *false*.

The file selection display is then redrawn with only those files and subdirectories for which *accept* has returned a *true* displayed. For *SelectFileFilter* to be complete, there are certain methods that must be defined, even though some of them are never used in this particular program.

Thumbnail Graphics Display

We would like to include in the file selection display a thumbnail display of whatever picture in the file list we have selected with the mouse cursor. To accomplish this, we define a *previewer* in the *ViewPic* class with the statement:

```
FilePreviewer previewer;
```

Then, in the fileDisplay method, we have the lines:

```
previewer = new FilePreviewer(chooser);
chooser.setAccessory(previewer);
```

which activate this capability. These all depend on the class *FilePreviewer*, which you will find defined slightly lower in the listing. This class begins by defining *thumbnail* to be of the *ImageIcon* type and defining *f* to be of the File type and nulling both of these. The constructor for this class sets the size of the component and adds a Property Change Listener. This listener detects when the mouse is clicked on one of the names listed in the file selection display and runs the method *propertyChange*. The method begins by getting the name of the property that was changed. If that was the *SELECTED_FILE_CHANGED_PROPERTY*, the method loads the newly selected file's information into *f* and then calls *loadImage* followed by *repaint*. The *loadImage* method does nothing if what was selected was not a file (perhaps it was a directory); otherwise, it gets a scaled-down image from the selected graphics file and stores it in *thumbnail*. The *repaint* method clears the display area and then calls *paint* to display a new image. If for any reason there is nothing in *thumbnail*, the *paint* method first calls *loadImage* to get a picture. Then, if there is a picture in *thumbnail*, the proper coordinates for the beginning of the picture are computed and *thumbnail.paintIcon* is called to draw the graphic in the proper place on the file selection display. At the same time, the name of the selected file is placed in the *File name* box at the bottom of the file selection display. This is all shown in Plate 4. Note that to produce this thumbnail, we only have to click the mouse on a file name; when we want to display a full-sized picture, we have to click on the file name and then click the *Open* box.

Displaying a Full-Sized Picture	Once the file selection display is shown, the *fileDisplay* method pauses until you have made a selection. Within this display, if we are using Windows 95 or 98, we would like to be able to click on the x in the top right hand corner of the display and have the program terminate. However, within this display, clicking on the x cannot be controlled, it continues the program with a file selection of *null*. We first run the file chooser *showDialog* method, which returns a 1 if we have a null file selected, upon which we terminate the program. This is also true if we clicked on the *Cancel* box. If we click on a graphic file and then click the *Open* box, the return value from *showDialog* is *APPROVE_OPTION*. An *if* statement now causes us to enter a section that draws a full-sized picture. First, we get the name of the selected file. If it is not *null*, we get the name and path for the selected file and use the *getImage* method to decode and transfer the picture data to the *Image* class object *display_image*. Next, we use the picture method to give a name to the window that will display the picture. Next, we use *picture* methods to set the size of the *picture* and display it, using the *picture.paint* method to call the graphics method *drawImage*.

Now we've got one picture; what happens next? If we click on the x at the top right corner of the picture display, we activate the window listener in the *Picture* constructor, causing the method *windowClosing* to be run. This first calls *dispose* to remove the window containing the full-sized picture and then runs *fileDisplay* to repeat the process of selecting and displaying a file again. Note that triggering the x in the top right-hand corner of the full-sized picture display does not end the program; to terminate, you must trigger the x from the file selection display. Plate 5 is a *GIF* file as it would appear using the *ViewPic* program.

10

Viewing BMP File Images

The *BMP* files are used by Windows to store graphics, They do not use any form of compression so they take up a lot of file space and this means that they do not often appear on the Internet. But since they require no decoding, they are about the fastest way to get from a stored graphic to an actual display. Unfortunately, Java makes no provision for handling them. In this chapter we'll discuss the *BMP* file format and show how you can display *BMP* files with Java. By using the *Image* class, we can display a *BMP* file fairly quickly, but not quite as fast as Java can display a *GIF* or *JPG* file with its internal processing, even though the processing required is much simpler. If you have other graphics files that you'd like to display with Java (such as the *PCX* file format that was once used extensively with DOS and Windows) you can use the same procedure shown in this chapter, but with adaptations to process the desired file format.

The *BMP* File Format

We're going to work with *BMP* files that make use of 4 bits per pixel, 8 bits per pixel, and 24 bits per pixel color representation and are compatible with Windows 3.1 and later versions. These are straight-forward bitmap files that don't use any form of data compression. They can thus be very large, but can be loaded by Windows very quickly. There are several other *BMP* file variations used with earlier Windows versions, but we'll ignore those in this chapter. If you are interested in the details of these formats, you can find them (and many other graphics file formats) in *Murray, James D. and vanRyper, William, "Encyclopedia of Graphics Formats," O'Reilly & Associates, Inc., 1994.*

The *BMP* File Header

Current *BMP* files have a header that consists of two parts. The first part, which is known as the *file header*, is shown in Table 10-1. It simply consists of the file identification characters, the file size, and the image offset, which is the

Table 10-1   BMP File Header Contents.

Byte #	Name	Description
00–01	Identification	Set to 424DH (ASCII letters BM).
02–05	File size	Length of file in bytes.
06–09	Reserved	Not used by current BMP files. Set to 00.
10–13	Image offset	Number of bytes from beginning of file to actual start of image data. May vary depending upon the amount of color information that follows the header.

number of bytes from the beginning of the file to the point where the graphic image begins. The second part of the header, which is known as the *file information header*, is shown in Table 10-2. In developing a program to display *BMP* images, we are only going to use a few pieces of information from these headers. First, we will use *Image offset* to determine where we should start reading graphics image information. Next, we will use *Width* and *Height* to determine the dimensions of the stored image in pixels. Finally, we will use *Bits per pixel* to determine how the file handles color information. All of the numbers in the *BMP* header are stored in a format used by Intel microprocessors, which calls for the least significant part of the number to be stored in the first byte, the next least significant part in the next byte, and so forth. This is sometimes called *little-endian*. Because of this, we can't just transfer a group of bytes from a *BMP* file to Java as an integer or long integer and expect to get the proper number, since Java doesn't define integers in the same way that the *BMP* file does. The first thing we need to do is convert each byte from the file number into an integer. The byte may originally represent a number from 0 to 255, but Java does not support unsigned bytes or integers so the number ends up expressed as a Java integer between –128 and +127. To convert this back to the original number, we must add 256 to the Java integer if it is negative. The result will then be the number originally represented by the first file byte. We then repeat the process for the next file byte. Then, this new integer is shifted 8 bits to the left and ORed with the integer created from the first file byte. The process is repeated for as many file bytes as are used to represent the number, except that the next byte is shifted 16 bits to the left, the following one 24 bits to the left, and so forth. When this process is completed, we have an integer that contains the same number in Java format that was originally represented by the file bytes in little-endian format.

Table 10-2   BMP File Information Header Contents.

Byte #	Name	Description
00–03	Header size	Length of information header. Should always be 28H (40 bytes).
04–07	Width	Width of graphic image in pixels.
08–11	Height	Height of graphic image in pixels.
12–13	Number of planes	Always set to 0001, since *BMP* files use only a single color plane.
14–15	Bits per pixel	Number of bits used to represent the color of a pixel. Acceptable values are 1, 4, 8, and 24.

continues

Table 10-2 BMP File Information Header Contents. *Continued*

Byte #	Name	Description
16–19	Compression	Always 0 for uncompressed files.
20–23	Size of bit map	Size of the bitmap in bytes.
24–27	Horizontal method	Horizontal resolution of device that generated the graphics image.
28–31	Vertical resolution	Vertical resolution of device that generated the graphics image.
32–35	Number of colors	Number of colors actually used in a picture. When set to 0, the number of colors is the maximum number of colors allowed by bits per pixel.
36–39	Number of significant colors	Colors that appear frequently in the image. If the display can handle this many colors, a good image will be produced.

Painting a *BMP* Picture with the *Image* Class

Listing 10.1 is the program to convert a *BMP* file into a displayed picture using the *Image* class that we used in the previous chapter. Note that in addition to importing *java.awt.* * and *java.awt.event*, we also import *java.io.* *, which contains the classes we need to read from the file stream, and *java.awt.image.* *, which contains the *Image* class and its methods. First, look at the beginning of the program, where we've used the *FileDialog* class to display a window showing a listing of files and to allow the user to change directories and select a file for display. In the previous chapter, we pointed out that the Java method for filtering file names so that only certain desired files appear doesn't work with Windows. There is a work-around, however, if you are only looking for one particular type of files. The statement:

```
d.setFile("*.bmp");
```

run before showing the list of files ensures that only names of files having a *.bmp* extension will be shown. Now let's look at the *paint* method, which contains a lot of things we haven't used before. First, observe that we have defined a parameter *flag* as part of our definition of the *ViewBmp* class and initialized it to be *false*. As you glance down through the *fileDisplay* method, you'll see that the method first displays a list of *BMP* files and then after a file has been selected runs *picture.show* to create and display the selected picture. This occurs the first time we run the method. On the next pass through the method, however, *picture.show* finds that it already has a picture ready for display, so it doesn't repaint the picture, even though we've displayed the name of a different file to display. To correct this, we need to run the *picture.repaint* method. However, we don't want to run this method on the first pass through *fileDisplay*; if we did, the picture would be displayed, erased, and then displayed again. To avoid this, we use an *if* statement that prevents running *picture.repaint* on the first pass, when *flag* is false. Immediately after this, we make *flag* true so that *picture.repaint* is used thereafter.

```
/*
   ViewBmp. ava
   BMP Image Viewer
*/

import java.awt.*;
import java.io.*;
import java.awt.image.*;
import java.awt.event.*;

public class ViewBmp extends Frame
{
   FileDialog d = new FileDialog(this,
      "Select File for Display",
      FileDialog.LOAD);
   boolean flag = false;
   String s,t;
   Image image;
   Picture picture = new Picture();

    ViewBmp()
   {
      fileDisplay();
   }

   public void fileDisplay()
   {
      d.setDirectory(".");
      d.setFile("*.bmp");
      d.show();
      s = d.getFile();
      if (s == null)
         System.exit(0);
      t = d.getDirectory();
      s = new String(t + s);
      picture.setTitle("Viewing File " + s);
      picture.setSize(640,480);
      picture.show();
      if (flag == true)
         picture.repaint();
```

LISTING *Program to Display BMP Images Point by Point. (continues)*
10.1

```
        flag = true;
    }

    class Picture extends Frame
    {
        Picture()
        {
            addWindowListener(new WindowAdapter()
            {
                public void windowClosing
                    (WindowEvent e)
                {
                    fileDisplay();
                }
            });
        }

        public void paint(Graphics g)
        {
            byte buf[] = new byte[64];
            int pixcol;
            int i, , xres, yres, temp, temp1, temp2,
xlength, offset;
            byte [] color16 = new byte[4];
            Color [] colors = new Color[256];
            try
            {
            RandomAccessFile in = new
RandomAccessFile(s,"r");
                in.read(buf, 0, 54);
                xres = (buf[18] >= 0) ? buf[18] :
buf[18] + 256;
                temp = (buf[19] >= 0) ? buf[19] :
buf[19] + 256;
                xres |= temp<<8;
                yres = (buf[22] >= 0) ? buf[22] :
buf[22] + 256;
                temp = (buf[23] >= 0) ? buf[23] :
buf[23] + 256;
                yres |= temp<<8;
                offset = (buf[10] >= 0) ? buf[10] :
buf[10] + 256;
                temp = (buf[11] >= 0) ? buf[11] :
buf[11] + 256;
                offset |= temp<<8;
                int pixels[] = new int[xres*(yres+1)];
                switch (buf[28])
                {
                    case 4:
```

LISTING *Program to Display BMP Images Point by Point. (continues)*
10.1

```
                        for (i=0; i<16; i++)
                        {
                            in.read(color16, 0, 4);
                            temp = (color16[2]<0) ?
color16[2] + 256:
                                color16[2];
                            temp1 = (color16[1]<0) ?
color16[1] + 256:
                                color16[1];
                            temp2 = (color16[0]<0) ?
color16[0] + 256:
                                color16[0];
                          colors[i] = new Color(temp,
temp1, temp2);
                        }
                        in.seek(offset);
                        xlength = xres/2;
                        while (xlength %4 != 0)
                            xlength++;
                        byte pixel[] = new
byte[xlength];

                        for (i=yres-1; i>=0; i—)
                        {
                            in.read(pixel, 0, xlength);
                            for ( =0;  <xres;  +=2)
{
                                pixcol = (pixel[ /2] >>
4) & 0x0F;

                                pixels[i*xres +  ] =
                                colors[pixcol].getRGB();
                                pixcol = (pixel[ /2]) &
0x0F;

                                pixels[i*xres +    + 1] =
                                colors[pixcol].getRGB();
                            }
                        }
                        break;
                    case 8:
                        for (i=0; i<256; i++)
                        {
                        in.read(color16, 0, 4);
                        temp = (color16[2]<0) ?
color16[2] + 256:
                            color16[2];
                        temp1 = (color16[1]<0) ?
color16[1] + 256:
                            color16[1];
                        temp2 = (color16[0]<0) ?
color16[0] + 256:
```

LISTING *Program to Display BMP Images Point by Point. (continues)*
10.1

```
                        color16[0];
                    colors[i] = new Color(temp,
temp1, temp2);
            }
            in.seek(offset);
            xlength = xres;
            while (xlength %4 != 0)
                xlength++;
            byte pixel1[] = new byte[xlength];
            for (i=yres-1; i>=0; i—)
            {
                in.read(pixel1, 0, xlength);
                for ( =0;  <xres;  ++)
                {
                    pixcol = pixel1[ ];
                    if (pixcol < 0)
                        pixcol += 256;
                    pixels[i*xres +  ] =
                    colors[pixcol].getRGB();
                }
            }
            break;

        case 24:
            in.seek(offset);
            xlength = 3*xres;
            while (xlength %4 != 0)
            xlength++;
            byte pixel2[] = new
byte[xlength+4];
            for (i=yres-1; i>=0; i—)
            {
                in.read(pixel2, 0, xlength);
                for ( =0;  <xlength;  +=3)
                {
                    temp = (pixel2[ +2]<0) ?
pixel2[ +2] + 256:
                        pixel2[ +2];
                    pixels[i*xres +  /3] = (255
<< 24) |
                        (temp << 16);
                    temp = (pixel2[ +1]<0) ?
pixel2[ +1] + 256:
                        pixel2[ +1];
                    pixels[i*xres +  /3] |=
(temp << 8);
                    temp = (pixel2[ ]<0) ?
pixel2[ ] + 256:
pixel2[ ];
```

LISTING *Program to Display BMP Images Point by Point. (continues)*
10.1

```
                    pixels[i*xres +   /3] |=
temp;
                }
            }
        }
        image = createImage(new
MemoryImageSource(xres, yres,
            pixels, 0, xres));
    }
    catch (Exception e)
    {
        System.out.println("Error: " +
e.toString());
    }
    g.drawImage(image, 0, 0, null);
    }
}

    public static void main(String args[])
    {
        Frame f = new ViewBmp();
    }
}
```

LISTING *Program to Display BMP Images Point by Point. (continued)*
10.1

Let's look at the *paint* method, which is a method of the *Picture* class. It begins by doing some reading from the *BMP* file that was selected by *FileDialog*. This is done by a class called *RandomAccessFile*. When we create an object of this class and use its methods to work with a file, there is a possibility that Java may report an *Exception*. A typical exception involving a file might be that the file you specify cannot be found, the file cannot be read, etc. To handle this situation, all of the code that involves our file handling must be included within a *try* statement. The *try* statement tells Java to run the code within the braces and if there is an *Exception* to then use the code that follows in a *catch* statement. If you look down to the end of the *try* statement, you'll see that our *catch* statement simply handles every *Exception* by printing out a line that says *Error:* and then gives the string that defines the error. Now that we've set up our *try* statement, we create and use an object of the *RandomAccessFile* class called *in* by specifying the file name and an *"r"* to indicate that we want the file opened for reading. This data stream works for any files that are on hard disk, since we can access any part of the file that we want. If we were to bring in a picture file from the Net, we would only be able to access the data stream sequentially and would therefore have to use *DataInputStream*. We now read 54 bytes into a buffer *buf*. This comprises the *BMP* file headers.

The next lines of code select the *Width, Height,* and *Image offset* members of the file headers and convert them to Java integers *xres, yres,* and *offset,* respectively, using the techniques just described. We'll select one of three methods to collect data for display, but regardless of the method used, we are going to write a string to the graphics window that says *Generating Picture* followed by the *BMP* file name. This is done because the program is going to create an empty window and then spend awhile working on creating the image before anything is drawn in the window. The legend just described is intended to encourage the user to believe that something is going on and to wait for the result to appear. When we get to the *for* loops that iterate for each row in the *switch* statement, we have added an *if* statement that causes a period to be appended to the legend after each 10 rows have been processed. Now we enter a *switch* statement that uses the *Bits per pixel* member of the header to determine how the data will be processed. First let's look at the case of 4 bits per pixel. For this case, the bytes following the header are 16 sets of 4 bytes, each of which defines one of 16 possible colors in terms of their blue, green, and red components. Each color occupies 1 byte and the 4th byte is always zero. We begin our processing of this case with a *for* loop that iterates once for each of the 16 possible colors. Each iteration reads a color quadruple from the file, converts the bytes to positive integers, and then creates a member of an array *colors* that contains the red, green, and blue color values in the format acceptable to Java. Next, we set the file pointer to the beginning of the file graphics image data. We then determine *xlength* the number of bytes in an image line of the file. This is equivalent to the width of the image divided by 2 (since each byte contains color data for 2 pixels). However, each image line must begin on a double word boundary so we next use a *while* loop to add bytes to *xlength* until this is so. We then define an array of bytes (*pixel*) whose length is sufficient to contain a line of image data. Next, a *for* loop begins that iterates once for each line of the image. Since *BMP* files begin with the bottom line of an image and work toward the top line, we begin the *for* loop with this last line and decrease the line number by 1 for each iteration. At each iteration, a line of data is read into the buffer array *pixel*. We then enter a second *for* loop that iterates once for every other pixel of the image line. The loop begins by taking the first pixel (most significant 4 bits) from the proper member of the *pixel* array, shifting it 4 bits to the right, ORing it with 0x0F (to strip any unwanted bits), and using the result to select the proper member of the *colors* array. The color of the selected member of the *colors* array is stored in the proper member of the *pixels* array. Next the loop takes the least-significant 4 bits of the previously selected member of the *pixel* array, ORs it with 0x0F, and uses the result to set the proper display color. The color information is then stored in the next member of the *pixel* array. The column index is then increased by 2 and the loop iterates again. The process repeats until the entire line has been drawn.

Now let's look at the case where 8 bits are used to define the color of each pixel. As before, we use a *for* loop to read in color quadruples and insert them in the *colors* array in proper Java format. However, in this case, we have 256 possible colors so the loop iterates 256 times. Similar to the previous case, the parameter *xlength* is then set up, in this case having at least as many bytes as there are pixels in the width of the image and to end on a double word boundary. The file bytes are then processed similarly to the 4-bit per pixel case except that a full byte is used to represent the color of a pixel in one of 256 colors.

Finally, let's look at the case where 24 bits are used to define the color of each pixel. There is now no color information at the beginning of the file. This case also sets up the *xlength* parameter, with its size in bytes 3 times the number of pixels in the image width plus as many bytes as needed to end on a double word boundary. The file bytes are then processed similarly to the two previous cases, except that there are three bytes to represent the color of a single pixel. Each is converted to a positive integer, shifted to its proper position for that color and ORed into the 32-bit integer that represents a color pixel. The 8 most significant bits of the integer must also be set to 1 during this process. The resulting integer value is in the proper position for that pixel in the array *pixels*. This results in an image that may contain 16 million colors.

After the *for* loops in whatever case was selected have completed, we use the *createImage* method to create an image of the desired size from the *pixels* array, the image being of the *MemoryImageSource* class. We then draw this image to the screen.

The constructor for the *Picture* class includes a *WindowListener* and the *WindowClosing* method to handle a windows event. If one clicks the mouse on the x at the top right corner of a *Picture* screen, the method simply runs *fileDisplay* again to show the directory, allow selection of a file, and display that file. Finally, note that in the *fileDisplay* method, if the name of the selected file is a null, we terminate the program. This covers both the selection of the x in the top right corner of the list of files display and the selection of the *Cancel* button. Plate 6 was made from a photograph originally stored as a 256 color *BMP* file.

CHAPTER

11 Animation

A s you surf the Web, you'll come across a lot of little animated pictures that add life and interest to Web pages. Animation can be performed in just the same way as movies. A series of frames is displayed in sequence, with the picture nearly the same in each one, but with small differences in position that make objects appear to move. The first animations simply used a whole series of graphics files, often in *GIF* format. They usually had the same file name with the last couple characters being a unique frame number. Your Java program then had to display the first of these frames, then change the file name to the next frame and display it, and so forth. If necessary, some time delay was added between frames. There are some pretty complex programs to do this, including the animator included as a demo program with Java. However, today, Web animations seem to be standardizing on a *GIF* format that contains all of the frames in one file. A *GIF* file is capable of storing as many frames as you need. If you are using Java 1.2, you have the capability to display such files.

Animation *GIF* Files

If you use a Webcrawler to search for *GIF Animation*, you'll find many sites that have such files available. One good source is *http://member.aol.com/royaleflgifanim.htm*, which provides a whole gallery of *GIF* animations, many of them available free with no strings attached. The CD-ROM contains three *GIF* animation files: *FIDDLER.GIF*, *STARROLL.GIF*, and *SUNGLASS.GIF*, which I downloaded from this Website. If you try to view these files with the *ViewPic* program from Chapter 16, you'll see one frame, or maybe a blank screen. This is because the *imageUpdate* method is set up to wait until the whole file has been loaded before displaying a frame. If you now replace the *imageUpdate* method with the following:

```
public boolean imageUpdate(Image img, int flags, int
   x, int y, int w, int h)
{
   if ((flags & FRAMEBITS) != 0)
{
   repaint();
 }
 return (true);
}
```

you'll find that the program will properly show the animated displays. This works because the *FRAMEBITS* parameter goes *true* each time a frame of the *GIF* file has finished loading, causing the *imageUpdate* method to run *repaint* and paint the latest frame to the screen. You will note that there is a lot of objectionable flashing on the screen, however. Now we'll look at a more sophisticated program for viewing animated *GIF* image files.

An Advanced Animation Viewer

Listing 11.1 is an improved program for viewing animated *GIF* multiframe files. As with previous viewing programs, we've begun by defining an object *d* of the *FileDialog* class. In initializing our *ViewAnim* object, we first use *d* to set up a directory window and allow the user to select a file from the desired directory. We then set up an object *tracker* of class *MediaTracker*. This handles all processing of the *GIF* file without our intervention. We get the selected file into the *Image* class object *display_image* through the use of the *FileDialog* class, which displays a list of files and then waits for the user to select one of them. As you'll note in the *fileDisplay* method, we begin our use of *FileDialog* by the statement:

```
d.setFile(*.gif);
```

which limits the display to directories and files having extensions of the type *gif*. When we're looking at the *FileDialog* display, we might want to click on the x in the top right corner of the window to close down the program. *FileDialog* doesn't work this way, however. If you select the x, it simply reports back the selection of a file whose name is *null*. We've included a null string, and an *if* statement in the *fileDisplay* method that causes the program to quit if this is the same name reported by the selection process. If a real file is selected, we set up *tracker*, get the data from the file selected into *display_*image, and then use the *tracker.addImage* method to place it under the jurisdiction of *tracker*. Next, enclosed in a *try* statement, we use the *tracker* method *waitforID* to pause until an image is complete; then we call *repaint* to display the image on the screen.

```
/*
   ViewAnim.java
   Program for Viewing Animated Multi-frame GIF
Files
*/

import java.awt.*;
import java.io.*;
import java.awt.event.*;
```

LISTING *Advanced Animation Viewer for Multiframe GIF Files. (continues)*
11.1

```java
public class ViewAnim extends Frame
{
    FileDialog d = new FileDialog(this,
        "Select File for Display",
        FileDialog.LOAD);
    Image display_image;
    int offset;
    String s, t, oldTitle=null;

    ViewAnim()
    {
        addWindowListener(new WindowAdapter()
        {
            public void windowClosing(WindowEvent e)
            {
                System.exit(0);
            }
        });
        addMouseListener(new MouseAdapter()
        {
            public void mousePressed(MouseEvent e)
            {
                fileDisplay();
            }
        });

        fileDisplay();
        setSize(300,240);
        show();
    }

    public void fileDisplay()
    {
        String st = null;
        d.setFile("*.gif");
        d.setDirectory(".");
        d.show();
        s = d.getFile();
        if (s.equals(st))
            System.exit(0);
        setTitle("Animation Viewer - " + s);
        t = d.getDirectory();
        s = new String(t + s);
        MediaTracker tracker = new MediaTracker(this);
        display_image =
Toolkit.getDefaultToolkit().getImage(s);
        tracker.addImage(display_image, 0);
        try
        {
```

LISTING *Advanced Animation Viewer for Multiframe GIF Files. (continues)*
11.1

```
            tracker.waitForID(0);
            repaint();
        }
        catch (InterruptedException e)
        {
        }

    }

    public void paint(Graphics g)
    {
        offset =50;
        g.drawImage(display_image, offset, offset++,
Color.white, this);
    }

    public void update(Graphics g)
    {
        if (s.equals(oldTitle))
            paint(g);
        else
        {
            oldTitle = s;
            g.setColor(Color.white);
            g.fillRect(0,0,320,240);
        }
    }

    public static void main(String args[])
    {
        Frame f = new ViewAnim();
    }
}
```

LISTING *Advanced Animation Viewer for Multiframe GIF Files. (continued)*
11.1

The *paint* method makes use of the *drawImage* method to paint each image to the screen. Many of the *GIF* animation images are built with a transparent background. When running as an animation, this causes the current image to displayed on top of all other images that have been previously viewed, giving an undesirable hodgepodge. To avoid this, we use a version of the *drawImage* method that specifies a background color as the last parameter passed to the method. We've used white in the program; you can use any color you want, but make sure it isn't the same as the color being used to paint the principal features of the image, or you'll lose a lot of detail.

In the constructor for the *ViewAnim* class, we've included a window listener, together with an embedded class that handles a window closing event in the displayed animation and causes it to terminate the program. We've also included a mouse listener. Its embedded class is activated by the *mouseClicked* event and simply runs *fileDisplay* to go through the whole file selection and animation display process.

One final thing. Normally, when a *repaint* occurs, *update* is called, which clears the screen and then calls *paint* to produce a new display. This causes a lot of flicker on the animated display. We avoid this simply by overriding *update* with a new version that doesn't clear the screen each time, but instead only calls *paint* to draw another frame. As long as the animation frame background is not transparent, the previous frame is completely covered by the new frame and everything works fine. However, if we terminate an animation by a mouse click and then select a different one whose size is smaller than the first, the new animation will only cover part of the frame; the rest will still contain the last frame of the previous animation that was displayed. To avoid this, we keep track of the animation title and if it changes, we do not allow the *paint* method to be called on the next run of *update*. Instead, we paint a white rectangle the size of the whole frame on the display. Future frames are then displayed against the white rather than against a distracting picture.

If you care to experiment, you'll find that this *ViewAnim* program also does a good job of displaying ordinary *GIF* files that contain only a single picture. Therefore, you might want to use only this one program for all of your *GIF* display requirements. Note, however, that we have sized the window to be about right for most of the sample animation files that are available; you'll need to make it bigger if you want to display full-sized pictures.

Using Sprites

A *sprite* is a small graphic that moves in some path around the display screen. It usually consists of a series of images to provide animation, as well as movement. Sprite manipulation can get pretty complicated. We're only going to present a very simple case. If you looked carefully at the *paint* method in Listing 11.1, you may have noticed something that didn't make sense. Each time paint runs, we reset the parameter *offset* to 0. Then when we call *drawImage* we specify that the top left-hand corner of the image be at coordinates (offset,offset), which is always (0,0). This was included to give you some experience with sprites. If you now comment out the line:

```
offset = 0;
```

and compile and run the program, you'll observe that *offset* starts at 0 but is incremented each time *paint* is run. Your animation will start at the top left corner of the display and move down in a slanting path until it disappears off the screen. You can get a lot more complicated than this by using more mathematics to define the offset for each time *drawImage* is called. It would be quite easy, for example, to make the sprite move around the perimeter of the display. One thing that you need to be concerned about is that your sprite includes enough background around the edges so that it doesn't leave unwanted traces of images as it moves across the display. All this works fine as long as you're not covering up other objects as the sprite moves around the screen. If you need to allow for this, you need to use a sprite with a transparent background and then make provisions for restoring anything covered by the sprite before each new frame is written.

Making Your Own Animation Files

Suppose you have a sequence of images that you want to use for an animation. You may have drawn these frame by frame, or perhaps you have a card that can capture video camera frames. There is a fine program that will permit you to create a multiframe *GIF* file from these images. It is called *GIF Construction Set for Windows*. It is shareware and is available from

Alchemy Mindworks, Inc.
P. O. Box 500
Beeton, Ontario
Canada L0G 1A0

Alchemy Mindworks also has an excellent shareware program for working on all kinds of graphics files. It is called *Graphics Workshop* and is available in DOS, Windows, and Windows 95 versions. You can download any of this software from *http://www.mindworkshop.com*. A more advanced *Graphics Workshop* and the *GIF Construction Set for Windows* are included as part of *Graphics Workshop Pro*, which is included on the CD-ROM. One thing you need to consider in making your own animations and that is that the animation continually recycles. Therefore, you want to have the series of frames that make up your animation begin and end with pictures that are very similar; otherwise, there will be a noticeable jump each time a new cycle occurs. One way to do this, if backward motion isn't objectionable, is to follow the first set of frames with a second set that is the same as the first except that it is reversed.

Pseudo-Animation

The new Java 2D capabilities for rotation, scaling, translation, and skewing, as well as gradient color, make it possible for a Java display to appear to be animated, even though it doesn't use a lot of separate frames. Essentially, what you do is start a thread and have it run as long as the program exists. You include a statement that causes the thread to rest for a convenient time between itera-tions. At each iteration, you include a statement that causes one or more of the parameters listed previously to change. Another statement causes the display to be redrawn with the new parameters. This causes a moving appearance on the display. If you want to see how such code actually works, go back and look at the use of gradient color in Chapter 7. In this example, the thing that is mov-ing is the gradient color control points, causing the distribution of two colors that make up the display background to be changed.

Anfy Java

Anfy Java is a set of 30 animated Java applets by Fabio Ciucci that you can use to enhance your Web pages. They also give you a good idea of how you can use Java to create your own applets. This program is included on the CD-ROM that accompanies this book. When you run it, you can preview each of the ap-plets to see how each looks and whether it meets your requirements. You can control the text message that appears in each applet as well as the picture that appears as the background of some of them, and also a number of other char-acteristics. When you have an applet to your liking, you can copy all the asso-ciated files to a separate directory and ultimately to your Web page. We've chosen two applets as samples. The first is of a lake containing a rippling re-flection of a scene. A snapshot of this applet is shown in Plate 8. It was created by properly cropping a photograph of the Grand Teton mountains with a photo processing program and then adding it to the applet. The applet makes it appear that this scene is at the side of a lake and provides a rippling reflection of the mountains in the lake. As the applet runs, the lake continues to ripple and the selected text comes up a line at a time; first as small lettering in the background and then the lettering grows larger and appears to move toward the front of the scene until it disappears. To create this applet, you run the Anfy Java program and select the *Lake* applet at the beginning. Then click on *next* and you will be led through a series of screens that give you the opportunity to change the applet characteristics. The final screen shows the resulting *html* pro-gram. The one for our version of the lake applet is shown in Listing 11.2.

When you reach this last screen, which shows the *html* file, you need to click on the box that says *Copy all files to...* You can then select the directory where you want this applet to be stored. Then type in a name for the *html* file, and finally click on *Save*. To run this applet, choose a DOS window, go to the directory where the applet is stored, and then type *AppletViewer* followed by the name you gave to the *html* file. We've saved the *Lake* applet for you under *Programs\Chap11\AnfyLake\Lake.html*.

```
<applet code="AnLake.class" width=711 height=538>
<param name=credits value="Applet by Fabio Ciucci
(www.anfiteatro.it/java.html)">
<param name=res value="1">
<param name=image value="Tetons.jpg">
<param name=wavspeed value="30">
<param name=perspective value="10">
<param name=farwaving value="200">
<param name=wind value="10">
<param name=windvarval value="5">
<param name=windvarmin value="5">
<param name=windvarmax value="15">
<param name=overimg value="NO">
<param name=overimgX value="140">
<param name=overimgY value="150">
<param name=textscroll value="lakescr.txt">
<param name=texttype value="zooming">
<param name=textvspace value="0">
<param name=textminfont value="36">
<param name=textmaxfont value="172">
<param name=textoffset value="240">
<param name=textspeed value="2">
<param name=textfont value="Helvetica">
<param name=textbold value="NO">
<param name=textitalic value="NO">
<param name=textsize value="24">
<param name=textshadow value="YES">
<param name=TextSColR value="20">
<param name=TextSColG value="20">
<param name=TextSColB value="50">
<param name=TextColR value="255">
<param name=TextColG value="255">
<param name=TextColB value="155">
<param name=TextJumpAmp value="0">
<param name=TextJumpSpd value="0">
<param name=TextSineAmp value="0">
<param name=TextSineSpd value="0">
<param name=TextSineAngle value="0">
<param name=regcode value="NO">
<param name=reglink value="NO">
<param name=regnewframe value="NO">
<param name=regframename value="_blank">
<param name=statusmsg value="AnLake applet">
<param name=memdelay value="1000">
<param name=priority value="3">
<param name=MinSYNC value="10">
Sorry, your browser doesn't suppor Java.
</applet>
```

LISTING *HTML Program for Lake Applet.*

11.2

The second applet we've chosen for demonstration is one called *Anfy3D*. Plate 9 shows a snapshot of this applet. In the plate, the lettering is in the process of moving from the bottom of the screen to the top. You have several options as to how the text can be handled. As we've set up the applet, the text is streaming across the bottom of the display, moving from right to left. The applet has been stored in *programs\chap11\anfy3D\3D.html*.

If you need a special applet and don't feel comfortable with programming it yourself, Fabio Ciucci will create one for you at a reasonable price. The directions for contacting him are included in the Anfy Java program.

E ven if you've been using the Internet regularly, you may still not realize that most providers allow you to have your own Web page without any additional charge. This feature is not generally known because most providers do not advertise it, but it is there if you're willing to dig deep enough. In this chapter, you'll learn how to create a Web page on FlashNet, which is the provider that I use. I'll try to point out all the pitfalls, so that you can use the same general techniques for your own provider without encountering any difficulties.

The first step in creating a Web page is to go to the homepage of your provider. In my case, this is

```
http://www.flash.net
```

When the homepage comes up, you'll see about half way down on the right side a box labeled *FlashNet Features*. Go to the item labeled *About FlashNet*. Click this item and when the page comes up, you'll see a heading *FlashNet Sites*. Under this heading is an item called *Make-A-Page*. When you click this item, a page comes up that describes how to make your own page. You are asked to enter your name and your username. You then click *Continue*. The next page that comes up aids you in creating a basic page of your own. You don't need to pay much attention to this stuff, since we want to create a whole page from scratch, rather than using the preformatted page. However, we need to go through the procedure to get a page established in the first place. Go down to the bottom of the page and click on *Test*. You'll be shown a sample of what FlashNet proposes as your page. Click on *Send* and the page will be registered for you. Make sure you record the address of your Web page. For FlashNet, it is the FlashNet address followed by a tilde and your username. For example,

```
http://www.flash.net.~rtsteve
```

A Sample Web Page Program

Before proceeding further on the Web, we're going to create our desired Web page with Java. To do this, we need to create a Java applet as was briefly demonstrated in Chapter 5. We do this by compiling a class that is an extension of the *Applet* class with the *javac* compiler. There must be an *HTML* program that is used by the *AppletViewer* or a network browser to run the applet. Listing 12.1 is the *html* program used for the sample Web page program described in this chapter.

```
<APPLET CODE = "Page.class" WIDTH=640 HEIGHT=480>
```

LISTING *HTML Program to Activate Page Applet.*
12.1

Listing 12.2 is the Java program used to create our example Web page. The applet comprises a class called *Page*. It's a pretty simple program, defining a number of text strings and two external picture files.

```
/*
   Page.java
   Creating Your Own Web Page
*/

import java.awt.*;
import java.applet.*;
import java.awt.event.*;
import java.net.*;

public class Page extends Applet
{
    Image pic1, pic2;

    public void paint(Graphics g)
    {
        pic1 = getImage(getDocumentBase(),
"Aspen2.jpg");
        pic2 = getImage(getCodeBase(), "Aspen40.jpg");
        Font f = new Font("TimesRoman", Font.BOLD,
24);
        g.setFont(f);
        g.drawString("A Graphics Tip",230,25);
        g.drawString("By Roger T. Stevens",200,50);
        Font f1 = new Font("TimesRoman", Font.PLAIN,
14);
        g.setFont(f1);
        g.drawString("Have you ever been told that if
you convert a JPEG graphics file to another format
for editing and", 20, 80);
        g.drawString("then convert it back to JPEG
again and repeat this several times, the accumulated
loses of the JPEG ", 20, 95);
        g.drawString("conversions will leave your
picture unuseable? This is simply not true. True,
the first JPEG", 20, 110);
```

LISTING *Java Program to Create Web Page. (continues)*
12.2

```
        g.drawString("conversion causes some loss of
detail, but succeeding conversions cause no
additional losses because", 20, 125);
        g.drawString("the algorithm attempts to remove
the very same detail that was already removed by the
first conversion." , 20, 140);
        g.drawString("That detail is already gone.
Nothing else is removed. To demonstrate this, I took
a BMP graphics file", 20, 155);
        g.drawString("and converted it to JPEG. The
resulting picture is shown below on the left. I then
converted this file",20,170);
        g.drawString("back to BMP format and then
converted back to JPEG again and repeated this
process 20 times. The", 20, 185);
        g.drawString("JPEG picture is shown below on
the right. As you can see, there is no discernible
difference in quality",20,200);
        g.drawString("after 20 JPEG
conversions.",20,215);
        g.drawImage(pic1, 0, 240, this);
        g.drawImage(pic2, 320, 240, this);

    }
}
```

LISTING *Java Program to Create Web Page. (continued)*
12.2

For the program to run properly, you must first compile it with *javac*. The two graphics files must be in the same subdirectory as the compiled program. Then run *AppletViewer* with the corresponding *html* file as a parameter. For example,

```
AppletViewer Page.html
```

Make sure that you include the *html* extension, or the program will not run. Alternately, you may run your Web browser in the offline mode and select as a file name the whole path including the file name and the extension *html*. A word of warning: If you are running Windows 95 or Windows 98, either the browser or the *AppletViewer* program will disregard case in file names. However, this is not true when you upload the program to your Web page. To run on the Web, the program shown must call the two graphics files with the capitals and small letters corresponding exactly to the way in which the file names are stored. If this is not true, the program may run perfectly well on the

AppletViewer or browser, but when you try to view the Web page, the two pictures will be missing.

Transferring Your Page to the Web

In order to put your page on the Web, you'll need some special software. If you're using Netscape 3.0 or above as your browser, you'll find that it includes file transfer software. Otherwise, there are several other programs that will do the job. The one I used is *ws_ftp*. You can down load this from

```
http://www.csra.net/junodj/ws_ftp32.htm
```

Scan down the page that appears until you find the line

```
Download LE4.60 32 bit Self-Extracting
```

either under the heading *Primary Site* or *Alternate Site*. Click this line to download and run the program to set the program up for operation. When you run the program, you'll first need to make a connection to your Internet server. Once this is complete, the first thing that you get is a screen that asks you for basic setup information. This screen is shown in Figure 12.1. To fill in this screen, the most important thing that you need to know is the name of the Host, which is usually not the name that you use in accessing your server. For example, the address of my server is *flash.net*, but the Host name that I need to use to set files to my Web page is *ftpusers.flash.net*. I discovered this by looking at a FlashNet Web page called

```
http://www.flash.net/surf/web.html
```

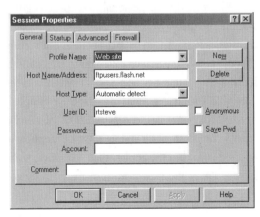

FIGURE *The ws_ftp Program Setup Screen.*
12.1

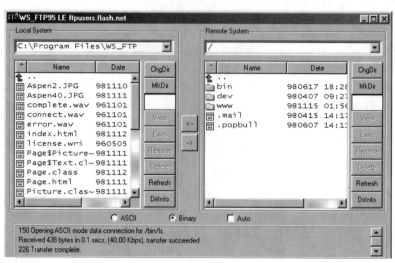

FIGURE   *The ws_ftp Program Operating Screen.*
12.2

If you're working with some other server, you'll need to search around a bit, beginning with the homepage of the server, to determine what Host name you need to use for uploading. You may also need to enter the username and password under which your Web page is registered.

When you've okayed this page, the display shown in Figure 12.2 will appear. You're now ready to transfer files to your Web page. You don't need to transfer the *Page.java* file that you created. Instead, you transfer the *Page.class* file that was produced when you compiled *Page.java*. In addition, you need to transfer the *Page.html* file that you created to permit you to view the program with the *AppletViewer*. If your personal Web page is going to consist of only a single screen, you need to rename *Page.html* to *index.html* before you do the file transfer. If you want to have more than one screen, you need an *index.html* file that contains code that enables you to select and run more that one applet. Finally, if there are other class files or graphics files associated with your applet, you need to transfer them also. In the example, two *JPEG* graphics files are needed, *Aspen2.JPG* and *Aspen40.JPG*. Remember that the use of capital and small letters in these file names must be identical to the way in which they were referred to within the applet. Plate 10 shows what the sample Web page looks like. You may also view it from the Internet by going to

```
http://www.flash.net/~rtsteve
```

13 Plotting Points, Lines, and Rectangles

T he Java AWT package provides methods in its *Graphics* class for drawing single pixel wide straight lines, rectangles, rounded rectangles, and
three-dimensional rectangles. It also has methods for creating filled
rectangles. All of these are independent of the characteristics of the platform on
which you are using Java. These methods will cover a lot of the situations you
encounter in which lines and rectangles must be drawn. However, if you want
to draw wide lines, or patterned lines (such as dotted lines, dashed lines, or center lines) you need to extend beyond these basic capabilities. This used to be
pretty difficult, but since the inclusion of the Java 2D graphics package, all this
and more has become quite simple. This chapter will show you how to do just
about everything you want to with lines and rectangles.

Drawing Lines

First we're going to look at drawing lines with the original Java AWT. Listing
13.1 is a program to draw a burst of lines radiating from the center of the display window.

```
/*
Lines1.java
Program to draw a line pattern
*/

import java.awt.*;
import java.util.*;
import java.awt.event.*;

class Lines1Canvas extends Canvas
{
    Lines1Canvas()
    {
    }

    public void paint(Graphics g)
    {
        int i, ndex, row, col, xres=640, yres=480;

        for(i=30; i<yres-10; i+=25)
        {
            g.setColor(new Color(0, 0, 255));
            g.drawLine(7,9,xres-7,i);
            g.setColor(new Color(255, 0, 0));
            g.drawLine(xres-7, yres-5, 7,i);
            g.setColor(new Color(0,255,0));
```

LISTING *Line Drawing Program. (continues)*
13.1

```
                g.drawLine(7, yres-5, xres-7, i);
                g.setColor(new Color(255, 0, 255));
                g.drawLine(xres-7, 9, 7, i);
        }
    }
}

public class Lines1 extends Frame
{
    public Lines1()
    {
        super("Line Pattern");
        addWindowListener(new DWAdapter());
        setBackground(Color.white);
        setLayout( new BorderLayout());
        add("Center", new Lines1Canvas());
        setSize(640, 480);
        show();
    }

    class DWAdapter extends WindowAdapter
    {
        public void windowClosing(WindowEvent event)
        {
            System.exit(0);
        }
    }

    public static void main(String args[])
    {
        Lines1 f = new Lines1();
    }
}
```

LISTING *Line Drawing Program. (continued)*
13.1

As you can see, the program is pretty simple. We use just one *for* loop to draw four sets of radiating lines. For each line we use one iteration of a *g.setColor* statement to set the correct line color and then one iteration of a *g.drawLine* statement to do the actual line drawing. These are included in the *paint* method. The rest of the program is very similar to the examples in previous chapters. The resulting display is shown in Figure 13.1.

Drawing straight lines is easy, but we can use the *drawLine* function for a lot more than this. In fact, we can create very complex curves by composing them from a lot of short line segments. Listing 13.2 is a program to draw a graph of the function *sinc(x)* or *(sine x)/x*. The program is very similar in structure to the

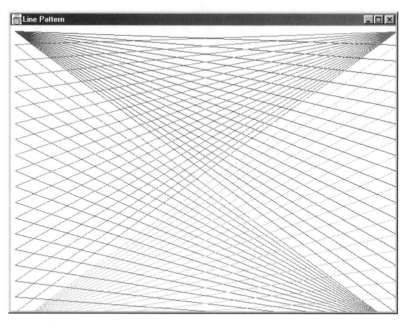

FIGURE *Drawing a Pattern of Straight Lines.*
13.1

program in Listing 13.1; the principal difference is in the *paint* method. The method begins by using the *drawLine* method to draw horizontal and vertical straight lines through what is to be the origin of the graph, dividing the graph into four equal rectangles. Next, we enter a *for* loop that iterates once for each column value (*col*) of the display. The loop first calculates a value for the *x* coordinate of the graph. It is set up so that the range of *x* is –26.667 radians to +26.667 radians, with the zero value of *x* at the middle of the graph. Next, the method computes the value of the *y* coordinate of the function *(sin x)/x*. One point, where *x* is 0, it cannot be computed by the computer, which can't divide by 0. Using more advanced mathematical techniques, however, we can find that the value of *y* at that point is 1, so we use an *if* statement to take care of that point. Next we find a value for *row* such that the maximum *y* point will be at the top of the screen. Then we use an *if* statement to avoid drawing a line at the first iteration of the loop (which is used solely to fill the line starting coordinates by setting *old_col* to *col* and *old_row* to *row*). For each of the rest of the loop iterations, we draw a straight line between the old and new values of *row* and *col*. Figure 13.2 shows the resulting display; a very nice representation of the *sinc* curve.

```
/*
   Sinc. ava = Program to draw sinc(x)
*/

import  ava.awt.*;
import  ava.awt.event.*;

class SincCanvas extends Canvas
{
   SincCanvas()
   {
   }

   public void paint(Graphics g)
   {
      double x, y;
      int col, row, old_col=0, old_row=0;

      g.drawLine(0,240,639,240);
      g.drawLine(320,0,320,479);
      for (col=0; col<640; col++)
      {
         x = ((double)(col-320))/12.0;
         if (x == 0)
            y = 1;
         else
            y = Math.sin(x)/x;
          row = 240 - (int)(y * 240.0);
         if (col>0)
            g.drawLine(old_col, old_row, col, row);
         old_col = col;
         old_row = row;
      }

   }
}

public class Sinc extends Frame
{
   public Sinc()
   {
      super("Sinc(x) curve");
      addWindowListener(new DWAdapter());
      setBackground(Color.white);
      setLayout( new BorderLayout());
      add("Center", new SincCanvas());
      setSize(640, 480);
      show();
   }
```

LISTING *Program to Draw the sinc Function with Short Line Segments. (continues)*
13.2

```
class DWAdapter extends WindowAdapter
{
   public void windowClosing(WindowEvent event)
   {
      System.exit(0);
   }
}

public static void main(String args[])
{
   Sinc f = new Sinc();
}
}
```

LISTING *Program to Draw the sinc Function with Short Line Segments. (continued)*
13.2

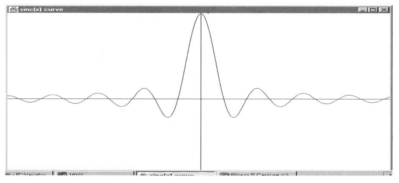

FIGURE *Display of the sinc Curve.*
13.2

Drawing Rectangles

There are eight methods for creating rectangles using the Java *Graphics* class, four for drawing the rectangle outlines and four for making filled rectangles. These are shown in monochrome in Figure 13.3. As you look at the figure, you'll see that some of these methods are not very useful. This sample display was created using the program of Listing 13.3. Looking at the listing, you'll see that we have defined six classes that are extensions of the class *Canvas*. Each uses one of the rectangle drawing methods. The first is the class *RectCanvas*. For this class we have defined a *paint* method that begins by setting the painting color to black and then draws a rectangle with the expression

```
g.drawRect(10, 10, 120, 80);
```

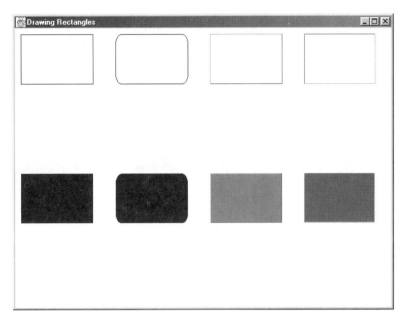

FIGURE *Drawing Rectangles.*
13.3

If you are used to functions that specify the top left and lower right corners to define a rectangle, please note that this is **not** the way this method works. The first two parameters passed to the method are indeed the *x* and *y* coordinates of the top left corner of the rectangle, but the last two coordinates are the rectangle width and height, respectively (the actual number of pixels in the width and height lines, respectively). If you're thinking in terms of the bottom right coordinates, you have to subtract the top left coordinates from them and add 1 to each to get the width and height.

```
/*
   Rectangles. ava
   Program to draw rectangles
*/

import  ava.awt.*;
import  ava.awt.event.*;

class RectCanvas extends Canvas
```

LISTING *Program to Draw Rectangles. (continues)*
13.3

```
{
   public void paint(Graphics g)
   {
      g.setColor(Color.black);
      g.drawRect(10, 10, 120, 80);
   }
}

class RoundRectCanvas extends Canvas
{
   public void paint(Graphics g)
   {
      g.setColor(Color.black);
      g.drawRoundRect(10, 10, 120, 80, 20, 30);
   }
}
class Rect3DCanvas extends Canvas
{
   boolean raiseorlower;
   Rect3DCanvas(boolean B)
   {
      raiseorlower = B;
   }

   public void paint(Graphics g)
   {
      g.setColor(Color.gray);
      g.draw3DRect(10, 10, 120, 80, raiseorlower);
   }

}

class FillRectCanvas extends Canvas
{
   public void paint(Graphics g)
   {
      g.setColor(Color.black);
      g.fillRect(10, 10, 120,80);
   }
}

class FillRoundRectCanvas extends Canvas
{
   public void paint(Graphics g)
   {
      g.setColor(Color.black);
      g.fillRoundRect(10, 10, 120, 80, 20, 30);
   }
}
```

LISTING *Program to Draw Rectangles. (continues)*
13.3

```
class FillRect3DCanvas extends Canvas
{
   boolean raiseorlower;
   FillRect3DCanvas(boolean B)
   {
      raiseorlower = B;
   }

   public void paint(Graphics g)
   {
      g.setColor(Color.gray);
      g.fill3DRect(10, 10, 120, 80, raiseorlower);
   }

}
public class Rectangles extends Frame
{

   public Rectangles()
   {
      super("Drawing Rectangles");
      addWindowListener(new DWAdapter());
      setLayout( new GridLayout(2,4) );
      add(new RectCanvas());
      add( new RoundRectCanvas());
      add(new Rect3DCanvas(true));
      add(new Rect3DCanvas(false));
      add(new FillRectCanvas());
      add( new FillRoundRectCanvas());
      add(new FillRect3DCanvas(true));
      add(new FillRect3DCanvas(false));
      setSize(640, 480);
      show();
   }

   class DWAdapter extends WindowAdapter
   {
      public void windowClosing(WindowEvent event)
      {
         System.exit(0);
      }
   }

   public static void main(String args[])
   {
      Frame f = new Rectangles();
   }
}
```

LISTING *Program to Draw Rectangles. (continued)*
13.3

The second class to be defined is the *RoundRectCanvas* class. It uses the expression

```
g.drawRoundRect(10, 10, 120, 80, 20, 30);
```

to draw a rounded rectangle. As with the *drawRect* method, the first four parameters passed to this method are the *x* and *y* coordinates of the top left corner and the width and height of a rectangle. These values, however, are those of a regular rectangle, before its corners are rounded. The last two coordinates are the height and width of a bounding box that is used to define an ellipse. Each quarter of this ellipse is properly positioned and used to draw one rounded corner for the rectangle. Before we proceed, let's look at a little program that shows how the rectangle and ellipses interact. This program is listed as Listing 13.4. The program first draws a rounded rectangle. It then draws an ellipse (circle and ellipse drawing will be described in detail in Chapter 17). The bounding box for this ellipse has its top left corner at the same coordinates as the top left corner of the rounded rectangle. Its width and height are the same as those specified for the rounded corners of the rounded rectangle. Next, three more ellipses are drawn, each having the same width and height as the first ellipse. The coordinates of the bounding box for each of these ellipses are set so that one corner of the bounding box will be the same as one corner of the rectangle prior to rounding. Figure 13.4 shows the figure that is produced by the program. Note that a quarter of each ellipse is the same as a rounded corner of the rounded rectangle. This will give you an idea of how the rounded rectangle method works internally. Fortunately, you don't have to go through all of the calculations; the method handles it all for you.

```
    /*
    RndRect. ava
    Shows How Rounded Rectangle is Drawn
 */

import   ava.awt.*;
import   ava.awt.event.*;

class RndRectCanvas extends Canvas
{
    RndRectCanvas()
    {
    }
```

LISTING *How Rounded Rectangles Are Drawn. (continues)*
13.4

```
    public void paint(Graphics g)
    {
       g.drawRoundRect(10,10,620,460,62,46);
       g.drawOval(10,10,62,46);
       g.drawOval(568,10,62,46);
       g.drawOval(568,424,62,46);
       g.drawOval(10,424,62,46);
    }
}

public class RndRect extends Frame
{
    public RndRect()
    {
       addWindowListener(new DWAdapter());
       setTitle("Rounded Rectangle Construction");
       setLayout( new BorderLayout());
       add("Center", new RndRectCanvas());
       setSize(680, 520);
       show();
    }

    class DWAdapter extends WindowAdapter
    {
       public void windowClosing(WindowEvent event)
       {
          System.exit(0);
       }
    }

    public static void main(String args[])
    {
       RndRect f = new RndRect();
    }
}
```

LISTING *How Rounded Rectangles Are Drawn. (continued)*
13.4

Now let's continue with our description of the *Rectangles* program. The next class that we define is the *Rect3DCanvas* class. We first define a constructor for this class that includes having a parameter passed to a new object of the class when it is created. Within the class, the *paint* method is defined. It sets the drawing color to gray and then calls the method

```
g.draw3DRect(10, 10, 120, 80, raiseorlower);
```

The first four parameters passed to this method are the coordinates of the top left corner of the rectangle and its width and height. The 3D rectangle is

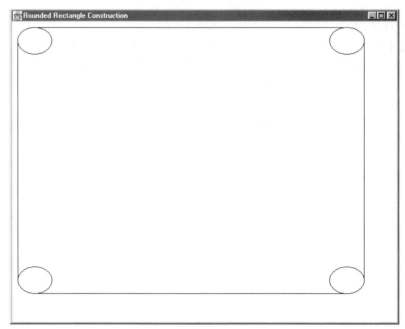

FIGURE *Drawing the Rounded Rectangle with Ovals.*
13.4

supposed to give a three-dimensional effect by drawing two adjacent sides in a darker shade of color than the other two. The boolean parameter *raiseorlower* determines which sides are darker. When the parameter is *true*, the right and bottom sides are darker; when it is *false*, the left and top sides are darker. Don't draw a 3D rectangle colored black or white, since darker and lighter shades are not available. You'll see from the color plate that the three-dimensional effect is minimal and probably won't ever be of much use to you.

The next three classes that are defined create filled versions of the rectangle (*fillRect*), the rounded rectangle (*fillRoundRect*), and the three-dimensional rectangle (*fill3DRect*). Their parameters are the same as for the respective line-drawn versions. Observe from the figure that the three-dimensional effect for 3D filled rectangles is even less obvious than for drawn 3D rectangles. When the parameter *raiseorlower* is *true*, the right and bottom sides are darker than the rest of the rectangle; when the parameter is *false*, the entire rectangle except for the right and bottom sides is darker.

Next, the program defines a *Rectangles* class that sets up a title for the window, establishes a 2 × 4 grid layout, and adds an object of each of the rectangle classes to the display. The program also includes the usual method for terminating the display. Finally is the *main* method that is called when Java interprets the class.

Drawing Lines with Java 2D

You've now seen how to draw lines and rectangles using the original Java AWT, but these capabilities are quite primitive. Fortunately, Java 2D vastly increases the drawing capabilities of Java. As an example of the new capabilities, we're going to show you a program that has the capability to draw wide lines, offers several different ways to join wide lines, and provides for anti-aliasing. This program is listed in Listing 13.5.

```
/*
    Triangle1. ava
    Draws a Triangle
*/

import  ava.applet.Applet;
import  ava.awt.*;
import  ava.awt.event.*;
import  ava.awt.geom.GeneralPath;

public class Triangle1 extends Applet implements
Ad ustmentListener, ItemListener
{
    static String label = "Line width: ";
    TriangleCanvas canvas;
    Scrollbar slider = new Scrollbar();
    TextField field = new TextField();
    Checkbox antialiastoggle, round, miter, bevel ;

    public void init()
    {
        setLayout(new BorderLayout());
        setBackground(new Color(180, 180, 255));
        Panel p1 = new Panel();
        Panel p2 = new Panel();
        CheckboxGroup group = new CheckboxGroup();
        slider = new Scrollbar(Scrollbar.HORIZONTAL,
0, 20, 0, 120);
        slider.addAd ustmentListener(this);
        antialiastoggle = new Checkbox("Antialias",
false);
        antialiastoggle.addItemListener(this);
        p1.setLayout(new GridLayout(1,4));
        p2.setLayout(new GridLayout(1,4));
        p1.add(antialiastoggle);
        p1.add(new Label("Line width: "));
        p1.add(slider);
        p2.add(new Label("Line  oin method: "));
```

LISTING *Drawing Wide Triangles. (continues)*

13.5

```java
      p2.add(miter = new Checkbox ("Miter", group,
true));
      p2.add(round = new Checkbox ("Round", group,
false));
      p2.add(bevel = new Checkbox ("Bevel", group,
false));
      round.addItemListener(this);
      miter.addItemListener(this);
      bevel.addItemListener(this);

      add ("North", p2);
      add("South", p1);
      add("Center", canvas = new
TriangleCanvas(this));
   }

   public String roundstr(double value) {
      return Double.toString(Math.round(value *
100.0) / 100.0);
   }

   public double sliderval()
   {
      Scrollbar s = slider;
      int val = s.getValue();
      double ret = (val / 100.0 * 20.0);
      field.setText(roundstr(ret));
      return ret;
   }
   public void
adjustmentValueChanged(AdjustmentEvent e)
   {
      Object target = e.getSource();
      if (target == slider)
   {
      canvas.penwidth = sliderval();
         canvas.repaint();


      }
   }

   public void itemStateChanged(ItemEvent e)
   {
      e.getStateChange();
      if (e.getSource().equals(round))
         canvas.join = BasicStroke.JOIN_ROUND;
      if (e.getSource().equals(miter))
         canvas.join = BasicStroke.JOIN_MITER;
      if (e.getSource().equals(bevel))
```

LISTING *Drawing Wide Triangles. (continues)*
13.5

```
            canvas. oin = BasicStroke.JOIN_BEVEL;
        if (e.getSource().equals(antialiastoggle))
        {
            canvas.antialias =
antialiastoggle.getState();
        }
        canvas.repaint();
    }

    public static void main(String argv[])
    {
        Frame f = new Frame("Drawing Lines with Java
2D");
        final Triangle1 demo = new Triangle1();
        f.add(demo);
        f.addWindowListener(new WindowAdapter() {
            public void windowClosing(WindowEvent e)
                {System.exit(0);}
        });
        f.pack();
        f.setSize(new Dimension(500,400));
        demo.init();
        f.show();
    }
}

class TriangleCanvas extends Canvas
{
    Triangle1 applet;
    double penwidth;
    boolean antialias;
    int  oin;

    public TriangleCanvas(Triangle1 app)
    {
        applet = app;
        setBackground(new Color(220, 220, 255));
    }

    public Dimension getPreferredSize()
    {
        return new Dimension(300, 300);
    }

    public void update(Graphics g) {
        paint(g);
    }

    public void paint(Graphics g)
```

LISTING *Drawing Wide Triangles. (continues)*
13.5

```
    {
        Graphics2D g2;
        int width = getSize().width;
        int height = getSize().height;
        g2 = (Graphics2D) g;
        g2.clearRect(0, 0, width, height);

g2.setRenderingHint(RenderingHints.KEY_ANTIALIASING,
        (antialias ?
RenderingHints.VALUE_ANTIALIAS_ON
        : RenderingHints.VALUE_ANTIALIAS_OFF));

g2.setRenderingHint(RenderingHints.KEY_RENDERING,
        (antialias ?
RenderingHints.VALUE_RENDER_QUALITY

        : RenderingHints.VALUE_RENDER_SPEED));
        BasicStroke bs;
        bs = new BasicStroke((float) penwidth,
           BasicStroke.CAP_ROUND,  oin, 10.0f);
        g2.translate(width / 2.0, height / 2.0);
        GeneralPath p = new GeneralPath(0);
        p.moveTo(- width / 2.5f, + height / 5.0f);
        p.lineTo(0.0f, - height / 2.2f);
        p.lineTo(width / 2.5f, + height / 5.0f);
        p.closePath();
        g2.setStroke(bs);
        g2.draw(p);
        g2.dispose();
    }
}
```

LISTING *Drawing Wide Triangles. (continued)*
13.5

First let's look at the initialization method *init*. It begins by setting up a *BorderLayout* and then setting the background color to a light blue. It is then going to set up the layout for the buttons that control the management of the graphic. At the top (North) of the display will be three choices that determine how the lines are to be joined together. For these, we create a *CheckboxGroup* so that only one box can be chosen at a time. The three choices are *Miter, Round,* and *Bevel.* For each we add a checkbox to the group with *Miter* set to *true* initially. These are arrayed together with a generic definition label in a *GridLayout.* At the bottom (South) of the display, we have another *GridLayout,* which contains a checkbox for the anti-aliasing action and a slider, which controls the line width. Listeners are provided for all the actions. Finally, the graphic is added to the center of the display by creating a new *TriangleCanvas* object.

When a change is made in the slider, the *adjustmentValueChanged* method is called. It then uses the methods *sliderval* and *roundstr* to obtain a number for the line width from the slider position. This is stored in *canvas.penwidth*. The canvas is then repainted at the new line width. When a new way of joining the lines is selected, the method *itemStateChanged* is selected. The *canvas.join* object is then set to the proper value for the selection. Similarly, if the anti-aliasing button is toggled, this method changes the *canvas.antialias* parameter to the proper value.

The *main* program is similar to those we've given in other examples. It creates a new frame and adds the *Triangle1* class object *demo* to it. The window listener to close the program when a close window action is taken is added. The display information is packed, the window size is set, the *demo* object is initiated, and the display then takes place.

The *TriangleCanvas* object supervises the actual creation of the graphics, which takes place in its *paint* method. This method begins by getting the width and height of the window. It then creates a graphics object *g2* of class *Graphics2D*. It next clears the window. Then the rendering hints are set up. These are either anti-aliasing or no anti-aliasing, and if anti-aliasing is chosen, whether the method selected should emphasize speed or quality. These rendering hints determine how all lines will be drawn. Next, the object *bs* of class *BasicStroke* is created. The parameters of this object determine for all lines to be drawn what the width shall be, how the ends of unclosed subpaths shall be terminated, how line segments shall be joined, and the limit for miter joins. The *translate* method is then called to move the center of the coordinate system from the top right corner of the display to the center of the display.

We then set up an object *p* of class *GeneralPath*. This object stores all of the coordinates for the lines that are to be drawn. We then create the line segments. The method *moveTo* establishes the coordinates of the beginning of a path. Then, for each *lineTo* statement, a line is drawn from the current position on the path to the coordinates specified as parameters in the method. Finally, if you want to close the path, the method *closePath* draws a line from the current position back to the starting point of the path. We've used these statements to draw a large triangle. Once the path is done, the method *setStroke* assures that the line will be drawn with all of the characteristics specified by the *bs* object. The Graphics2D *draw* method is then used to draw all the lines that are part of *p*. Finally, we dispose of the *g2* object since it is no longer needed.

Anti-Aliasing

Because a computer display has a discrete number of picture elements, usually when we attempt to draw a slanting line, we find that there are many cases where no picture element is at exactly the place where we'd like to have one as part of our line. Consequently, we have to make do with activating the pixels that are nearest to our line even if they aren't in exactly the right position. The resulting line has "jaggies," a step-like characteristic that makes the line look like a tiny staircase rather than a smooth straight line. The mathematical discipline that deals with this kind of situation is called *sampled data theory*. It tells us that when we sample a continuous piece of data (such as a straight line) at discrete intervals, we not only lose some of the information about the line, but also introduce new and unwanted information at multiples of the sampling frequency. This is those stair steps that we'd rather not see. Such information is called *aliases*.

If you're drawing a single pixel wide line, you pretty much have to live with this situation. But if you want a wider line, although you can't make the actual situation any better, you can trick the eye into believing the line is smooth by proper pixel manipulation. The trick is to paint all pixels that are totally in the line's path black and those that are only partially in the line's path with some shade of gray. This is called *anti-aliasing*. In the preceding paragraph, we showed how a Java program could specify anti-aliasing, but didn't go into the details of how it works. We don't need these details either; all you need to do is specify what you want in the rendering hints and Java 2D takes care of the rest. The best way to see how this works is to run the program previously discussed. First set the line to be fairly wide—about a quarter inch or so. With anti-aliasing off, you'll see the characteristic stair steps. Then click anti-aliasing on and you'll swear the line has suddenly become smooth, even though we've warned you that this is just an optical illusion.

While running the program, you can try selecting the different ways to join lines together and note the difference in the way each pair of sides of the triangle are joined. The display that results from running this program is shown in Figure 13.5.

Dashed and Dotted Lines

You can't use the line drawing method from the AWT to create dashed or dotted lines. Before Java 2D you needed to develop a complete line drawing program if you wanted anything but solid lines. The Java 2D line drawing methods, however, do have the capability to create lines with any pattern you want. Listing 13.6 gives a program to display two different sets of patterned

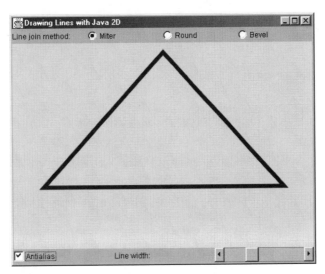

FIGURE   *First Triangle Display.*
13.5

lines. Mostly, the program is just like Listing 13.5. However, the buttons for determining the line segment joining method have been removed and the join type has been fixed. Two new general path objects have been used. The first creates a pair of lines, one horizontal and one vertical, that intersect at the center of the display. We now add to the parameters passed to the *BasicStroke* object a final parameter consisting of a floating point array. This array consists of the value for a line segment length, followed by a value for a space, followed by the value for a line segment length, followed by another space. You can have as many members of the array as you want; when the line is drawn it will follow the pattern to the end and then repeat as many times as necessary. For the first pattern, we've used a center line. This is a line that has a short line segment, followed by a short space, followed by a long line segment, followed by a space. Normally, center lines intersect at the middle of one of the short line segments, but this can't be simply controlled in Java. If you need this type of intersection, you'd need to start a center line at the intersection and then go in each of the four directions. You'd also have to modify the pattern. You could have half a short line, followed by a short space, followed by a long line, followed by a short space, followed by half a short line.

The second general path object draws a rectangle around the perimeter of the display. This pattern consists of alternate lines and spaces of the same size. These are only samples. You can create any line pattern that your imagine can invent. Figure 13.6 show the result of running this program.

```
/*
   Lines.java
   Draws dashed and center lines
*/

import java.applet.Applet;
import java.awt.*;
import java.awt.event.*;
import java.awt.geom.GeneralPath;

public class Lines extends Applet implements
AdjustmentListener
{
   static String label = "Line width: ";
   DisplayCanvas canvas;
   Scrollbar slider = new Scrollbar();
   TextField field = new TextField();

   public void init()
   {
      setLayout(new BorderLayout());
      setBackground(new Color(180, 180, 255));
      Panel p1 = new Panel();
      slider = new Scrollbar(Scrollbar.HORIZONTAL,
0, 20, 0, 120);
      slider.addAdjustmentListener(this);
      p1.setLayout(new GridLayout(1,2));
      p1.add(new Label("Line width: "));
      p1.add(slider);
      add("South", p1);
      add("Center", canvas = new
DisplayCanvas(this));
   }

   public String roundstr(double value)
   {
      return Double.toString(Math.round(value *
100.0) / 100.0);
   }

   public double sliderval()
   {
      Scrollbar s = slider;
      int val = s.getValue();
      double ret = (val / 100.0 * 20.0);
      field.setText(roundstr(ret));
      return ret;
   }
}
```

LISTING *Program to Draw Patterned Lines. (continues)*
13.6

```
    public void
adjustmentValueChanged(AdjustmentEvent e)
   {
      Object target = e.getSource();
      if (target == slider)
      {
         canvas.penwidth = sliderval();
            canvas.repaint();


      }
   }

   public static void main(String argv[]) {
      Frame f = new Frame
         ("Drawing Dashed and Center Lines with Java
2D");
      final Lines demo = new Lines();
      f.add(demo);
      f.addWindowListener(new WindowAdapter()
      {
         public void windowClosing(WindowEvent e)
         {
            System.exit(0);
         }
      });
      f.pack();
      f.setSize(new Dimension(500,400));
      demo.init();
      f.show();
   }
}

class DisplayCanvas extends Canvas
{
   Lines applet;
   double penwidth;

   public DisplayCanvas(Lines app)
   {
      applet = app;
      setBackground(new Color(220, 220, 255));
   }

   public Dimension getPreferredSize()
   {
      return new Dimension(300, 300);
   }

   public void update(Graphics g)
```

LISTING *Program to Draw Patterned Lines. (continues)*
13.6

```
    {
        paint(g);
    }

    public void paint(Graphics g)
    {
        Graphics2D g2;
        int width = getSize().width;
        int height = getSize().height;
        g2 = (Graphics2D) g;
        g2.clearRect(0, 0, width, height);

g2.setRenderingHint(RenderingHints.KEY_ANTIALIASING,
        (RenderingHints.VALUE_ANTIALIAS_OFF));
        BasicStroke bs;
        bs = new BasicStroke((float) penwidth,
            BasicStroke.CAP_BUTT, 0, 10.0f,
            new float[]{10,10,30,10},0);
        g2.translate(width / 2.0, height / 2.0);
        GeneralPath p = new GeneralPath(0);
        p.moveTo(0.0f / 2.5f, + height / 2.2f);
        p.lineTo(0.0f, - height / 2.2f);
        p.moveTo(-width / 2.5f, 0.0f);
        p.lineTo(width / 2.5f, 0.0f);
        g2.setStroke(bs);
        g2.draw(p);
        bs = new BasicStroke((float) penwidth,
            BasicStroke.CAP_BUTT, 0, 10.0f,
            new float[] {10, 10, 10, 10} ,0);
        p.moveTo(-width/2.5f, -height/2.2f);
        p.lineTo(width/2.5f, -height/2.2f);
        p.lineTo(width/2.5f, height/2.2f);
        p.lineTo(-width/2.5f, height/2.2f);
        p.closePath();
        g2.setStroke(bs);
        g2.draw(p);
        g2.dispose();
    }
}
```

LISTING *Program to Draw Patterned Lines. (continued)*
13.6

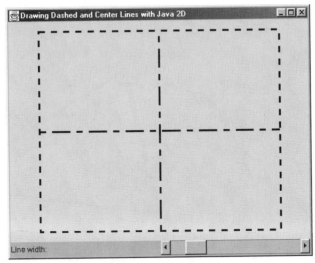

FIGURE *Program to Generate Patterned Lines.*
13.6

Scaling, Rotating, Skewing, and Translating Lines

A set of affine transformation capabilities in Java 2 allows a *Graphics2D* object to be translated, scaled, rotated, or skewed by any desired amount. This can be extremely useful. For example, suppose you want a square that is rotated 45 degrees. Previously, you had to figure out the coordinates of each corner of the square and then draw lines between adjacent points. If there was an error in your math, you might get a strange figure instead of what you want. Now, you insert a 45-degree rotation of the graphics object and then draw an ordinary square as a *Graphics2D* object with the ordinary orientation of sides along the x and y axes. Java will rotate the square 45 degrees for you without you needing to make any calculations. (Well, actually, you have to convert the rotation angle to radians, but that's quite easy.) Listing 13.7 is a program to allow you to try these operations. It is similar to the last two programs, except that it has sliders for rotation, skewing, and scaling. The necessary methods are there to translate the returned slider positions into numbers. If you look in the *paint* method, the only difference you'll notice is a set of methods. The method *g2.scale* changes the size of the object. It can do this in each of the x and y coordinates, but we use the same value for each to preserve the shape relationship during this operation. The method *g2.shear* allows you to skew the object. The method *g2.rotate* allows you to rotate the object. Figure 13.7 shows the result of running this program and performing some affine transforms. Try running the program and making some changes yourself to become familiar with the capabilities available.

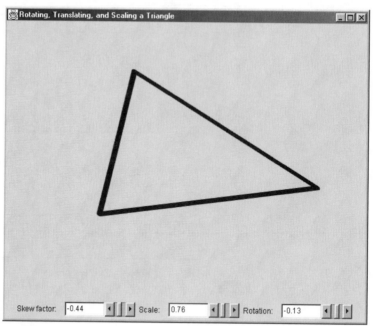

FIGURE   *Affine Transformation Display.*
13.7

```
/*
   Triangle2.java
   Program to Rotate, Scale, and Skew a Triangle
*/

import java.applet.Applet;
import java.awt.*;
import java.awt.event.*;
import java.awt.geom.GeneralPath;
import javax.swing.*;

public class Triangle2 extends Applet implements
AdjustmentListener
{
   static final int SKEW = 1;
   static final int SCALE = 2;
   static final int ROTATE = 3;

   static String labels[] =
   {
```

LISTING   *Program to Demonstrate Affine Transformations. (continues)*
13.7

```
            "Line width:",
            "Skew factor:",
            " Scale:",
            " Rotation:",
        };

        static final int MIN = 0;
        static final int DEF = 1;
        static final int MAX = 2;

        static double limits[][] =
        {
            {0.0, 4.0, 20.0},
            {-2.0, 0.0, 2.0},
            {0.01, 0.8, 3.0},
            {-Math.PI, 0.0, Math.PI},
        };

        TextField fields[] = new
    TextField[labels.length];
        Scrollbar sliders[] = new
    Scrollbar[labels.length];
        triCanvas canvas;

        public void init()
        {
            setLayout(new BorderLayout());
            setBackground(new Color(220, 220, 255));
            add("Center", canvas = new triCanvas(this));
            Panel p = new Panel();
            Panel px = new Panel();
            px.setLayout(new BoxLayout(px,
    BoxLayout.X_AXIS));
            for (int i = 1; i < fields.length; i++)
            {
                Label label = new Label(labels[i]);
                px.add(label);
                fields[i] = new TextField("", 6);
                px.add(fields[i]);
                sliders[i] = new
    Scrollbar(Scrollbar.HORIZONTAL, 0, 20, 0, 120);
                sliders[i].addAdjustmentListener(this);
                px.add(sliders[i]);
            }
            p.add(px);
            add("South", p);
            resetValues();
        }
```

LISTING *Program to Demonstrate Affine Transformations. (continues)*
13.7

```java
public void resetValues()
{
    for (int i = 1; i < limits.length; i++)
    {
        double def = limits[i][DEF];
        fields[i].setText(roundstr(def));
        sliders[i].setValue(sliderset(i, def));
        handleValue(i, def);
    }
    canvas.repaint();
}

public void handleValue(int index, double val)
{
    switch (index)
    {
        case SKEW:
            canvas.skew = val;
            break;
        case SCALE:
            canvas.scale = val;
            break;
        case ROTATE:
            canvas.rotate = val;
            break;
    }
}

public String roundstr(double value)
{
    return Double.toString(Math.round(value *
100.0) / 100.0);
}

public int sliderset(int fieldindex, double val)
{
    return (int) (100.0 * ((val -
limits[fieldindex][MIN])
        / (limits[fieldindex][MAX]
        - limits[fieldindex][MIN])));
}

public double fieldval(int fieldindex)
{
    TextField t = fields[fieldindex];
    String val = t.getText();
    double ret;
    try
    {
```

LISTING *Program to Demonstrate Affine Transformations. (continues)*
13.7

```
        ret = Double.valueOf(val).doubleValue();
    }
    catch (NumberFormatException e)
    {
        ret = limits[fieldindex][DEF];
    }
        ret = Math.max(limits[fieldindex][MIN],
            Math.min(limits[fieldindex][MAX], ret));
        t.setText(roundstr(ret));

sliders[fieldindex].setValue(sliderset(fieldindex,
ret));
        return ret;
    }

    public double sliderval(int fieldindex)
    {
        Scrollbar s = sliders[fieldindex];
        int val = s.getValue();
        double ret = (limits[fieldindex][MIN]
            + val / 100.0 * (limits[fieldindex][MAX]
                - limits[fieldindex][MIN]));
        fields[fieldindex].setText(roundstr(ret));
        return ret;
    }

    public void
adjustmentValueChanged(AdjustmentEvent e) {
        Object target = e.getSource();
        for (int i = 0; i < sliders.length; i++) {
            if (target == sliders[i]) {
                handleValue(i, sliderval(i));
                canvas.repaint();
                break;
            }
        }
    }

    public static void main(String argv[])
    {
        Frame f = new Frame("Rotating, Translating,
and Scaling a Triangle");
        final Triangle2 demo = new Triangle2();
        f.add(demo);
        f.addWindowListener(new WindowAdapter() {
            public void windowClosing(WindowEvent e)
{System.exit(0);}
        });
            f.pack();
```

LISTING *Program to Demonstrate Affine Transformations. (continues)*
13.7

```
        f.setSize(new Dimension(600,500));
        demo.init();
        f.show();
    }
}

class triCanvas extends Canvas
{
    Triangle2 applet;
    double scale;
    double rotate;
    double skew;

    public triCanvas(Triangle2 app)
    {
        applet = app;
        setBackground(new Color(220, 220, 255));
    }

    public Dimension getPreferredSize()
    {
        return new Dimension(400, 300);
    }

    public void update(Graphics g)
    {
        paint(g);
    }

    public void paint(Graphics g)
    {
        Graphics2D g2;
        int width = getSize().width;
        int height = getSize().height;
        g2 = (Graphics2D) g;
        g2.clearRect(0, 0, width, height);

g2.setRenderingHint(RenderingHints.KEY_ANTIALIASING,
        (RenderingHints.VALUE_ANTIALIAS_ON));

g2.setRenderingHint(RenderingHints.KEY_RENDERING,
        (RenderingHints.VALUE_RENDER_QUALITY));
        g2.translate(width / 2.0, height / 2.0);
        g2.scale(scale, scale);
        g2.rotate(rotate);
        g2.shear(-skew, 0.0);
        BasicStroke bs;
        bs = new BasicStroke(10.0f,
BasicStroke.CAP_ROUND, 1, 10.0f);
```

LISTING *Program to Demonstrate Affine Transformations. (continues)*
13.7

```
        GeneralPath p = new GeneralPath(0);
        p.moveTo(- width / 2.5f, + height / 5.0f);
        p.lineTo(0.0f, - height / 2.2f);
        p.lineTo(width / 2.5f, + height / 5.0f);
        p.closePath();
        g2.setStroke(bs);
        g2.draw(p);
        g2.dispose();
    }
}
```

LISTING *Program to Demonstrate Affine Transformations. (continued)*
13.1

14 Clipping Techniques

I f you've created graphics in a DOS framework, you are aware of the importance of clipping. Most DOS graphics applications accessed display memory directly; if you specified graphics parameters outside the screen parameters, horrible things were apt to happen. For example, suppose you were using a 640 × 480 pixel display mode and attempted to draw a line from (0, 200) to (800, 275). When your line drawing function reached the horizontal pixel values in excess of 640, it might count out the new horizontal value from the beginning of the current row (placing the pixel in a wrong location in the next line). Worse yet, if you were near the end of a display memory page, it might try to write a pixel to a totally different memory location, which might contain important program instructions or other information. In DOS, you, as the programmer, are responsible for assuring that your program never attempts to draw pixels outside the screen boundaries, either through the use of programming techniques that create such restrictions, or by use of a function that clips all lines at the boundaries of a specified clipping rectangle.

Things are much different if you are using Java. Once you've established a display window of the *Frame* class, Java takes care of assuring that your graphics don't extend beyond the window boundaries. Let's see how this works in practice.

Random Straight Lines

Listing 14.1 is a simple program to generate 500 straight lines whose starting and ending coordinates are determined randomly. Except for the use of the *Random* class in the *paint* method, the program contains nothing different from previous programs we've written. We first create an object *r* of the *Random* class. We next have a *for* loop that iterates 500 times. For each iteration, the beginning and ending *x* and *y* coordinates, we use the method *nextInt* to

```
/*
    RandomLines.java
    Program to Generate Random Lines
*/

import java.awt.*;
import java.util.*;
import java.awt.event.*;

class RLCanvas extends Canvas
```

LISTING *Program to Generate Random Lines. (continues)*
14.1

```
{
    RLCanvas()
    {
    }

    public void paint(Graphics g)
    {
        int i, xs, ys, xe, ye;
        Random r = new Random();

        for (i=0; i<500; i++)
        {
            xs = Math.abs(r.nextInt())%800;
            ys = Math.abs(r.nextInt())%600;
            xe = Math.abs(r.nextInt())%800;
            ye = Math.abs(r.nextInt())%600;
            g.drawLine(xs, ys, xe, ye);
        }

    }
}

class RandomLines extends Frame
{
    public RandomLines()
    {
        super("Random Straight Lines");

        addWindowListener(new DWAdapter());
        setBackground(Color.white);
        setLayout( new BorderLayout());
        add("Center", new RLCanvas());
        setSize(640, 480);
        show();
    }

class DWAdapter extends WindowAdapter
    {
        public void windowClosing(WindowEvent event)
        {
            System.exit(0);
        }
    }

    public static void main(String args[])
    {
        RandomLines f = new RandomLines();
    }
```

LISTING *Program to Generate Random Lines. (continued)*
14.1

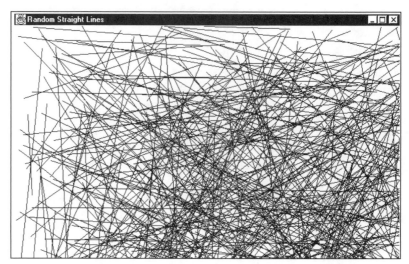

FIGURE **14.1** *Display of Randomly Oriented Lines that Can Go Off the Right and Bottom Sides Only.*

obtain a random integer and then use modulo arithmetic to obtain from the random integers a random integer between 0 and 800 in the *x* direction and between 0 and 600 in the *y* direction. Note that since the lowest values of our coordinates are 0, we can't ever go off the screen on the top and left sides. We then use the *Graphics* method *drawLine* to draw a line between the beginning and ending coordinates. The resulting display is shown in Figure 14.1. Observe that Java copes with the fact that many of the lines run off the edge of the window at the bottom and right by simply truncating each line at the proper point without any untoward effects. If you think this display is a little skewed (which it is) you can subtract 100 from each of the *x* and *y* coordinates (giving an *x* distribution from –100 to +700 and a *y* distribution from –100 to +500). The result, which is shown in Figure 14.2, is a prettier display and demonstrates that Java can effectively handle excursions beyond the top and left boundaries and that it is not phased by negative numbers.

Using a Clipping Rectangle

We've seen that as far as clipping at the edges of a specified window, Java does a fine job without any intervention. In fact, Java even takes care of situations where the window is positioned so near one or more edges of the display that the entire window isn't shown. However, suppose that we have a picture that we want to clip so that it will only fill part of our display. Java has a way of doing this, but we must use it with care. Listing 14.2 is a program to display two clipped pictures within our original frame. Look closely at the *paint* method,

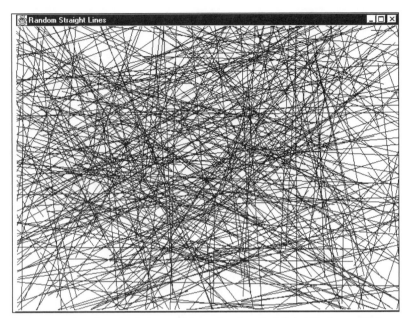

FIGURE *Display of Randomly Oriented Lines that Can Go Off the Window on All Four*
14.2 *Sides*

which is where all of the important new techniques appear. First, note that the
Graphics class has a method called *clipRect*. Four integer parameters are passed
to this method. The first two are the location of the *x* and *y* coordinates, respectively, of the top left corner of the clipping rectangle. The third parameter
is the clipping rectangle width, and the fourth parameter is the clipping rec-

```
/*
   RandomClippedLines. ava
   Program to Generate Random Clipped Lines
*/

import   ava.awt.*;
import   ava.util.*;
import   ava.awt.event.*;

class RCLCanvas extends Canvas
{
   RCLCanvas()
   {
```

LISTING *Program Showing Use of Clipping Rectangles. (continues)*
14.2

```
    }

  public void paint(Graphics g)
  {
      int i, xs, ys, xe, ye;
      Random r = new Random();

      Graphics clipped_g1 = g.create();
      Graphics clipped_g2 = g.create();
      clipped_g1.clipRect(0, 0, 300, 200);

      for (i=0; i<500; i++)
      {
          xs = Math.abs(r.nextInt()%800);
          ys = Math.abs(r.nextInt()%600);
          xe = Math.abs(r.nextInt())%800;
          ye = Math.abs(r.nextInt())%600;
          clipped_g1.drawLine(xs, ys, xe, ye);
      }
      clipped_g1.dispose();
      clipped_g2.clipRect(320, 240, 300, 200);

      for (i=0; i<500; i++)
      {
          xs = Math.abs(r.nextInt()%800);
          ys = Math.abs(r.nextInt()%600);
          xe = Math.abs(r.nextInt())%800;
          ye = Math.abs(r.nextInt())%600;
          clipped_g2.drawLine(xs, ys, xe, ye);
      }
      clipped_g2.dispose();
      g.drawString
          ("We still can draw anywhere in the
original frame.", 320, 80);
      g.drawString
          ("That includes this quadrant down here.",
20, 280);
      }
  }

  class RandomClippedLines extends Frame
  {
      public RandomClippedLines()
      {
          super("Random Clipped Straight Lines");

          addWindowListener(new DWAdapter());
```

LISTING *Program Showing Use of Clipping Rectangles. (continues)*
14.2

```
            setBackground(Color.white);
            setLayout( new BorderLayout());
            add("Center", new RCLCanvas());
            setSize(640, 480);
            show();
    }

    class DWAdapter extends WindowAdapter
    {
        public void windowClosing(WindowEvent event)
        {
            System.exit(0);
        }
    }

    public static void main(String args[])
    {
        RandomClippedLines f = new
RandomClippedLines();
    }
}
```

LISTING *Program Showing Use of Clipping Rectangles. (continued)*
14.2

tangle height. Unfortunately, once you have specified a clipping rectangle, it is associated with that Graphics object forever; you cannot change it. To get around this limitation, we make use of another *Graphics* class method that we have not mentioned before. This method is called *create()*. What it does is make a copy of the current Graphics object. Now look at the *paint* method listing. It begins by creating two copies of the current graphics object, one called *clipped_g1* and the other *clipped_g2*. Next, we set up a clipping rectangle for *clipped_g1*, having its top left corner at (0,0), and width and height of 300 and 200, respectively. We next use a *for* loop to draw 500 randomly oriented lines just as we did for Listing 14.1. We then dispose of *clipped_g1*. We then set up a clipping rectangle for *clipped_g2*. This has the same width and height as the other clipping rectangle, but has its top left corner at (320,240). Another *for* loop draws 500 lines within this clipping rectangle, after which it is disposed of. Finally, we write some text in a couple locations of the original Graphics object, and outside the boundaries of the two clipping rectangles to show that this can still be done. The resulting display is shown in Figure 14.3. You can see that each set of lines is confined to be within the boundaries of its clipping window and that the text is properly written outside the clipping windows.

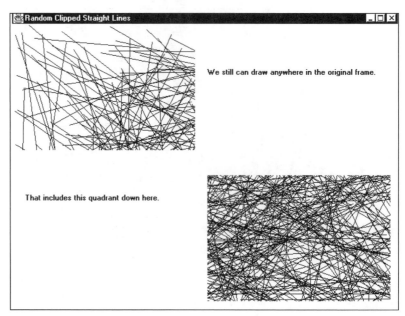

FIGURE *Display Including Clipping Windows.*
14.3

Clipping with Java 2D

Java 2D has the capability to let you specify any complex closed shape and then specify an image or other kind of background that will be clipped to fit within the specified shape. Listing 14.3 shows how this is done.

```
/*
   Clip. ava
   Program to Demonstrate Clipping
*/

import   ava.awt.*;
import   ava.awt.event.*;
import   ava.awt.geom.Line2D;
import   ava.awt.geom.AffineTransform;
import   ava.awt.font.TextLayout;
import   ava.awt.font.FontRenderContext;
import   avax.swing.*;

public class Clip extends JApplet
{
   public void init()
```

LISTING *Clipping with Java 2D. (continues)*
14.3

```
      {
        Demo demo = new Demo();
        getContentPane().add(demo);
      }

    static class Demo extends JPanel
      {
        public void drawDemo(int w, int h, Graphics2D
g2)
          {
            FontRenderContext frc =
g2.getFontRenderContext();
            Font f = new Font("serif",Font.BOLD,32);
            String s = new String("CLIP");
            TextLayout tl = new TextLayout(s, f, frc);
            double sw = tl.getBounds().getWidth();
            double sh = tl.getBounds().getHeight();
            double sx = (w-40)/sw;
            double sy = (h-40)/sh;

            AffineTransform Tx =
AffineTransform.getScaleInstance(sx, sy);
            Shape shape = tl.getOutline(Tx);
            sw = shape.getBounds().getWidth();
            sh = shape.getBounds().getHeight();
            Tx =
AffineTransform.getTranslateInstance(w/2-sw/2,
h/2+sh/2);
            shape = Tx.createTransformedShape(shape);
            Rectangle r = shape.getBounds();
            g2.clip(shape);
            g2.setColor(Color.blue);
            g2.fill(shape.getBounds());
            g2.setColor(Color.white);
            f = new Font("serif",Font.BOLD,10);
            tl = new TextLayout("Text", f, frc);
            sw = tl.getBounds().getWidth();
            int x = r.x;
            int y = (int) (r.y + tl.getAscent());
            sh = r.y + r.height;
            while ( y < sh )
              {
                tl.draw(g2, x, y);
                if ((x += (int) sw) > (r.x+r.width))
                  {
                    x = r.x;
                    y += (int) tl.getAscent();
                  }
              }
          }
```

LISTING *Clipping with Java 2D. (continues)*
14.3

```
            g2.setClip(new Rectangle(0, 0, w, h));
            g2.setColor(Color.black);
            g2.draw(shape);
        }

    public void paint(Graphics g)
    {
        Graphics2D g2 = (Graphics2D) g;
        Dimension d = getSize();
        g2.setBackground(getBackground());
        g2.clearRect(0, 0, d.width, d.height);


g2.setRenderingHint(RenderingHints.KEY_ANTIALIASING,
RenderingHints.VALUE_ANTIALIAS_ON);
            drawDemo(d.width, d.height, g2);
        }
    }

    public static void main(String argv[])
    {
        final Clip demo = new Clip();
        demo.init();
        Frame f = new Frame("Clipping with Java 2D");
        f.addWindowListener(new WindowAdapter() {
            public void windowClosing(WindowEvent e)
{System.exit(0);}
        });
        f.add("Center", demo);
        f.pack();
        f.setSize(new Dimension(640, 480));
        f.show();
    }
}
```

LISTING *Clipping with Java 2D. (continued)*
14.3

You'll find this program is quite similar to some of our previous Java 2D programs. The *paint* method manages the production of the display. It begins by setting up the *Graphics2D* class object *g2*. It gets the size of the window, sets the window background color, and then clears a rectangle the size of the whole window. It sets the rendering hints to use anti-aliasing. It then calls the method *drawDemo*, which creates the actual display.

The first thing that *drawDemo* does is to create an object *frc* of class *FontRenderContext* and an object *f* of class *font*, which is passed the parameters to be of the type font *serif*, the style *BOLD*, and of 32-point size. These two statements are necessary to fully define the type to be used. This type is going to produce very large letters across the display, which are then to be filled using the Java 2D clipping technique. First we set up an object *tl* of class *TextLayout* that contains the string "CLIP", the font *f*, and the font rendering context *frc*. Next we use the *getBounds* method to determine the height and width of the text. We now determine the factors by which the text should be scaled up to fill the page. To do this we first subtract a little from the window height and width to allow for some margin and then divide by the type height and width to find scale factors in each direction. Finally, we define the object *Tx* of class *AffineTransform* and then use the method *AffineTransform.getScaleInstance* to scale up the whole display by the scale factors that we found previously. We create an object *shape* of class *Shape* and get the outline of our text to put in it. We now have the large text letters to use as clipping boundaries, but they aren't in the right place to be centered on the screen. To accomplish this, we use the method *getBounds().getWidth()* to get the width of our scaled text, and the method *getBounds().getHeight()* to get the height of our scaled text. We then divide these by 2 to get the center of the text and divide the window dimensions by 2 to find the center of the window. Subtracting the center of the text from the center of the window tells us how much we have to translate the text for it to appear in the proper place in the window.

FIGURE *Clipping with Java 2D.*
14.4

We then apply the method *AffineTransform.getTranslateInstance* to perform this translation.

We are now going to set a color for our display. Using the method *setColor* we set the color to blue. If we just did this and then went on to fill and draw the shape, we'd end up with the whole window painted blue. However, first, we use the method *g2.clip(shape)*. This very simple statement limits the blue color to within the outlines of the text characters.

We're going to make things a little more complicated by continuously repeating the display of the characters *Text* on the blue background. You'll see in the listing that we set up a new serif type font in 10 point bold. We then place this with the string *Text* in our *TextLayout* class object *tl*. We come up with some parameters to limit the rectangle in which this text will be printed and the spacing with which it is repeated, using a *while* loop to do the repetition. Now note that the *g2.clip(shape)* method that we used before clips this repeated text as well as the background so that none of it appears outside the shape boundaries. The resulting display is shown in Figure 14.4. As you can see, this clipping capability is very powerful. You have wide latitude in defining the clipping shape and the type of background to be used inside the clipping shape.

15 User Interfaces

I n this chapter, we're going to look at some more ways in which the user can interact with the computer program. Specifically, we're going to look at the situation where we allow the user to enter various data and use that to control the display that is generated. Our first specific example will be a display that shows a Mandelbrot set. At the top of the window are four boxes that show the values of the left, right, top, and bottom boundaries of the Mandelbrot display. When the program is first run, these boundaries are set to default values. The user can then select one or more of these boxes with the mouse and type in a new limit. When the boundaries have been set to the desired new values, the user can click on a *Repaint* button near the top right of the display and the Mandelbrot set will be redrawn using the new boundaries. In this way the user can select boundaries that allow him or her to zoom in and show an enlarged view of any desired portion of the Mandelbrot set. You may want to zoom in by steps to zero in on the exact picture that you want. When you get a picture that you like, record its boundaries so that you can reproduce it if you desire. In Chapter 4, we described how events are handled by Java. This chapter will give you some more practical experience in interacting with events.

The Mandelbrot Set

The Mandelbrot set is the most well-known of all fractal curves. It was discovered by the mathematician Benoit Mandelbrot. The Mandelbrot set is a map of the complex plane over some specified range. (The range that we start with is from –2.2 to +1.6 for the real part the number, and from –1.6 to +1.6 for the imaginary part of the number). To determine the color of a pixel on the screen, we iterate the following equation for the value of the complex number c represented by that pixel:

$$Z_{n+1} = Z_n + c \qquad \text{(Eq. 15-1)}$$

where z is also a complex number (starting with $z_0=0$) until the sum of the squares of the real and imaginary parts of z is greater than or equal to 4. At this point, we stop and color the pixel represented by the current value of c in accordance with the number of iterations that have taken place. The Mandelbrot set program is listed in Listing 15.1.

```
/*
   Mandelbrot. ava = Program to generate Mandelbrot
Set
      using an Image file.
*/

import  ava.awt.*;
import  ava.util.*;
import  ava.awt.image.*;
import  ava.awt.event.*;

class MandelCanvas extends Canvas implements
Observer
{
    Bounds bounds;

    MandelCanvas(Bounds s)
    {
      bounds = s;
      s.addObserver(this);
    }

    public void update(Observable o, Ob ect arg)
    {
      repaint();
    }

    public void paint (Graphics g)
    {
      Image image;
      double left, right, top, bottom;
      double Q, deltaP, deltaQ, x, y, xsq, ysq;
      int index, oldrow=0, row, col, xres=640,
yres=480;
      int pixels[] = new int[xres*(yres+1)];
      Color[] color = new Color[16];

      color[0] = Color.black;
      color[1] = new Color(0, 0, 168);
      color[2] = new Color(0, 168, 0);
      color[3] = new Color(0, 168, 168);
      color[4] = new Color(168, 0, 0);
      color[5] = new Color(168, 0, 168);
      color[6] = new Color(168, 84, 0);
      color[7] = new Color(168, 168, 168);
      color[8] = new Color(84, 84, 84);
      color[9] = new Color(84, 84, 255);
      color[10] = new Color(84, 255, 84);
      color[11] = new Color(84, 255, 255);
```

LISTING *Program to Draw Mandelbrot Sets (continues)*
15.1

```
        color[12] = new Color(255, 84, 84);
        color[13] = new Color(255, 84, 255);
        color[14] = new Color(255, 255, 84);
        color[15] = Color.white;

        left = bounds.limits[0];
        right = bounds.limits[1];
        top = bounds.limits[2];
        bottom = bounds.limits[3];
        deltaP = (right - left)/xres;
        deltaQ = (top - bottom)/yres;
            g.drawString("Generating Mandelbrot Image
Line ",20,20);
        for (row=0; row<yres; row++)
        {
            if (row%10 == 0)
            {
               g.clearRect(240,0,400,100);
                  g.drawString("" + row + " of " +
yres,240,20);
            }
            Q = top - row*deltaQ;
            for (col=0; col<xres; col++)
            {
                x = y = 0.0;
                for (index=0; index<512; index++)
                {
                   xsq = x*x;
                   ysq = y*y;
                   if (xsq + ysq > 4)
                      break;
                   y = 2*x*y + Q;
                   x = xsq - ysq + left + col*deltaP;
                }
                    pixels[row*xres + col] =
color[index%16].getRGB();
            }
        }
        image = createImage(new
MemoryImageSource(xres, yres,
            pixels, 0, xres));
        g.drawImage(image, 0, 0, null);
    }
}

class Bounds extends Observable
{
    public double[] limits;
```

LISTING *Program to Draw Mandelbrot Sets (continues)*
15.1

```
   Bounds()
   {
      limits = new double[4];
      limits[0] = -2.2;
      limits[1] = 1.6;
      limits[2] = 1.6;
      limits[3] = -1.6;
   }

   public double getValues(String c)
   {
         if (c.equals("left"))
            return limits[0];
         if (c.equals("right"))
            return limits[1];
         if (c.equals("top"))
            return limits[2];
         if (c.equals("bottom"))
            return limits[3];
         return 0;
      }

   public void setValues(String c, double f)
   {
      if (c.equals("left"))
         limits[0] = f;
      if (c.equals("right"))
         limits[1] = f;
      if (c.equals("top"))
         limits[2] = f;
      if (c.equals("bottom"))
         limits[3] = f;
   }

   public void newPicture(String c)
   {
      setChanged();
      notifyObservers(this);
    }
}

class ValuesField extends Panel implements
Observer, ActionListener
{
   String name;
   Bounds bounds;
   TextField field;
   static Button b;
```

LISTING *Program to Draw Mandelbrot Sets (continues)*
15.1

```
        ValuesField(Bounds cs, String s)
        {
            b = new Button("Repaint");
            b.addActionListener(this);
            name = s;
            bounds = cs;
            add( new Label(name +":"));
                add(field = new
TextField(Double.toString( cs.getValues(s)), 4));
            cs.addObserver(this);
        }

        public void update(Observable o, Ob ect arg)
        {
            double value =
Double.valueOf(field.getText()).doubleValue();
            bounds.setValues(name, value);
         }

        public void actionPerformed(ActionEvent event)
        {
            bounds.newPicture(name);
        }
    }

    public class Mandelbrot extends Frame
    {
        public Mandelbrot()
        {
            super("Mandelbrot Set Generator");
            addWindowListener(new DWAdapter());
            setBackground(Color.lightGray);
            setLayout( new BorderLayout());
            Bounds cs = new Bounds();
            Panel p = new Panel();
            MandelCanvas canvas = new MandelCanvas(cs);
            p.setLayout( new GridLayout(1, 5));
            p.add(new ValuesField(cs, "left"));
            p.add(new ValuesField(cs, "right"));
            p.add(new ValuesField(cs, "top"));
            p.add(new ValuesField(cs, "bottom"));
            p.add(ValuesField.b);
            add("North", p);
            add("Center", canvas);
            setSize(640, 520);
            show();
        }

    class DWAdapter extends WindowAdapter
```

LISTING *Program to Draw Mandelbrot Sets (continues)*
15.1

```
{
    public void windowClosing(WindowEvent event)
    {
        System.exit(0);
    }
}

public static void main(String args[])
{
Mandelbrot f = new Mandelbrot();
}
```

LISTING *Program to Draw Mandelbrot Sets (continued)*
15.1

Observer and Observable

Note that at the beginning of the program in addition to importing the *java.awt.** and *java.awt.event.** classes, we include *import java.util.*;*, which includes definitions for the *Observer* and *Observable* classes, and *import java.awt.image.*;*, which includes the definition for *Image*. As with several of our other graphics programs, we begin by defining an object of class *Canvas*, in this case called *MandelCanvas*. Unlike previous programs, however, this object implements the class *Observer*. The *Observer* and *Observable* classes are what makes it possible to exchange information between classes and keep our display up to date. The *Observable* class must have a statement like:

```
class Bounds extends Observable
```

Then somewhere within the class a method must be defined that includes the statements:

```
setChanged();
notifyObservers();
```

These two statements set a flag and notify all the classes registered as *Observers* that changes have been made that require them to perform an update. Each *Observer* class must include in its class definition statement the words *implements Observer*. The constructor must include a statement of the form:

```
cs.addObserver(this);
```

which registers the class as an observer of the class *cs*. Finally, the class must include an update method that is defined like this:

```
public void update(Observable o, Ob ect arg)
```

Within this method is the code that controls what updating actions the *Observer* should take when it is notified to do so by the *Observable* class.

For this program we have an *Observable* class called *Bounds* that handles the four bounds of the Mandelbrot set: left, right, top, and bottom. You'll note that *Bounds* has an array of four limit variables that are initialized in the constructor. *Bounds* includes a method *getValues* , which is passed a string containing one of the label strings "left", "right", "top", or "bottom". The method returns the proper limit value for that string as a double floating point number. *Bounds* also includes a method *setValues*. Parameters passed to this method are one of the four strings just described and a double floating point number. If the changed value corresponds to any of the four strings, the proper limit for the selected string is changed to the new value.

The class *Observer* class *ValuesField* is used to create the four labels (Left, Right, Top, and Bottom) at the top of the screen, as well as the text fields that contain the numerical values for each from *Bounds*. It also creates the *Repaint* button. The four fields are made into a panel for display in *Mandelbrot*. The class has an object *bounds* (of class *Bounds*), an object *name* (of class *String*), and an object *field* (of class *TextField*). The constructor is passed a *Bounds* object *cs* and a *String* object *s* (which is one of "left", "right", "top", or "bottom"). The parameter *name* is set to *s* and *bounds* to *cs*. Then a *Label* is added to the display, containing *name* and a colon. An 8-character long *TextField* is added to the display. Initially, we use the *Bounds* method *getValues* to get the value of the limit from the *cs* object, convert this to a string, and display it as the contents of the *TestField*. Finally, we use the *addObserver* method to register *ValuesField* with the *Bounds* observable. As with all classes that implement *Observer*, *ValuesField* must have an *update* method. In this method we first define an object *cs* of class *Bounds* and set it equal to the passed parameter *arg* after converting it to the *Bounds* class (we can't use *arg* directly, since it isn't passed as a *Bounds* type). We set *s* by getting the proper *limit* value from the *Bounds* object *cs* and converting it to a string of characters. Next, we use the method *setText* to replace the existing text in the *TextField* with the new value from the *Bounds* object *cs* (which is in *s* in the form of a string of characters).

It isn't intuitively obvious how everything fits together when we actually are using the program. As you type in a new value for one or more of the four limits at the top of the screen, the value on the display changes. This is done by Java; our program really does nothing yet with the new information. However, when we click the mouse on the *Repaint* button, an Action event is detected, resulting in the appropriate method in *ValuesField* calling the *newPicture* method of *Bounds*. This notifies the observers that an update is required. The update method in *ValuesField* gets the text from each limit that was changed, converts it to a double floating point number, and stores it in the appropriate member of the *limits* array. Then, the update method of the *MandelCanvas* class calls *repaint*, which draws a complete new Mandelbrot display.

The *MandelCanvas* class is another class that implements *Observer*. Its *update* method simply repaints the canvas. The method *paint* actually draws the Mandelbrot set. This method begins by doing some initialization and definition of parameters. Note that *xres* and *yres* define a 640 × 480 pixel rectangle to define the size of the Mandelbrot set display. In the *Mandelbrot* class, we define the window size as 640 × 520 pixels, which allows for the title block, the four labels and text boxes, and the *Repaint* button that appear at the top of the display and still leaves plenty of room for the Mandelbrot set graphic. Next, the *paint* method sets up the 16 PC colors as described in Chapter 7. Next, we obtain the current bounds for the set from the *bounds* object. The *deltaP* and *deltaQ* parameters represent the increment in *P* and *Q* values (the real and imaginary parts of *c* in Equation 15-1) for each pixel. We now draw the beginning of the legend that will show progress while the graphic is being generated. Then we precompute the *P* values and place them in an array. The method then begins a *for* loop that iterates once for each row of the display. It first clears an area on the screen and displays the current row for every tenth row. Then it determines the value of *Q* for that row. Then, we enter another *for* loop that iterates once for each column of the display. It sets *x* and *y* to zero and then enters another *for* loop that nominally iterates 512 times. Within this loop, we compute new values of *x* and *y* (the real and imaginary parts of *z* in Equation 9-1). After each computation, we check the sum of the squares of *x* and *y* and if this sum exceeds 4, we break out of the inner *for* loop. We then set the color to be the number of iterations of the inner *for* loop modulo 16, convert this to a color integer, and save it in the proper member of the *pixel* array. We're then ready for another iteration of the column *for* loop. When all three nested *for* loops have finished, our pixel array is complete. We then convert it to an *Image* and display the resulting image.

The Mandelbrot Display

The *Mandelbrot* class is the main program class. It includes the *main* method. The constructor begins by setting the display title. It then sets the background color and layout type (*Border* layout). A new *Bounds* object *cs* is created. We now set up a *MandelCanvas* object (which creates the Mandelbrot set with the default boundary parameters and displays it in the center of the window). A new *Panel* called *p* is then created. Its layout is set to be a grid one cell high and five cells wide. Next, a *ValuesField* object is created for each of the first four cells and the *Repaint* button for the fifth cell. The resulting panel is added to the *North* side of the display. Then the size of the window is set and it is displayed.

The process for handling the *WindowClosing* event and the *main* method are just the same as for previous programs.

Plate 3 shows the original Mandelbrot set. One of the characteristics of a fractal is self-similarity, where an expanded portion of the fractal is similar in shape to the original fractal. Let's make sure you know how to use this program. When you run the program, the default boundary values for the Mandelbrot set will be shown at the top of the display and the Mandelbrot set itself will appear in the remainder of the display. To create a new display, click on the "left" *Textfield* with the mouse. Then, using the backspace and numeric keys, set the value you want for the "left" boundary. Repeat this procedure for each of the other three boundaries. The Mandelbrot display will not change until you click on the *Repaint* button. Then, the new Mandelbrot set will be drawn.

This is just one example of how you can make display sections containing text values interact with a graphics display. If you've paid close attention to how *Observers* and *Observables* are used in this chapter, you shouldn't have any trouble generating your own controllable displays. Figure 15.1 is an example of the Mandelbrot display.

A Simpler Mandelbrot Set Program

The Mandelbrot set program just described makes it possible to specify any desired values for the right, left, top, and bottom limits of a Mandelbrot set and draw the newly specified picture. Just because Java makes it easy for you to design a program such as this shouldn't mean that you create such a program without giving some thought to exactly what your goals are and how simple you can make the program. The purpose of our original program was to be able to look at a Mandelbrot set display and choose a portion of it to expand. Another way to do this is to use the mouse click to select a point on the Mandelbrot display and have the program draw an expanded Mandelbrot set centered about the mouse location with limits half those of the previous display. This gives you good control over the display, but doesn't allow you to jump to huge expansions in a single step. On the other hand, as each new expansion is created, you have the opportunity to refine the selection of the point that is to be the center of the display. Listing 15.2 is a program to draw Mandelbrot sets in this manner.

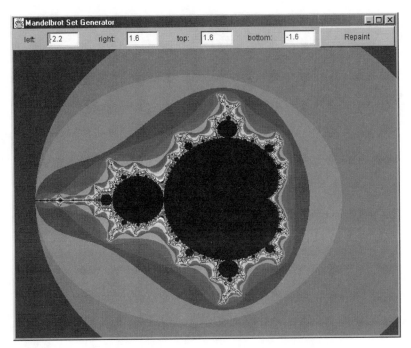

FIGURE   *The Mandelbrot Set.*
15.1

```
/*
   Mandelbrot1.java
   Program to generate and zoom in on Mandelbrot Set
*/

import java.awt.*;
import java.awt.event.*;
import java.util.*;
import java.awt.image.*;

public class Mandelbrot1 extends Frame
{

   double left=-2.05, right=1.8, top=1.6, bottom=-
1.6,
      deltaP=0.0059375F, deltaQ=0.00666667F;
   int row, col, xres=640, yres=480;

   double P, Q;
```

LISTING *A Simpler Program to Draw Mandelbrot Sets. (continues)*
15.2

```java
    Color[] color = new Color[15];

    public Mandelbrot1()
    {
        color[0] = new Color(0, 168, 0);
        color[1] = new Color(0, 0, 168);
        color[2] = Color.black;
        color[3] = new Color(0, 168, 168);
        color[4] = new Color(168, 0, 0);
        color[5] = new Color(168, 0, 168);
        color[6] = new Color(168, 84, 0);
        color[7] = new Color(84, 84, 255);
        color[8] = new Color(84, 255, 84);
        color[9] = new Color(84, 255, 255);
        color[10] = new Color(255, 84, 84);
        color[11] = new Color(255, 84, 255);
        color[12] = new Color(255, 255, 84);
        color[13] = Color.yellow;
        color[14] = Color.orange;

        add("Center", new ManCanvas());
        setSize(640, 500);
        show();
    }

    public static void main(String args[])
    {
        Mandelbrot1 f = new Mandelbrot1();
    }

    class ManCanvas extends Canvas
    {
        Image image;

        int row, col, xres=640, yres=480;
        int pixels[] = new int[xres*(yres+1)];

        ManCanvas()
        {
            addWindowListener(new DWAdapter());
            addMouseListener(new MAdapter());
        }

        class DWAdapter extends WindowAdapter
        {
            public void windowClosing(WindowEvent
event)
            {
                System.exit(0);
            }
        }
```

LISTING *A Simpler Program to Draw Mandelbrot Sets. (continues)*
15.2

```
        }

    public void paint(Graphics g)
    {
        double x=0.0, y=0.0, xsq = 0.0, ysq = 0.0;
        int index;

            setTitle("Mandelbrot Set: Left = " +
(float)left + " Right = " + (float)right
            + " Top = " + (float)top + " Bottom = "
+ (float)bottom);
        for (col=0; col<xres; col++)
        {
            P = left + col*deltaP;
            for (row = 0; row<yres; row++)
            {
                Q = top - row*deltaQ;
                x = y = 0.0;
                for (index=0; index<512; index++)
                {
                    xsq = x*x;
                    ysq = y*y;
                    if (xsq + ysq > 4)
                        break;
                    y = 2*x*y + Q;
                    x = xsq - ysq + P;
                }
                    pixels[row*xres + col] =
color[index%15].getRGB();
            }
        }

        image = createImage(new
MemoryImageSource(xres, yres,
            pixels, 0, xres));
        g.drawImage(image, 0, 0, null);
    }

    class MAdapter extends MouseAdapter
    {
        public void mousePressed(MouseEvent event)
        {
            int x, y;
            double xcoord, ycoord;
            x = event.getX();
            y = event.getY();
            xcoord = left + x*deltaP;
            ycoord = top - y*deltaQ;
            deltaP /= 2.;
```

LISTING *A Simpler Program to Draw Mandelbrot Sets. (continues)*
15.2

```
                    deltaQ /= 2.;
                    left = xcoord - 320*deltaP;
                    top = ycoord + 240*deltaQ;
                    right = left + 640*deltaP;
                    bottom = top - 480*deltaQ;
                    repaint();
                }
            }
        }
    }
```

LISTING *A Simpler Program to Draw Mandelbrot Sets. (continued)*
15.2

Working Between Two Graphics: The Julia Set

In this section we're going to look at a different approach to user interaction. The Julia set is a different way of looking at Equation 15-1. Whereas the Mandelbrot set is a map of what happens when we do repeated iteration of the equation over a range of values of c, beginning each set of iterations with $z=0$, the Julia set is constructed by selecting a constant value for c and doing sets of iterations over a range of starting values for z. The Mandelbrot set is said to be a map of the Julia sets, since it can be used to determine which values of c will yield interesting Julia sets. The best Julia sets occur at points on the Mandelbrot set where cusps occur. Our programming problem is that we would like to display the Mandelbrot set and then select a point on it with the cursor. When the mouse is clicked on this point, we want to draw a picture of the Julia set that has c corresponding to the value of c on the Mandelbrot set at the point where the cursor was located. We're going to do this by using the *Card* layout. We'll have two cards; on one we have the Mandelbrot set and on the other we draw the desired Julia set. Listing 15.3 shows how this is done. The *Julia* class defines two canvases, *mandel* and *julia*.

```
/*
   Julia.java
   Program to generate Julia Set
      from Mandelbrot Set
*/

import java.awt.*;
import java.awt.event.*;
```

LISTING *Program to Draw a Mandelbrot Set and then a Julia Set from It. (continues)*
15.3

```
import java.util.*;
import java.awt.image.*;

public class Julia extends Frame
{

   double left=-2.05, right=1.8, top=1.6, bottom=-
1.6,
      deltaP=0.0059375F, deltaQ=0.00666667F;
   int row, col, xres=640, yres=480;

   MandelbrotCanvas mandel = new MandelbrotCanvas();
   JuliaCanvas julia = new JuliaCanvas();
   double P, Q;
   Panel p = new Panel();
   CardLayout c = new CardLayout();
   Color[] color = new Color[15];

   public Julia()
   {
      color[0] = new Color(0, 168, 0);
      color[1] = new Color(0, 0, 168);
      color[2] = Color.black;
      color[3] = new Color(0, 168, 168);
      color[4] = new Color(168, 0, 0);
      color[5] = new Color(168, 0, 168);
      color[6] = new Color(168, 84, 0);
      color[7] = new Color(84, 84, 255);
      color[8] = new Color(84, 255, 84);
      color[9] = new Color(84, 255, 255);
      color[10] = new Color(255, 84, 84);
      color[11] = new Color(255, 84, 255);
      color[12] = new Color(255, 255, 84);
      color[13] = Color.yellow;
      color[14] = Color.orange;
      addWindowListener(new DWAdapter());
      p.setLayout(c);
      mandel.init();

      add(p);
      p.add("Man", mandel);
      p.add("Jul", julia);

      setSize(640, 500);
      show();
   }

   class DWAdapter extends WindowAdapter
   {
```

LISTING *Program to Draw a Mandelbrot Set and then a Julia Set from It. (continues)*
15.3

```
        public void windowClosing(WindowEvent event)
        {
            System.exit(0);
        }
    }

    public static void main(String args[])
    {
        Julia f = new Julia();
    }

    class MandelbrotCanvas extends Canvas
    {
        Image image;

        int row, col, xres=640, yres=480;
        int pixels[] = new int[xres*(yres+1)];

        MandelbrotCanvas()
        {
            addMouseListener(new MAdapter());
        }

        public void init()
        {
            double x=0.0, y=0.0, xsq = 0.0, ysq = 0.0;
            int index;
            for (col=0; col<xres; col++)
            {
                P = left + col*deltaP;
                for (row = 0; row<yres; row++)
                {
                    Q = top - row*deltaQ;
                    x = y = 0.0;
                    for (index=0; index<512; index++)
                    {
                        xsq = x*x;
                        ysq = y*y;
                        if (xsq + ysq > 4)
                            break;
                        y = 2*x*y + Q;
                        x = xsq - ysq + P;
                    }
                    pixels[row*xres + col] =
                        color[index%15].getRGB();
                }
            }
        }
```

LISTING **15.3** *Program to Draw a Mandelbrot Set and then a Julia Set from It. (continues)*

```
    public void paint(Graphics g)
    {
        setTitle("Select point for Julia Set and

           click mouse");
        image = createImage(new MemoryImageSource
           (xres, yres,
        pixels, 0, xres));
        g.drawImage(image, 0, 0, null);
    }

    class MAdapter extends MouseAdapter
    {
        public void mousePressed(MouseEvent event)
        {
            int x, y;

            x = event.getX();
            y = event.getY();
            P = left + x*deltaP;
            Q = top - y*deltaQ;
            JuliaCanvas julia = new JuliaCanvas();
            julia.repaint();
            c.next(p);
        }
    }
}

class JuliaCanvas extends Canvas
{

 JuliaCanvas()
{
   addMouseListener(new MAdapter());
}

public void paint(Graphics g)
{
    double x=0.0, y=0.0, xsq = 0.0, ysq = 0.0,
       old=0.;
    int index;

    setTitle("Click mouse to return to Mandelbrot
       set");
    for (col=0; col<xres; col++)
    {
        for (row = 0; row<yres; row++)
        {
            x = left + (double)col * deltaP;
```

LISTING *Program to Draw a Mandelbrot Set and then a Julia Set from It. (continues)*
15.3

```
                y = top - (double)row * deltaQ;
                for (index=0; index<128; index++)
                {
                    xsq = x*x;
                    ysq = y*y;
                    if (xsq + ysq > 4)
                        break;
                    y = 2*x*y + Q;
                    x = xsq - ysq + P;
                }
                if (index >= 128)
                {
                    g.setColor(color[(int)((xsq + ysq)
                        * 16.0) % 15]);
                }
                else
                    g.setColor(Color.lightGray);
                g.drawLine(col,row,col,row);
            }
        }
    }

    class MAdapter extends MouseAdapter
    {

        public void mousePressed(MouseEvent event)
        {
            c.next(p);
        }
    }
}
```

LISTING *Program to Draw a Mandelbrot Set and then a Julia Set from It. (continued)*
15.3

Within the *Julia* constructor, we define our colors, add the *WindowListener* to detect when we want to end the program, set up the layout, run *mandel.init* to create the Mandelbrot set graphic, add listeners for a mouse action from each of the canvases, and create the two card pages. We then set the display size and show the first card (the Mandelbrot set display).

The *init* method for the *MandelbrotCanvas* is quite similar to the *paint* method for generating a Mandelbrot set in the previous listing except that there is no provision for changing the limit values. We use *init* for the whole Mandelbrot set calculation so that we only need to go through it once. For *paint* or *repaint* operations, we only draw the Mandelbrot set image, which has been stored in an array.

When the mouse is clicked on the *MandelbrotCanvas* page, the mouse listener sends an event to the *Madapter* embedded class, which gets the mouse *x* and *y* coordinates at the time it was clicked and converts them to *P* and *Q* values for the Julia set. A new Julia canvas is created and the *JuliaCanvas repaint* method is called to create the newly defined Julia set. The method *c.next(p)* is called to display the Julia set card page. Note that when the mouse is clicked while the Julia set card page is being displayed, the event activates the version of *Madapter* that is part of the *JuliaCanvas* class. This only switches the display back to the Mandelbrot set card page. You'll note that by using the *Card* layout, we have been able to eliminate the use of *Observer* and *Observable*, and all the associated interactions. Plate 12 is a typical Julia set drawn by this program.

16

Drawing and Filling Polygons

I f you've ever tried your hand at writing software functions to draw and fill polygons, you'll be very pleased with the simple and effective methods used to perform these actions in Java. However, you do need to know a little bit about how these methods work internally, so as to understand just what they can and cannot do. With this knowledge, you'll be able to get the most out of the polygon methods without encountering any unpleasant surprises. This chapter will supply the knowledge you need to work with polygons effectively.

The Polygon Drawing Method

A polygon is defined as "a closed plane figure bounded by straight lines." The *drawPolygon* method actually draws a series of straight line segments connecting specified coordinates and then connects the end of the last line segment to the beginning of the first line segment. To use this method, you first specify the coordinates of each point that you want to use. The *drawPolygon* method then draws a line from the first point to the second point, from the second point to the third point, and so forth for all specified points. In the first versions of Java, the *drawPolygon* method stopped at this point and could thus be used to draw figures that were not closed; the newer versions also draw a final line from the last point specified back to the first point. If you have been careful to assure that none of the lines are going to cross each other, you will have a well-behaved polygon. If you don't take these precautions, you have some sort of geometric figure, but it may not be anything like a polygon. Let's see how this works in real life. Listing 16.1 is a program that draws three figures using the *drawPolygon* method. It produces three geometric figures, which are shown in Figure 16.1. The program is a lot like our other graphics programs except for the *paint* method, which actually creates the three figures. This method begins by creating three objects of the *Polygon* class, *poly1, poly2,* and *poly3*. Then, using the *addPoint* method repeatedly, the consecutive points for each polygon are set up. The coordinates of each point are defined using the convention normally used of display screens, where the origin is at the top left corner, with increasing values of the *x* coordinate (the first coordinate of the pair) moving toward the right, and increasing values of the *y* coordinate (the second coordinate of the pair) moving toward the bottom of the screen. After all the points are defined, we use the *drawPolygon* method three times to draw the three figures. Now look at Figure 16.1. The bottom left geometric figure is a well-behaved polygon, namely a pentagon. But what about the geometric figure at the top of the picture? We can see several different geometric figures within it that meet the dictionary definition of a polygon. So is it a polygon, or isn't it? For most practical purposes, it doesn't matter. But we shall see later that things are a lot more critical when we come to filling polygons. Finally, the geometric figure at the bottom right is a commonly used method of drawing a star using five straight lines. Each of the lines forms two boundaries of the star and also has a part of the line that is within the interior of the star. Later, we'll see what this does to us when we try to fill this figure.

```java
/*
   Polydraw.java
   Drawing figures
*/

import java.awt.*;
import java.awt.event.*;

class PCanvas extends Canvas
    {
    PCanvas()
    {
    }

    public void paint(Graphics g)
    {
        Polygon poly1 = new Polygon();

        Polygon poly2 = new Polygon();
        Polygon poly3 = new Polygon();

        poly1.addPoint(210, 90);
        poly1.addPoint(410, 90);
        poly1.addPoint(310, 270);
        poly1.addPoint(210, 200);
        poly1.addPoint(310, 20);
        poly1.addPoint(410, 200);
        poly2.addPoint(55, 300);
        poly2.addPoint(157, 225);
        poly2.addPoint(257, 300);
        poly2.addPoint(213, 420);
        poly2.addPoint(100, 420);
        poly3.addPoint(380, 300);
        poly3.addPoint(582, 300);
        poly3.addPoint(424, 420);
        poly3.addPoint(481, 225);
        poly3.addPoint(538, 420);
        g.setColor(Color.black);
        g.drawPolygon(poly1);
        g.drawPolygon(poly2);
        g.drawPolygon(poly3);
```

LISTING *Drawing Figures with the drawPolygon Method. (continues)*
16.1

```
        }
    }

    class PolyDraw extends Frame
    {
        public PolyDraw()
        {
            super("Drawing Polygons and Other Figures");
            setBackground(Color.white);
            setLayout( new BorderLayout());
            add("Center", new PCanvas());
            setSize(640, 480);
            show();
            addWindowListener(new DWAdapter());
        }
        class DWAdapter extends WindowAdapter
        {
            public void windowClosing(WindowEvent event)
            {
                System.exit(0);
            }
        }
        public static void main(String args[])
        {
            PolyDraw f = new PolyDraw();
        }
    }
```

LISTING *Drawing Figures with the drawPolygon Method. (continued)*
16.1

Drawing Polygons with Java 2D

The preceding program draws polygons using a single pixel wide line. If you want to control the line width, specify how line segments are joined, or use anti-aliasing, all of these can be done with Java 2D. The program to do this is shown in Listing 16.2. You will see that it is a little different from the previous listing. First, at the beginning of the program, we import the package *java.awt.geom.GeneralPath*, which provides methods for creating a curve composed of several line segments. Next, in the *paint* method, we create the object *g2* of class *Graphics2D*. We then use *setRenderingHint* to enable the anti-aliasing feature. We then create an object *bs* of class *BasicStroke* to define the characteristics of the lines to be drawn and set it up to create lines that are 3 pixels wide. Next, we create three objects, *poly1, poly2,* and *poly3* of class *GeneralPath*. In the previous program, we used the *addPoint* method to add the coordinates of every point in a polygon. Here, we use the *moveTo* method to establish the first point of the curve, the *lineTo* to define further points on the curve, and the

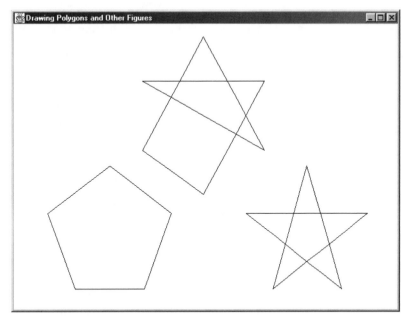

FIGURE *Three Geometric Figures Drawn by drawPolygon Method.*
16.1

```
/*
   PolyDraw2D. ava
   Drawing polygon figures with Java 2D
*/

import  ava.awt.*;
import  ava.awt.event.*;
import  ava.awt.geom.GeneralPath;

class PCanvas extends Canvas
{
   PCanvas()
   {
   }

   public void paint(Graphics g)
   {
      Graphics2D g2;
      g2 = (Graphics2D) g;

g2.setRenderingHint(RenderingHints.KEY_ANTIALIASING,
```

LISTING *Drawing Polygon Figures with Java 2D. (continues)*
16.2

```
            (RenderingHints.VALUE_ANTIALIAS_ON));
      BasicStroke bs;
      bs = new BasicStroke((float) 3,
BasicStroke.CAP_BUTT, 0, 10.0f);
      GeneralPath poly1 = new GeneralPath(0);
      GeneralPath poly2 = new GeneralPath(0);
      GeneralPath poly3 = new GeneralPath(0);
      poly1.moveTo(210, 90);
      poly1.lineTo(410, 90);
      poly1.lineTo(310, 270);
      poly1.lineTo(210, 200);
      poly1.lineTo(310, 20);
      poly1.lineTo(410, 200);
      poly1.closePath();
      poly2.moveTo(55, 300);
      poly2.lineTo(157, 225);
      poly2.lineTo(257, 300);
      poly2.lineTo(213, 420);
      poly2.lineTo(100, 420);
      poly2.lineTo(55, 300);
      poly2.closePath();
      poly3.moveTo(380, 300);
      poly3.lineTo(582, 300);
      poly3.lineTo(424, 420);
      poly3.lineTo(481, 225);
      poly3.lineTo(538, 420);
      poly3.lineTo(380, 300);
      poly3.closePath();
      g.setColor(Color.black);
      g2.setStroke(bs);
      g2.draw(poly1);
      g2.draw(poly2);
      g2.draw(poly3);
      g2.dispose();
   }
}

class PolyDraw2D extends Frame
{
   public PolyDraw2D()
   {
      super("Drawing Polygons and Other Figures");
      setBackground(Color.white);
      setLayout( new BorderLayout());
      add("Center", new PCanvas());
      setSize(640, 480);
      show();
      addWindowListener(new DWAdapter());
   }
```

LISTING *Drawing Polygon Figures with Java 2D. (continues)*
16.2

```
class DWAdapter extends WindowAdapter
{
   public void windowClosing(WindowEvent event)
   {
      System.exit(0);
   }
}

public static void main(String args[])
{
   PolyDraw2D f = new PolyDraw2D();
}
}
```

LISTING *Drawing Polygon Figures with Java 2D. (continued)*
16.2

closePath method to close the geometric figure by drawing a line from the current position back to the initial point of the figure. Finally, we can simply use the *draw* method to draw each shape rather than the *drawPolygon* method.

Drawing Complex Curves with the Polygon Class

In Chapter 13, we showed how to draw a complex curve as a series of short line segments. An alternative method that is somewhat simpler is to use the *GeneralPath* technique shown in the previous. Listing 13.3 shows how this is done for the sinc curve that we drew in Chapter 13. You'll see that we've been able to eliminate the *if* statement that skips drawing a line on the first loop iteration and that we no longer have to save the coordinates of each previous point to use in a *drawLine* statement with the new point that is calculated. Instead, just use *moveTo* to enter the starting point and *lineTo* to add each successive point to the path. After the path is complete, we use *draw* to plot the whole figure. Figure 16.2 shows the sinc curve produced by this program, which is basically the same as the sinc curve produced by drawing a number of short line segments, except that we have widened the lines.

```
/*
   Sinc. ava
   Program to draw sinc(x)
*/

import  ava.awt.*;
```

LISTING *Drawing a sinc Curve with the Polygon Class. (continues)*
16.2

```
import  ava.awt.event.*;
import  ava.awt.geom.GeneralPath;

class SincCanvas extends Canvas
{
    SincCanvas()
    {
    }

    public void paint(Graphics g)
    {
        double x, y;
        int col, row;
        Graphics2D g2;
        g2 = (Graphics2D) g;

g2.setRenderingHint(RenderingHints.KEY_ANTIALIASING,
        (RenderingHints.VALUE_ANTIALIAS_ON));
        BasicStroke bs;
        bs = new BasicStroke((float) 3,
BasicStroke.CAP_BUTT,
        BasicStroke.JOIN_MITER, 10.0f);
        g.drawLine(0,240,639,240);
        g.drawLine(320,0,320,479);
        GeneralPath pol = new GeneralPath(0);
        for (col=0; col<640; col+=2)
        {
            x = ((double)(col-320))/12.0;
            if (x == 0)
                y = 1;
            else
                y = Math.sin(x)/x;
            row = 240 - (int)(y * 240.0);
            if (col==0)
                pol.moveTo(col, row);
            else
                pol.lineTo(col, row);
        }
        g2.setStroke(bs);
        g2.draw(pol);
        g2.dispose();
    }
}

public class Sinc extends Frame
{
    public Sinc()
    {
        super("sinc(x) curve");
```

LISTING *Drawing a sinc Curve with the Polygon Class. (continues)*
16.2

```
        setBackground(Color.white);
        setLayout( new BorderLayout());
        add("Center", new SincCanvas());
        setSize(640, 480);
        addWindowListener(new DWAdapter());
        show();
    }

    class DWAdapter extends WindowAdapter
    {
        public void windowClosing(WindowEvent event)
        {
            System.exit(0);
        }
    }

    public static void main(String args[])
    {
        Sinc f = new Sinc();
    }
}
```

LISTING *Drawing a sinc Curve with the Polygon Class. (continued)*
16.2

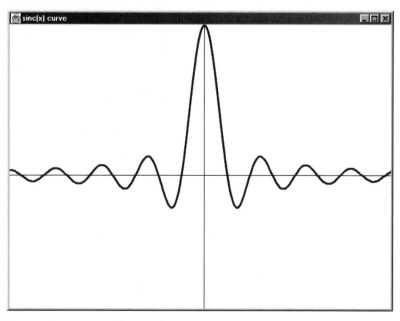

FIGURE *Creating a sinc Curve with Java 2D.*
16.2

Filling Polygons

The *fillPolygon* method works in the same way as the *drawPolygon* method, except that the geometric figure is filled with color instead of being outlined. To use it, you first set up an object of class *Polygon* and then use the *addPoint* method to define each of the points. This works just fine with a well-behaved polygon. To understand what happens in more complicated cases, you need to know a bit about what's going on inside the method. Figure 16.3 depicts a somewhat complex polygon with a horizontal line drawn through it. The simplest technique that you might use to fill a polygon is to draw a series of horizontal lines, each going from the farthest left boundary point on the polygon to the farthest right boundary point. As you can see, this technique would be all right for the bottom of this polygon, but it wouldn't work for the top, where the fill would go right over the empty space between two polygon sections. What the *fillPolygon* method actually does is scan horizontal lines and count the number of polygon boundary crossings. At every odd-numbered boundary crossing it begins to draw a line, and at every even-numbered boundary crossing it stops drawing. As you can see by following the sample horizontal line and imagining others, this works well for the polygon shown.

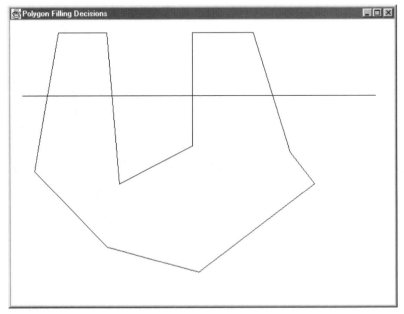

FIGURE *How the Polygon Filling Technique Works.*
16.3

Now let's look at some simple filled polygons that illustrate some more points about filling polygons. Listing 16.3 is a program to create some simple filled polygons. The program is much like Listing 16.1, except for changes in the *paint* method. At the beginning of this method, we've set the color to magenta and created a couple of filled circles. Just accept them for now; in the next chapter we'll go into drawing circles and ovals in detail. The result of running the program is shown in Figure 16.4. For each polygon, we have not only filled it in color, but also have drawn the lines that define the polygon sides in black. Look first at the six-pointed star. Depending upon how you draw this, you could get into trouble when you wanted to fill it in. The technique we used is to break it up into two completely separate triangles. Each is a well-behaved polygon that can be filled with no trouble. This is a technique you should keep in mind. If you're faced with a complicated polygon that will give you fits to fill, try breaking it up into separate, more simple polygons.

```
/*
   StarDemo. ava
   Some Filled Polygons
*/

import  ava.awt.*;
import  ava.awt.event.*;

class StarCanvas extends Canvas
{
    StarCanvas()
    {
        addMouseListener(new M());
    }

    public void paint(Graphics g)
    {
        g.setColor(Color.magenta);
        g.fillOval(374, 225, 213, 213);
        g.fillOval(50, 225, 213, 213);
        Polygon poly1 = new Polygon();

        Polygon poly2 = new Polygon();
        Polygon poly3 = new Polygon();
        Polygon poly4 = new Polygon();
        poly1.addPoint(210, 90);

        poly1.addPoint(410, 90);
```

LISTING *Sample Filled Polygons. (continues)*
16.3

```
        poly1.addPoint(310, 270);
        poly1.addPoint(210, 90);
        poly2.addPoint(210, 200);
        poly2.addPoint(310, 20);
        poly2.addPoint(410, 200);
        poly2.addPoint(210, 200);
        poly3.addPoint(380, 300);
        poly3.addPoint(582, 300);
        poly3.addPoint(424, 420);
        poly3.addPoint(481, 225);
        poly3.addPoint(538, 420);
        poly3.addPoint(380, 300);
        poly4.addPoint(55, 300);
        poly4.addPoint(135, 300);
        poly4.addPoint(157, 225);
        poly4.addPoint(179, 300);
        poly4.addPoint(257, 300);
        poly4.addPoint(192, 349);
        poly4.addPoint(213, 420);
        poly4.addPoint(157, 376);
        poly4.addPoint(100, 420);
        poly4.addPoint(123, 349);
        poly4.addPoint(55, 300);
        g.setColor(Color.blue);
        g.fillPolygon(poly1);
        g.fillPolygon(poly2);
        g.setColor(Color.yellow);
        g.fillPolygon(poly3);
        g.fillPolygon(poly4);
        g.setColor(Color.black);
        g.drawPolygon(poly1);
        g.drawPolygon(poly2);
        g.drawPolygon(poly3);
        g.drawPolygon(poly4);
    }

    class M extends MouseAdapter
    {
        public void mouseClicked(MouseEvent event)
        {
            System.out.println("x: " + event.getX() + "
y: " + event.getY());
        }
    }
}

class StarDemo extends Frame
{
    public StarDemo()
    {
```

LISTING *Sample Filled Polygon. (continues)*
16.3

```
            super("Drawing a Star");
            setBackground(Color.white);
            setLayout( new BorderLayout());
            add("Center", new StarCanvas());
            setSize(640, 480);
            show();
            addWindowListener(new DWAdapter());
        }

        class DWAdapter extends WindowAdapter
        {
            public void windowClosing(WindowEvent event)
            {
                System.exit(0);
            }
        }

        public static void main(String args[])
        {
            StarDemo f = new StarDemo();
        }
    }
```

LISTING *Sample Filled Polygon. (continued)*
16.3

FIGURE *Demonstration of Filled Polygons.*
16.4

Now look at the five-pointed star in the bottom right of the color plate. This is drawn by five straight lines using a popular technique. This polygon is closed, but it isn't well behaved, because the lines cross in the interior. When we use the *fillPolygon* method with this figure, there is a small pentagon in the center that does not get filled. How do we fill the whole star? Well, one way is to re-draw it with lines that only compose the outside boundaries. You can see this in the bottom left of the color plate. The black lines show how the sides are drawn, with no interior content. How do we do this? To draw the other five-pointed star, we needed to know the coordinates of the five points of the star, but that was all. Now we need to know the coordinates of five other points where the star's sides meet. The best way to get this information is to include a *MouseListener* in the program and have it associated with a method that prints out to the DOS window the coordinates of the cursor location when the mouse clicking event occurs. To use it, we first set up the program to draw the star on the left in the same manner that we used to draw the star on the right. Then we run this program and click the mouse on each of the five side intersection points that we need to know to draw the star differently. When the program is finished, we have the coordinates of each of the five points listed in the DOS window. Using this information, we can rewrite the star point coordinates so that only the sides of the star are drawn. The result, as shown in the color plate, is that the star is completely filled by the *fillPolygon* routine. This is another good trick that you can use if you need the coordinates of some points that aren't too easily calculated mathematically. Just insert this simple *MouseListener*, click on the points whose locations you want to know, and they will be re-ported to the DOS window in the proper coordinate system for use in your Java program.

Creating Filled Polygons with Java 2D

As with drawing polygons, the techniques using Java 2D are very similar to the Java AWT technique. Listing 16.4 shows the program to do this. You can note the differences between it and the previous program listing. Observe that we have chosen to draw the straight lines that outline the polygons with a 3 pixel width, which makes them easier to distinguish than those in Figure 16.4. We've also selected anti-aliasing, which gets rid of the "jaggies" that are characteristic of the figure.

```
/*
   StarDemo. ava
   Some Filled Polygons
*/

import   ava.awt.*;
import   ava.awt.event.*;
import   ava.awt.geom.GeneralPath;

class StarCanvas extends Canvas
{
   StarCanvas()
   {
   }
   public void paint(Graphics g)
   {
      Graphics2D g2 = (Graphics2D) g;

g2.setRenderingHint(RenderingHints.KEY_ANTIALIASING,
         (RenderingHints.VALUE_ANTIALIAS_ON));
      BasicStroke bs;
      bs = new BasicStroke((float) 3,
BasicStroke.CAP_BUTT, 0, 10.0f);
      GeneralPath poly1 = new GeneralPath(0);
      GeneralPath poly2 = new GeneralPath(0);
      GeneralPath poly3 = new GeneralPath(0);
      GeneralPath poly4 = new GeneralPath(0);
      g.setColor(Color.magenta);
      g.fillOval(372, 223, 218, 218);
      g.fillOval(48, 223, 218, 218);
      poly1.moveTo(210, 90);
      poly1.lineTo(410, 90);
      poly1.lineTo(310, 270);
      poly1.closePath();
      poly2.moveTo(210, 200);
      poly2.lineTo(310, 20);
      poly2.lineTo(410, 200);
      poly2.closePath();
      poly3.moveTo(380, 300);
      poly3.lineTo(582, 300);
      poly3.lineTo(424, 420);
      poly3.lineTo(481, 225);
      poly3.lineTo(538, 420);
      poly3.closePath();
      poly4.moveTo(55, 300);
      poly4.lineTo(135, 300);
      poly4.lineTo(157, 225);
      poly4.lineTo(179, 300);
      poly4.lineTo(257, 300);
```

LISTING *Creating Filled Polygons with Java 2D. (continues)*
16.4

```java
        poly4.lineTo(192, 349);
        poly4.lineTo(213, 420);
        poly4.lineTo(157, 376);
        poly4.lineTo(100, 420);
        poly4.lineTo(123, 349);
        poly4.closePath();
        g.setColor(Color.blue);
        g2.fill(poly1);
        g2.fill(poly2);
        g2.setColor(Color.yellow);
        g2.fill(poly3);
        g2.fill(poly4);
        g.setColor(Color.black);
        g2.setStroke(bs);
        g2.draw(poly1);
        g2.draw(poly2);
        g2.draw(poly3);
        g2.draw(poly4);
        g2.dispose();

    }
}

class StarDemo2D extends Frame
{
    public StarDemo2D()
    {
        super("Drawing a Star");
        setBackground(Color.white);
        setLayout( new BorderLayout());
        add("Center", new StarCanvas());
        setSize(640, 480);
        show();
        addWindowListener(new DWAdapter());
    }

    class DWAdapter extends WindowAdapter
    {
        public void windowClosing(WindowEvent event)
        {
            System.exit(0);
        }
    }

    public static void main(String args[])
    {
        StarDemo2D f = new StarDemo2D();
    }
}
```

LISTING *Creating Filled Polygons with Java 2D. (continued)*
16.4

Using an Array to Supply Polygon Data

The technique we used so far to create polygons works very well when only a few points need to be defined. But it certainly becomes cumbersome for a large, complex polygon with 100 or more points. Imagine having to include over 100 *addPoint* statements in our program. To avoid this, we can create two separate arrays, one for the *x* coordinate values of points and one for the *y* coordinate values. Arrays are easily initialized with a large number of values. Once we have the arrays, we can use a *for* loop to set all of the polygon points. There are two ways of defining an array in Java. One looks like this:

```
int [] c = new int[100];
```

The other way is:

```
int c[] = new int[100];
```

Either of these creates an array *c* of 100 integers. You don't need to use the *new* method to create an array if you are going to initialize it at the same time. An expression such as:

```
int [] c = {1,2,3,4,5,6,7,8};
```

will do just as well. It creates an array of eight members. The nice thing about this form is that you don't need to try to count the number of initial values; Java automatically sizes the array to include the number of values you have entered for initialization. However, when you come to use the array, you'll probably need to know how many values it contains. Now let's look at an example. Listing 16.5 is a program to create a map of South America. The polygon was created by tracing a map of South America onto an 8.5 × 11 inch sheet of graph paper. The outline was then broken up into 114 straight line segments and the coordinates of each recorded. Using this technique, you are likely to get a few coordinates wrong. This will be very apparent when you draw the map for the first time. If you see some obvious errors, here is one way to track them down. First, temporarily eliminate the *fill* method. This will draw an outline map, instead of a filled in one. Next, change the limits of the *for* loop that controls setting the points for the polygon. You can vary the starting and ending values until just a few line segments are drawn around the coordinate that is incorrect. At this point, you'll be able to count down in each array to find the actual values involved and modify as necessary to get them right. Usually, you read a value incorrectly from your graph paper. Correct this, and then change the *for* loop values to look at the next problem area. When all of the problem values have been fixed, you can go back to the full range of points and the *fill* method.

The resulting map is shown in Figure 16.5. If you want more accuracy than is given by this example, get a larger map and a larger piece of graph paper and break the outline into a lot smaller line segments.

```
/*
   SAmerica. ava
   Map of South America
*/

import  ava.awt.*;
import  ava.util.*;
import  ava.awt.event.*;
import  ava.awt.geom.GeneralPath;

class SACanvas extends Canvas
{
    SACanvas()
    {
    }

    public void paint(Graphics g)
    {
        Graphics2D g2;
        g2 = (Graphics2D) g;

g2.setRenderingHint(RenderingHints.KEY_ANTIALIASING,
        (RenderingHints.VALUE_ANTIALIAS_ON));
        BasicStroke bs;
        bs = new BasicStroke((float) 3,
BasicStroke.CAP_BUTT, 0, 10.0f);
        GeneralPath poly = new GeneralPath(0);
        int i;
        int [] x = {434, 437, 434, 416, 413, 413, 406,
392,
        385, 378, 374, 364, 357, 357, 350, 350,
        315, 308, 290, 290, 297, 297, 301, 294,
        266, 264, 259, 248, 248, 257, 242, 242,
        246, 234, 238, 245, 224, 231, 227,
        245, 231, 238, 227, 220, 213, 213, 206,
206,
        200, 189, 182, 182, 189, 189, 196, 196,
        197, 196, 189, 192, 196, 203, 203, 210,
        210, 196, 199, 189, 182, 175, 151, 147,
        140, 140, 140, 147, 147, 143, 140, 140,
        147, 164, 164, 154, 154, 168, 171, 189,
        203, 198, 203, 203, 210, 224, 231, 245,
        259, 273, 273, 280, 287, 308, 329, 329,
        336, 339, 332, 336, 350, 375, 373, 400,
        420, 434};
```

LISTING *Program to Generate a Map of South America. (continues)*
16.5

```
        int [] y = {126, 140, 150, 175, 182, 206, 220,
245,
          242, 245, 245, 253, 253, 259, 266, 284,
          329, 331, 322, 326, 330, 336, 340, 350,
          357, 372, 374, 373, 381, 385, 392, 399,
          413, 423, 426, 441, 455, 462, 472, 490,
          490, 504, 497,490, 483, 483, 476, 483,
          469, 465, 434, 420, 402, 402, 414, 399,
          378, 395, 378, 350, 315, 304, 280, 217,
          203, 199, 201, 175, 168, 147, 145, 147,
          143, 122, 115, 112, 115, 112, 105, 91,
          80, 60, 60, 52, 42, 35, 21, 15,
          28, 42, 28, 24, 28, 28, 35, 28,
          31, 42, 49, 56, 56, 63, 70, 77,
          87, 94, 98, 98, 105, 109, 112, 119,
          126, 126};

        poly.moveTo(x[0], y[0]);
        for (i=1; i<114; i++)
        {
            poly.lineTo(x[i], y[i]);
        }
        poly.closePath();
        g.setColor(Color.green);
        g2.setStroke(bs);
        g2.fill(poly);
        g2.draw(poly);
        g2.dispose();
    }
}

class SAmerica extends Frame
{
    public SAmerica()
    {
        super("South America");
        setBackground(Color.blue);
        setLayout( new BorderLayout());
        add("Center", new SACanvas());
        setSize(640, 520);
        show();
        addWindowListener(new DWAdapter());
    }

    class DWAdapter extends WindowAdapter
    {
        public void windowClosing(WindowEvent event)
        {
            System.exit(0);
```

LISTING *Program to Generate a Map of South America. (continues)*
16.5

```
        }
    }

    public static void main(String args[])
    {
        SAmerica f = new SAmerica();
    }
}
```

LISTING *Program to Generate a Map of South America. (continued)*
16.5

FIGURE *Map of South America.*
16.5

17

Drawing Circles, Ellipses, and Arcs

The Java *Graphics* class includes methods for drawing and filling circles, ellipses, and arcs that will take care of many of your requirements for drawing these figures. However, these methods have some severe limitations. You can't draw any of these figures with wide lines. Also, you can only draw ellipses oriented with their foci in the *x* or *y* directions. For a tilted ellipse, you're out of luck. There are work-arounds for these situations, but we recommend instead that you use the new Java 2D techniques for performing these operations. They offer you a lot more flexibility. We'll show you how to use them in this chapter.

Drawing and Filling Ellipses

The Java Graphics 2D method for drawing an ellipse defines the ellipse by specifying a box or rectangle. The ellipse is drawn within this rectangle so that it is tangent to each of the four sides of the rectangle. The method used is like this:

```
g2.draw(new Ellipse2D.Float(x, y, width, height);
```

where *g2* is a Graphics 2D object that you have already defined. The parameters passed to this method are *x* and *y*, the *x* and *y* coordinates of the top left-hand corner of the rectangle, and *width* and *height*, the width and height of the rectangle, respectively. When you see an ellipse defined in the geometry books, you may find it defined in terms of the center and the major and minor axes. This is a minor problem. You can define the *x* and *y* coordinates of the top left-hand rectangle corner in terms of *xcen* and *ycen*, the coordinates of the ellipse center, as follows:

```
x = xcen - width/2;
y = ycen + length/2;
```

The major axis is the longer diameter of the ellipse; the minor axis is the shorter one. If you set *width* equal to the major axis and *length* equal to the minor axis, you'll have an ellipse that is wider than it is tall. If you set *width* equal to the minor axis and *length* equal to the major axis, the ellipse will be taller than it is wide.

To fill ellipses, you use a very similar command:

```
g2.fill(new Ellipse2D.Float(x, y, width, height);
```

The same ellipse is created as with the *draw* command, but it is filled with the current color.

Drawing and Filling Circles

You may not realize it, but you already know how to draw and fill circles. A circle is just a degenerate case of the ellipse; one in which the width and length are the same. So if you use either of the methods just discussed with the *width* and *height* parameters the same, you'll get a circle.

Wide-Line Circles and Ellipses

Drawing circles and ellipses with the line wider than one pixel is easy. You simply insert the following line in your program:

```
g2.setStroke(new BasicStroke((float)(width));
```

where *width* is the line width you want.

Drawing and Filling Arcs

Java has a whole set of methods that are used to handle arcs. When Java defines an *Arc2D* object, it passes it a parameter that determines how the arc is to be filled if the *fill* method is called. To determine the size and location of the rectangle containing the arc, Java uses the *setFrame* method. The parameters passed to this method are the *x* and *y* coordinates of the upper left corner of the rectangle, and the width and height of the rectangle. If the width and height are the same, the arc will be part of the circumference of a circle; if they are not, the arc will be part of the circumference of an ellipse. The Java 2D method *setAngleStart* accepts a parameter that is the starting angle of the arc in degrees; the method *setAngleExtent* accepts a parameter that is the ending angle of the arc. If you want to draw the arc with a wide line, you need to add the method *setStroke* and pass it a *BasicStroke* parameter specifying the line width you want. In summary, the statements used for drawing an arc are:

```
Arc2D arc = new Arc2D.Float(fillParameter);
arc.setFrame(x, y, width, height);
arc.setAngleStart(start_angle);
arc.setAngleExtent(end_angle);
g2.setStroke(new BasicStroke(lineWidth));
g2.draw(arc);
```

You can fill an arc with the method:

```
g2.draw(arc);
```

If you're a stickler for mathematical exactness, you may be puzzled by just what is meant by filling an arc. After all, an arc is just a curved line that does not form a closed figure. So how do we "fill" it? Java provides three methods for drawing and filling an arc, depending upon the parameter that you specify when you create the *arc* object. If that parameter is 0, Java uses what it calls an *open* fill. When you draw such an arc, it is indeed an unclosed figure and when you fill it, it assumes that a chord is drawn between the ends of the arc and then fills the closed area that is thus formed. If the parameter is 1, Java uses what it calls a *chord* fill. When you draw such an arc, both the arc and a chord between its ends are drawn, and it is this closed figure that is filled by the *fill* method.. If the parameter is 2, Java uses what it calls a *pie* fill. When you draw such an arc, the arc itself is drawn and a straight line is then drawn from each end of the arc to the center of the underlying circle or ellipse. These form the bounds of the closed figure that is filled when you use the *fill* method. Listing 17.1 is a program to illustrate these three ways of drawing and filling an arc. The resulting display is shown in Figure 17.1.

```java
/*
   ArcFill.java
   Random Filled Circles
*/

import java.awt.*;
import java.util.*;
import java.awt.event.*;
import java.awt.geom.Ellipse2D;
import java.awt.geom.Arc2D;

class ArcCanvas extends Canvas
{
   ArcCanvas()
   {
   }

   public void paint(Graphics g)
   {
      Graphics2D g2 = (Graphics2D) g;

g2.setRenderingHint(RenderingHints.KEY_ANTIALIASING,
         RenderingHints.VALUE_ANTIALIAS_ON);
      Arc2D arc = new Arc2D.Float(0);
      arc.setFrame(50, 170, 130, 130);
      arc.setAngleStart(0);
      arc.setAngleExtent(300);
      g2.setStroke(new BasicStroke(5.0f));
      g.setColor(Color.black);
      g2.draw(arc);
      g.setColor(Color.gray);
      g2.fill(arc);
      arc = new Arc2D.Float(1);
```

LISTING *Program to Illustrate Three Ways of Drawing and Filling an Arc. (continues)*
17.1

```
        arc.setFrame(250, 170, 130, 130);
        arc.setAngleStart(0);
        arc.setAngleExtent(300);
        g2.setStroke(new BasicStroke(5.0f));
        g.setColor(Color.black);
        g2.draw(arc);
        g.setColor(Color.gray);
        g2.fill(arc);
        arc = new Arc2D.Float(2);
        arc.setFrame(450, 170, 130, 130);
        arc.setAngleStart(0);
        arc.setAngleExtent(300);
        g2.setStroke(new BasicStroke(5.0f));
        g.setColor(Color.black);
        g2.draw(arc);
        g.setColor(Color.gray);
        g2.fill(arc);
        g.setColor(Color.black);
        g.drawString("Open Fill",90, 350);
        g.drawString("Chord Fill",290, 350);
        g.drawString("Pie Fill",490, 350);
    }
}

class ArcFill extends Frame
{
    public ArcFill()
    {
        super("Ways of Filling an Arc");
        setBackground(Color.white);
        setLayout( new BorderLayout());
        add("Center", new ArcCanvas());
        setSize(640, 480);
        show();
        addWindowListener(new DWAdapter());
    }

    class DWAdapter extends WindowAdapter
    {
        public void windowClosing(WindowEvent event)
        {
            System.exit(0);
        }
    }

    public static void main(String args[])
    {
        ArcFill f = new ArcFill();
    }
}
```

LISTING *Program to Illustrate Three Ways of Drawing and Filling an Arc. (continued)*
17.1

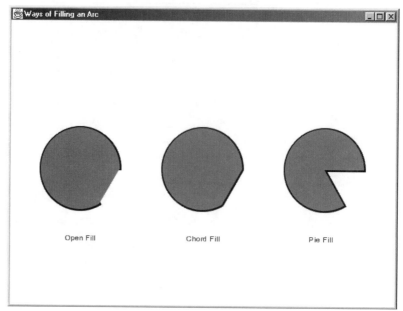

FIGURE *Three Ways of Drawing and Filling an Arc.*
17.1

Random Circles, Ellipses, and Arcs

The program in Listing 17.2 can be used to draw a display full of circles, ellipses, or arcs, either drawn with single pixel or wide lines or filled. All you have to do is change a few lines. Its features are similar to other Java programs we have written except for the *paint* method. This method starts by defining seven integers, an object *r* of class *Random*, and an object *g2* of class *Graphics2D*. The method then calls *setRenderingHint* to turn the anti-aliasing on. Next, we set up a *for* loop that will draw or fill 75 ellipses, circles, or arcs. At the beginning of this loop, on each iteration, we use the *Random* class method *r.nextDouble* to obtain three random double floating point numbers between 0 and 1.0. We multiply each by 255 and convert to an integer. This gives us three integers in the proper range to define a color, which we do with the method *setColor*. We then use the same technique to find two diameters for our circle or ellipse in the range 20 to 170. We also find random starting and ending angles for our arcs between 0 and 360. When we set up the *Circles* class, we call for a white background (same as *color[15]*) so each of the possible drawing or filling colors will show up on it. In a similar way, we set up random *x* values in the range 0–549, and *y* values in the range 0–349. At this point in the program, you'll see a number of lines that are commented out. Which of these lines we use determines

```
/*
   Circles.java
   Random Filled Circles
*/

import java.awt.*;
import java.util.*;
import java.awt.event.*;
import java.awt.geom.Ellipse2D;
import java.awt.geom.Arc2D;

class CirCanvas extends Canvas
{
   CirCanvas()
   {
   }

   public void paint(Graphics g)
   {
      int i, x, y, diameter1, diameter2, start_angle,
         end_angle;
      Random r = new Random();
      Graphics2D g2 = (Graphics2D) g;
      g2.setRenderingHint(RenderingHints.KEY_ANTIALIASING,
         RenderingHints.VALUE_ANTIALIAS_ON);
      for (i=0; i<95; i++)
      {
         g.setColor(new Color((int)(r.nextDouble() *
            255.0),(int)(r.nextDouble()
            * 255.0),(int)(r.nextDouble() * 255.0)));
         diameter1 = (int)(r.nextDouble() * 150.0 + 20.0);
         diameter2 = (int)(r.nextDouble() * 150.0 + 20.0);
         start_angle = (int)(r.nextDouble() * 360.0);
         end_angle = (int)(r.nextDouble() * 360.0);
         x = (int)(r.nextDouble() * 550.0);
         y = (int)(r.nextDouble() * 360.0);
//       g2.setStroke(new
//       BasicStroke((float)(r.nextDouble() * 20. + // 2.)));
//       g2.draw(new Ellipse2D.Float(x,y,diameter1,
//          diameter1));
//       g2.fill(new Ellipse2D.Float(x,y,diameter1,
//          diameter1));
//       g2.draw(new Ellipse2D.Float(x,y,diameter1,
//          diameter2));
//       g2.fill(new Ellipse2D.Float(x,y,diameter1,
//          diameter2));
         Arc2D arc = new Arc2D.Float((int)(r.nextDouble()
            * 2.5));
//       arc.setFrame(x,y,diameter1, diameter1);
```

LISTING *Program to Draw and Fill Circles, Ellipses, and Arcs. (continues)*
17.2

```
                arc.setFrame(x,y,diameter1, diameter2);
                arc.setAngleStart(start_angle);
                arc.setAngleExtent(end_angle);
                g2.setStroke(new BasicStroke(5.0f));
                g.setColor(Color.black);
                g2.draw(arc);
                g.setColor(new Color((int)(r.nextDouble() *
                    255.0),(int)(r.nextDouble()
                    * 255.0),(int)(r.nextDouble() * 255.0)));
                g2.fill(arc);
            }
        }
}

class Circles extends Frame
{
    public Circles()
    {
        super("Random Filled Arcs, Circles, and Ovals");
        setBackground(Color.white);
        setLayout( new BorderLayout());
        add("Center", new CirCanvas());
        setSize(640, 480);
        show();
        addWindowListener(new DWAdapter());
    }

    class DWAdapter extends WindowAdapter
    {
        public void windowClosing(WindowEvent event)
        {
            System.exit(0);
        }
    }

    public static void main(String args[])
    {
        Circles f = new Circles();
    }
}
```

LISTING **17.2** *Program to Draw and Fill Circles, Ellipses, and Arcs. (continued)*

what kind of display will be produced. We begin by commenting out the call to the *setStroke* method to draw and fill, the arc and associated methods all the way down to the end of the *for* loop, except for the first *g2.draw* method call, which specifies that the two diameters be equal, resulting in a display of circles. This display is shown in Figure 17.2. For the next run, we comment out the call to the *draw* method that we used before and use instead the next *g2draw*

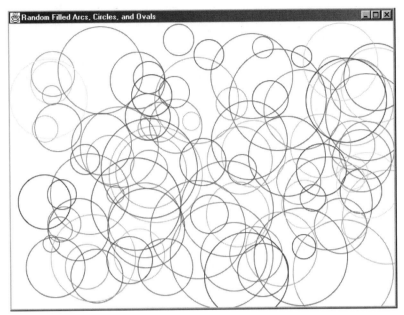

FIGURE   *Randomly Generated Circles.*
17.2

statement, which draws with two different diameters. This gives us a display of ellipses, which is shown in Figure 17.3. Next, we remove the comments from the *setStroke* method and run each of the two draw methods that we did in the two previous runs of the program. This produces wide line circles on the first run, as shown in Figure 17.4, and wide line ellipses on the second run, as shown in Figure 17.5. We then comment out the *setStroke* statement again as well as all the *draw* statements and uncomment the first *g2.fill* statement. When we run this, we get a display of filled circles, as shown in Figure 17.6. Substituting the second *g2.fill* statement for the first, we get a display of filled ellipses, as shown in Figure 17.7. Finally, we comment out all the *g2.draw* and *g2.fill* statements and uncomment all of the statements from the point where the *arc* object is created to the end of the *for* loop, except for the second *setFrame* statement. This gives us a display in which we have a bunch of circular arcs that are randomly of the open, chord, or pie types. Each arc is first drawn with a black line and then filled with a random color, using the appropriate method. The resulting display is shown in Figure 17.8. Finally, we comment out the first *setFrame* statement and uncomment the second. This gives us a display of arcs similar to the previous display except that we have elliptical arcs instead of circular arcs. The result is shown in Figure 17.9.

FIGURE *Randomly Generated Ellipses.*
17.3

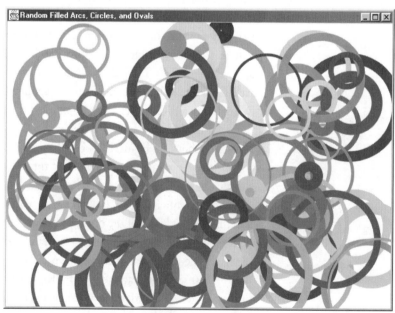

FIGURE *Randomly Generated Wide Line Circles.*
17.4

FIGURE *Randomly Generated Wide Line Ellipses.*
17.5

FIGURE *Randomly Generated Filled Circles.*
17.6

FIGURE *Randomly Generated Filled Ellipses.*
17.7

FIGURE *Randomly Generated Circular Arcs.*
17.8

FIGURE *Randomly Generated Elliptical Arcs.*
17.9

Balloons

Figure 17.10 shows a group of balloons in the sky. Listing 17.3 is the program that produced this display. By closely examining the *paint* method, you can see how we put together a number of *draw*, *fill*, and *drawLine* statements to generate this picture.

```
/*
   Balloons.java
   Program to draw balloons
*/

import java.awt.*;
import java.awt.event.*;
import java.awt.geom.Ellipse2D;
import java.awt.geom.GeneralPath;

class BalCanvas extends Canvas
{
```

LISTING *Program to Create Balloons Picture. (continues)*
17.3

```
BalCanvas()
{
}

public void paint(Graphics g)
{
    Graphics2D g2;
    int width = getSize().width;
    int height = getSize().height;
    g2 = (Graphics2D) g;
    g2.clearRect(0, 0, width, height);
    g2.setRenderingHint(RenderingHints.KEY_ANTIALIASING,
        (RenderingHints.VALUE_ANTIALIAS_ON));
    BasicStroke bs;
    bs = new BasicStroke((float) 2, BasicStroke.CAP_BUTT, 0,
        10.0f);
    g2.setStroke(bs);
    g.setColor(Color.green);
    g.fillRect(0,320,640,160);
    GeneralPath p = new GeneralPath(0);
    g.setColor(Color.white);
    p.moveTo(335, 110);
```

LISTING *Program to Create Balloons Picture. (continues)*
17.3

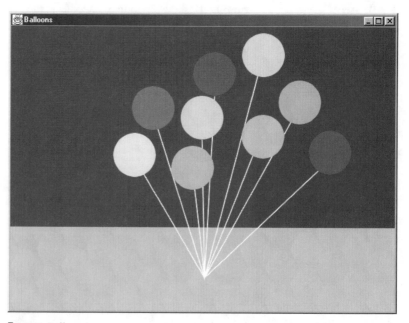

FIGURE *Balloons.*
17.10

```
        p.lineTo(320, 400);
        p.lineTo(315, 180);
        g2.draw(p);
        p = new GeneralPath(0);
        p.moveTo(475, 125);
        p.lineTo(320, 400);
        p.lineTo(400, 200);
        g2.draw(p);
        p = new GeneralPath(0);
        p.moveTo(520, 215);
        p.lineTo(320, 400);
        p.lineTo(240, 155);
        g2.draw(p);
        p = new GeneralPath(0);
        p.moveTo(410, 60);
        p.lineTo(320, 400);
        xp.lineTo(300, 230);
        g2.draw(p);
        p = new GeneralPath(0);
        p.moveTo(220, 235);
        p.lineTo(320, 400);
        g2.draw(p);
        g.setColor(Color.red);
        g2.fill(new Ellipse2D.Float(300, 40, 70, 70));
        g.setColor(Color.cyan);
        g2.fill(new Ellipse2D.Float(280, 110, 70, 70));
        g.setColor(Color.yellow);
        g2.fill(new Ellipse2D.Float(170, 170, 70, 70));

        g.setColor(Color.magenta);
        g2.fill(new Ellipse2D.Float(200, 95, 70, 70));
        g.setColor(Color.pink);

        g2.fill(new Ellipse2D.Float(440, 85, 70, 70));
        g.setColor(Color.green);
        g2.fill(new Ellipse2D.Float(380, 140, 70, 70));
        g.setColor(Color.red);
        g2.fill(new Ellipse2D.Float(490, 165, 70, 70));

        g.setColor(Color.cyan);
        g2.fill(new Ellipse2D.Float(380, 10, 70, 70));
        g.setColor(Color.orange);
        g2.fill(new Ellipse2D.Float(265, 190, 70, 70));
    }
}

class Balloons extends Frame
{
    public Balloons()
```

LISTING *Program to Create Balloons Picture. (continues)*
17.3

```
    {
        super("Balloons");
        setBackground(Color.blue);
        setLayout( new BorderLayout());
        add("Center", new BalCanvas());
        setSize(640, 480);
        show();
        addWindowListener(new DWAdapter());
    }

    class DWAdapter extends WindowAdapter
    {
        public void windowClosing(WindowEvent event)
        {
            System.exit(0);
        }
    }

    public static void main(String args[])
    {
        Balloons f = new Balloons();
    }
}
```

LISTING *Program to Create Balloons Picture. (continued)*
17.3

Pie Chart

Figure 17.11 shows a pie chart produced by using the *fillArc* method. Listing 17.4 is the program that produced this display. By closely examining the *paint* method, you can see how we put together a number of arc definitions and *fill* statements to generate this picture. If you want a pie chart that has each segment labeled and other text on it, you can easily add this with several *drawString* statements.

```
/*
    PieChart.java
    Pie Chart
*/

import java.awt.*;
import java.awt.event.*;
import java.awt.geom.Arc2D;

class PieCanvas extends Canvas
{
```

LISTING *Program to Generate Pie Chart. (continues)*
17.4

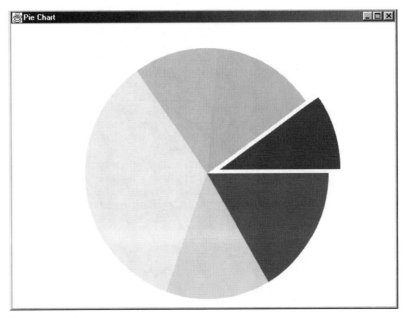

FIGURE *Pie Chart.*
17.11

```
    PieCanvas()
    {
    }

    public void paint(Graphics g)
    {
        Graphics2D g2 = (Graphics2D) g;

g2.setRenderingHint(RenderingHints.KEY_ANTIALIASING,
        RenderingHints.VALUE_ANTIALIAS_ON);

        Arc2D arc = new Arc2D.Float(2);
        g.setColor(Color.blue);
        arc.setFrame(140, 34, 400, 400);
        arc.setAngleStart(0);
        arc.setAngleExtent(35);
        g2.fill(arc);
        g.setColor(Color.orange);
        arc.setFrame(120, 40, 400, 400);
        arc.setAngleStart(35);
        arc.setAngleExtent(50);
        g2.fill(arc);
```

LISTING *Program to Generate Pie Chart. (continues)*
17.4

```
            g.setColor(Color.green);
            arc.setFrame(120, 40, 400, 400);
            arc.setAngleStart(85);
            arc.setAngleExtent(40);
            g2.fill(arc);
            g.setColor(Color.yellow);
            arc.setFrame(120, 40, 400, 400);
            arc.setAngleStart(125);
            arc.setAngleExtent(125);
            g2.fill(arc);
            g.setColor(Color.cyan);
            arc.setFrame(120, 40, 400, 400);
            arc.setAngleStart(250);
            arc.setAngleExtent(50);
            g2.fill(arc);
            g.setColor(Color.red);
            arc.setFrame(120, 40, 400, 400);
            arc.setAngleStart(300);
            arc.setAngleExtent(60);
            g2.fill(arc);
      }
}

class PieChart extends Frame
{
    public PieChart()
    {
        super("Pie Chart");
        setBackground(Color.white);
        setLayout( new BorderLayout());
        add("Center", new PieCanvas());
        setSize(640, 480);
        show();
        addWindowListener(new DWAdapter());
    }

    class DWAdapter extends WindowAdapter
    {
        public void windowClosing(WindowEvent event)
        {
            System.exit(0);
        }
    }

    public static void main(String args[])
    {
        PieChart f = new PieChart();
    }
}
```

LISTING *Program to Generate Pie Chart. (continued)*
17.4

Tilted Ellipses   The original Java *drawOval* and *fillOval* methods only allow you to create ellipses whose *length* and *height* axes are parallel to the *x* and *y* axes, respectively.
That's all that is ever needed for circles, which are the same for every tilt angle,
but when using ellipses (as, for example to represent the petals of flowers) we
would like to be able to rotate the ellipse to any desired angle. This is fairly simple with Java 2D. The *Violet.java* program draws a violet to show how this
technique is used. The result is shown in Figure 17.12. The program itself is
listed in Listing 17.5. In addition to the usual Java packages, we need to import
java.awt.geom.Ellipse2D and *java.awt.geom.GeneralPath*. The program is similar to others we've used, except for the *paint* method, which contains the special
things we need to make the tilted ellipses. However, before we start this method,
we set the background to blue to represent the sky. The *paint* method begins by
creating an object *g2* of class *Graphics2D*. It then uses *setRenderingHint* to turn
on quality anti-aliasing. We then set the color to green and create a *BasicStroke*
object *bs* that is set to create a line width of 10. We then set up the *GeneralPath*
object *p*, fill it with the initial and final points of the line representing the flower
stem, and call *g2draw* to draw the stem. Next, we change the color to magenta.
We get the width and height of the window and perform a *g2.translate* operation that moves the origin of the display from the top left corner to a position

FIGURE *Picture of a Violet.*
17.12

just slightly to the right of the center of the display. We now create an *Ellipse2D.Float* object called *petal*, which has its top left corner at coordinates (0, –25) and has a width of 170 and a height of 50. Next, we rotate our coordinate system 10 degrees and fill an ellipse. We then rotate backwards 20 degrees and fill another petal. We now enter a *for* loop that creates four more double petals. For each iteration, the coordinate system is rotated 52 degrees, a petal is filled, the system is rotated another 20 degrees and another petal is filled. Note that the rotation angles must be converted into radians before being passed to the *g2.rotate* method. Finally, we set the color to white and fill a circle at the center of the flower structure. We then dispose of the *g2* object.

```
/*
   Violet. ava
   Violets Using Tilted Ellipses
*/

import  ava.awt.*;
import  ava.awt.event.*;
import  ava.awt.geom.Ellipse2D;
import  ava.awt.geom.GeneralPath;

class TiltedEllipse
{
}

class Canvas4 extends Canvas
{
    Canvas4()
    {
    }
    public void paint(Graphics g)
    {
        int i,  , x, y, diameter1, diameter2;
        Graphics2D g2 = (Graphics2D) g;
g2.setRenderingHint(RenderingHints.KEY_ANTIALIASING,
        RenderingHints.VALUE_ANTIALIAS_ON);
g2.setRenderingHint(RenderingHints.KEY_RENDERING,
        (RenderingHints.VALUE_RENDER_QUALITY));
        g.setColor(Color.green);
        BasicStroke bs;
        bs = new BasicStroke(10.0f);
        GeneralPath p = new GeneralPath(0);
        p.moveTo(356,205);
        p.lineTo(292, 480);
        g2.setStroke(bs);
        g2.draw(p);
```

LISTING *Program to Draw a Violet with Tilted Ellipses. (continues)*
17.5

```
            g.setColor(Color.magenta);
            int width = getSize().width;
            int height = getSize().height;
            g2.translate(width / 2.0 + 37, height / 2.0);
            Ellipse2D.Float petal = new Ellipse2D.Float(0,-25, 170, 50);
            g2.rotate(.17453292);
            g2.fill(petal);
            g2.rotate(-.34906585);
            g2.fill(petal);
            for (i=0; i<4; i++)
            {
                g2.rotate(-.9075712);
                g2.fill(petal);
                g2.rotate(-.34906585);

                g2.fill(petal);
            }

            g.setColor(Color.white);
            g2.fill(new Ellipse2D.Float(-37, -37, 75, 75));
            g2.dispose();
        }
    }

    class Violet extends Frame
    {
        public Violet()
        {
            super("Violet from Tilted Ellipses");
            setBackground(Color.blue);
            setLayout( new BorderLayout());
            add("Center", new Canvas4());
            setSize(640, 480);
            show();
            addWindowListener(new DWAdapter());
        }

        class DWAdapter extends WindowAdapter
        {
            public void windowClosing(WindowEvent event)
            {
                System.exit(0);
            }
        }

        public static void main(String args[])
        {
            Violet f = new Violet();
        }
    }
```

LISTING *Program to Draw a Violet with Tilted Ellipses. (continued)*
17.5

18

Using Threads with Java

I t's easy to imagine that when we start running a program on our PC, the microprocessor begins chugging along, processing one instruction after another until it reaches the end of the program. Actually, this isn't the way it works at all. The computer has a lot of other things to do besides microprocessor operations: reading and writing to disks, sending data to display memory and displaying the results, reading from the keyboard, printing, and so forth. A lot of the time when these things are going on the microprocessor is just sitting there waiting. Burroughs on one of its early mainframe computers had a large panel of lights that showed the results of all kinds of computer operations. The company programmed the system so that whenever the central processor was idle, it lit up the lights to form a giant B for Burroughs. Unfortunately, there was so much processor idle time, that the B appeared to be lit almost all the time, advertising to the world how seldom the processor was being used.

With all this idle time begging for use, we can make substantial gains in computer speed by writing software that divides the available time up into slices and permits the microprocessor to be assigned to whichever of several different tasks requires its services most urgently in each particular time slice. Although the microprocessor is only doing one thing at a time, to the outside observer it appears that all of the tasks are being accomplished in parallel. This is known as *multitasking*. There are two kinds of multitasking. *Cooperative multitasking* requires that each task cooperate in letting go of the microprocessor so that it can take on another task. Windows 3.1 is a cooperative multitasking system. This is a less desirable way of multitasking, since a poorly designed program can hold onto the microprocessor for so long that the other tasks never get a chance to run. *Preemptive multitasking* uses the operating system to assign priorities and decide which of several tasks gains control of the microprocessor for each time slice. It's more difficult to implement, but is a lot more effective. Windows 95 and Windows 98 are examples of preemptive multitasking.

If you use Windows 95 or Windows 98, you've seen multitasking in action. Several programs can run simultaneously and you can interact with them as you desire. With most computer languages, you can't carry on this process at a higher level—the language is designed to allow you to run a single program and that's that. Java, however, allows you to use *multithreading*. With Java, you can design several *threads*, each of which runs in a separate context (although all threads can use some or all of the same variables). This is a complicated process; the operating system needs to make sure that two or more threads that are working with (and possibly changing) the same variables access them in such a way that the proper values are used for each operation. All this is transparent to the Java programmer, however.

In many Java books, you'll find a fairly simple-minded demonstration of the use of threads. A couple of threads are started up; one repeatedly prints *Thread 1* and the other repeatedly prints *Thread 2*. You compile and run this program and observe how the two lines are intermixed. This is a good demonstration of threads except that it has no practical application. In this chapter, we're going to get a little more practical. We'll use a program that allows the user to select one of three 256-color *BMP* files by clicking a button. The desired picture is then displayed. We're going to draw the picture one pixel at a time. Writing each pixel first requires creating a new *Color* object and then setting the display for the proper color. You wouldn't ordinarily use this method to display a *BMP* file; it is pretty slow. You can do a lot better with the program in Chapter 10. However, this program demonstrates very clearly a problem that you may often encounter. You select a picture button and the picture slowly begins to appear on the screen. Long before it's finished, you decide that you've chosen the wrong picture; you wanted another one instead. Or perhaps you decide you'd like to quit the program all together. With previous programs that we've described, you have no choice. Everything is frozen until the entire picture is written to the screen. When the picture is finally complete, you can, at last, take another action. Now we'll show you how to use threads to get around this limitation.

A Viewing Program with Threads

Listing 18.1 shows a *BMP* viewing program that uses threads as a key to resolving our problems. Our *main* method sets up a new object *f* of class *BmpThread*. The beginning of the initialization of this class is normal enough. First, we define an object *canvas* of class *Canvas*. We then set a string *s* to "goldengt.bmp". We set the display title. We then define three buttons, one for each of the three pictures we want to display. For each button we include an action listener, which detects when the button is clicked. Next we define a panel and set it for the *FlowLayout*. We display our three buttons on this panel, which is displayed at the north of the main display. The canvas is at the center of the principal display. Up to now, however, nothing is drawn on *canvas*. *The* last two lines of initialization define a new thread. There are several ways to create a thread in Java, but the very simplest is simply to create a class that is derived from the *Thread* class. We've added the words *extends Thread* following the definition of the class *PictureT*. This makes some significant changes in the way that *PictureT* is treated. In the next to last line of initialization for *BmpThread* we set up a new object *pic* of class *PictureT*. If *PictureT* were an ordinary class, it would begin to run as soon as the object was created and would preempt the rest of our program. Since *PictureT* is an extension of the *Thread* class, it doesn't start automatically. Instead, we start it with the call *pic.start();* in the last initialization line. The *pic* object then runs as a separate thread, completely independent of the rest of our program, which still can function as it would if *pic* were not there at all.

If you look at the *draw* method under *PictureT*, you'll see that we first get a *Graphics* object and then define and initialize some parameters. Next, we call *g.clearRect* which clears the entire center of the display window to the background color, erasing any previous whole or partial pictures that were there. The method then proceeds to get the header for the file whose file name is in *s*, sets up the parameters we need to extract from it, and then reads and displays the picture itself. The technique used is the same as for the *BMP* viewing program of Chapter 10, except that instead of building an array and making it into an image, we draw each pixel as it is encountered. We only use the procedure for 256-color *BMP* files, since our three *BMP* files are of that type. To make the thread run, we need a method called *run*. This method simply calls the *draw* method. Since the *pic* object is a separate thread, drawing the picture doesn't cause our mouse actions to hang up.

Now let's look at the *actionPerformed* method that appears under the *BmpThread* class. This method is run whenever a button is clicked. First, we have a series of *if* statements. Together, these set *s* to the desired file name whenever the mouse is clicked on one of the three buttons. If one of the buttons was clicked by the mouse, we set the flag in the currently running *PictureT* object (if there is one) to 1. Now, if you look at the *draw* method under *PictureT*, you'll see that there is a *for* loop that iterates once to draw each line of the picture. Each iteration of this loop begins by checking the flag; if it is 1, the loop control variable is set to the last line of the picture, so that the loop terminates and the method stops drawing the picture. Meanwhile, after setting the flag to 1, the *actionPerformed* method instantiates a new *pic* thread with the new value of *s*. It then calls *pic.start*, which starts running a new thread to draw the newly selected picture. We thus see that by this technique we can end the program or erase the principal window and draw a newly selected picture at any time, regardless of whether a picture has been completely drawn. Plate 13 shows two threads running simultaneously to generate pictures. To get this picture, we disabled the flag in Listing 18.1, which normally wipes out the first picture as soon as the second begins.

```
/*
   BmpThread. ava
   BMP Image Viewer with Threads
*/

import  ava.awt.*;
import  ava.io.*;
import  ava.awt.event.*;

public class BmpThread extends Frame implements
   ActionListener
   {
      String s;
      PictureT pic;
      private Canvas canvas;

      public BmpThread()
      {
         canvas = new Canvas();
         s = new String("goldengt.bmp");
         setTitle("Picture Viewer - " + s);
         Button button1 = new Button("Golden Gate");
         Button button2 = new Button("Rocks");
         Button button3 = new Button("Rose");
         button1.addActionListener(this);
         button2.addActionListener(this);

         button3.addActionListener(this);
         Panel panel = new Panel();
         panel.setLayout(new FlowLayout());
         panel.add(button1);
         panel.add(button2);
         panel.add(button3);
         add("North",panel);
         add("Center", canvas);
         addWindowListener(new WindowAdapter()
         {
            public void windowClosing(WindowEvent e)
            {
               System.exit(0);
            }
         });

         setSize(640, 480);
         show();
         pic = new PictureT(canvas,s);
         pic.start();
      }
```

LISTING *A Viewing Program Using Threads. (continues)*
18.1

```
      public void actionPerformed(ActionEvent e)
      {
         String name = new String(e.getActionCommand());
         if (name.equals("Golden Gate"))
            s = new String("goldengt.bmp");
         if (name.equals("Rocks"))
            s = new String("rocks1.bmp");
         if (name.equals("Rose"))
            s = new String("rose1.bmp");
         pic.flag = 1;
         setTitle("Picture Viewer - " + s);
         pic = new PictureT(canvas,s);
         pic.start();
      }
         public static void main(String[] args)
         {
         Frame f = new BmpThread();
      }
}

class PictureT extends Thread
{
   String name;
   private Canvas canvas;
   int i,  , xres, yres, flag = 0;
   public PictureT(Canvas c, String s)
   {
      canvas = c;
      name = s;
   }

   public void draw()
   {
      Graphics g = canvas.getGraphics();
      byte buf[] = new byte[64];
      int pixcol;
      int i, , xres, yres, temp, temp1, temp2, xlength,
         offset;
      byte [] color16 = new byte[4];
      Color [] colors = new Color[256];
      g.clearRect(0,0,640,480);
      try
      {
         RandomAccessFile in = new
            RandomAccessFile(name,"r");
         in.read(buf, 0, 54);
         temp = (buf[18] >= 0) ? buf[18] : buf[18] +
            256;
         xres = temp;
```

LISTING *A Viewing Program Using Threads. (continues)*
18.1

```
         temp = (buf[19] >= 0) ? buf[19] : buf[19] +
            256;
         xres |= temp<<8;
         temp = (buf[22] >= 0) ? buf[22] : buf[22] +
            256;
         yres = temp;
         temp = (buf[23] >= 0) ? buf[23] : buf[23] +
            256;
         yres |= temp<<8;
         temp = (buf[10] >= 0) ? buf[10] : buf[10] +
            256;
         offset = temp;
         temp = (buf[11] >= 0) ? buf[11] : buf[11] +
            256;
         offset |= temp<<8;
         for (i=0; i<256; i++)
         {
            in.read(color16, 0, 4);
            temp = (color16[2]<0) ? color16[2] + 256:
               color16[2];
            temp1 = (color16[1]<0) ? color16[1] + 256:
               color16[1];
            temp2 = (color16[0]<0) ? color16[0] + 256:
               color16[0];
            colors[i] = new Color(temp, temp1, temp2);
         }
         in.seek(offset);
         xlength = xres;
         while (xlength %4 != 0)
            xlength++;
         byte pixel1[] = new byte[xlength];
         for (i=yres-1; i>=0; i—)
         {
            if (flag != 0)
               i = 0;
            in.read(pixel1, 0, xlength);
            for ( =0;  <xres;  ++)
            {
               pixcol = pixel1[ ];
               if (pixcol < 0)
                  pixcol += 256;
               g.setColor(colors[pixcol]);
               g.drawLine( , i,  , i);
            }
         }
      }
      catch (Exception e)
      {
```

LISTING *A Viewing Program Using Threads. (continues)*
18.1

```
        System.out.println("Error: " +
e.toString());
        }
    }

    public void run()
    {
        draw();
    }
}
```

LISTING *A Viewing Program Using Threads. (continued)*
18.1

Animated Ellipses

Another way that we can use threads is to produce an animated display. Listing 18.2 shows a program to do this. We begin by setting up the *init* method, which sets up the data from *Demo* to be displayed; the method *start*, which begins the *Demo* thread running; and the method *stop*, which stops the *Demo* thread. Note that the *Demo* class implements *Runnable*. It also defines the thread *thread* and has methods for starting and stopping the thread, and a *run* method that causes the thread to repaint the display with new values from the *Demo* class, then sleep for 10 milliseconds, and then run the thread again.

Our *Demo* class begins by defining the arrays needed to create 50 ellipses. These are the *x* and *y* coordinates of the center for each ellipse, the color, the line width, two orthogonal diameters that dynamically change, two diameters that save the original diameter values, and a flag that tells the program whether the diameters should be increasing or decreasing with each run of the thread. The *Demo* constructor contains a *for* loop that on each iteration randomly selects the coordinates, diameters, and width for an ellipse. The *drawDemo* method is called from the *paint* method. It contains a *for* loop that sets the line width and color for each ellipse and then draws the ellipse. The *step* method is called each time the thread is run. It contains a *for* loop that iterates for each of the 50 ellipses. At each iteration, the method checks whether the flag indicates that the ellipse should have its diameters increasing or decreasing. If the former, the method randomly finds an amount of change *delta* in the positive direction, adds this to the current size of the diameters, and then checks whether either of the diameters has reached three times its original size. If so, the flag is changed to indicate that the diameters should be reduced on future passes. If the flag originally showed that change should be in a negative direction, the same procedure is followed except that the random change *delta* is made to be in a negative direction and that the test of diameter size checks whether the

diameters are smaller than their original values. If so, the flag is changed to indicate increasing size in future passes. The result is a display of 50 random ellipses that alternately increase and decrease in diameter. Since the changes are
not the same for each ellipse, all the ellipses are not changing in the same way
at any given time. This would be a good background display for a message on
the Web. Plate 14 shows a snapshot of the display.

```
/*
   AnimCir. ava
   Animated Random Circles
*/

import  ava.awt.*;
import  ava.util.*;
import  ava.awt.event.*;
import  ava.awt.image.BufferedImage;
import  ava.awt.geom.GeneralPath;
import  avax.swing.*;
import  ava.awt.geom.Ellipse2D;

public class AnimCir extends JApplet
{
    Demo demo;

    public void init()
    {
        getContentPane().add(demo = new Demo());
    }

    public void start()
    {
        demo.start();
    }

    public void stop()
    {
        demo.stop();
    }

    public class Demo extends JPanel implements Runnable
    {
        private Thread thread;
        private BufferedImage bimg;
        protected BasicStroke solid = new BasicStroke(10.0f,
            BasicStroke.CAP_BUTT, BasicStroke.JOIN_ROUND);
        int diameter1[] = new int[50];
```

LISTING *Program to Draw Random Animated Ellipses. (continues)*
18.2

```java
      int diameter2[] = new int[50];
      int dia1[] = new int[50];
      int dia2[] = new int[50];
      int x[] = new int[50];
      int y[] = new int[50];
      Color color[] = new Color[50];
      float width[] = new float[50];
      float delta[] = new float[50];
      int flag[] = new int[50];

      public Demo()
      {

         for (int i=0; i<50; i++)
         {
            color[i] = (new Color((int)(Math.random() *
               255.0),(int)(Math.random()
               * 255.0),(int)(Math.random() * 255.0)));
            dia1[i] = diameter1[i] = (int)(Math.random() *
               150.0 + 20.0);
            dia2[i] = diameter2[i] = (int)(Math.random() *
               150.0 + 20.0);
            x[i] = (int)(Math.random() * 750.0 - 200.0);
            y[i] = (int)(Math.random() * 560.0 - 200.0);
            width[i] = (float)(Math.random() * 20. + 2.);
         }
      }

      public void step(int w, int h)
      {
         for (int i=0; i<50; i++)
         {
            if (flag[i] == 0)
            {
               delta[i] = (float) (Math.random() * 6.0 +
                  4.0);
               diameter1[i] += delta[i];
               diameter2[i] += delta[i];
               if ((diameter1[i] >= 3.0*dia1[i]) ||
                  (diameter2[i] >= 3.0*dia2[i]))
                  flag[i] = 1;
            }
            else if (flag[i] == 1)
            {
               delta[i] = - (float) (Math.random() * 6.0 +
                  4.0);
               diameter1[i] += delta[i];
               diameter2[i] += delta[i];
               if ((diameter1[i] < dia1[i]) ||
```

LISTING *Program to Draw Random Animated Ellipses. (continues)*
18.2

```
                                (diameter2[i] < dia2[i]))
                                flag[i] = 0;
                    }

            }
    }

    public void drawDemo(int w, int h, Graphics2D g2)
    {
        g2.setRenderingHint(RenderingHints.KEY_ANTIALIASING,
            RenderingHints.VALUE_ANTIALIAS_ON);
        for (int i=0; i<50; i++)
        {
            g2.setStroke(new BasicStroke(width[i]));
            g2.setColor(color[i]);
            g2.draw(new
                Ellipse2D.Float(x[i],y[i],diameter1[i],
                diameter2[i]));
        }
    }

    public void paint(Graphics g)
    {
        Dimension d = getSize();
        step(d.width, d.height);
        Graphics2D g2 = null;
        bimg = (BufferedImage) createImage(d.width,
            d.height);
        g2 = bimg.createGraphics();
        g2.setBackground(getBackground());
        g2.clearRect(0, 0, d.width, d.height);
        g2.setRenderingHint(RenderingHints.KEY_ANTIALIASING,
            RenderingHints.VALUE_ANTIALIAS_ON);
        drawDemo(d.width, d.height, g2);
        g2.dispose();
        if (bimg != null)
        {
            g.drawImage(bimg, 0, 0, this);
        }
    }

    public void start()
    {
        thread = new Thread(this);
        thread.setPriority(Thread.MIN_PRIORITY);
        thread.start();
    }

    public synchronized void stop()
```

LISTING *Program to Draw Random Animated Ellipses. (continues)*
18.2

```
      {
         thread = null;
      }

      public void run()
      {
         Thread me = Thread.currentThread();
         while (thread == me)
         {
            repaint();
            try
            {
               thread.sleep(10);
            } catch (Exception e) { break; }
         }
         thread = null;
      }
   }

   public static void main(String argv[])
   {
      final AnimCir demo = new AnimCir();
      demo.init();
      Frame f = new Frame("Animated Bezier Curves");
      f.addWindowListener(new WindowAdapter() {
         public void windowClosing(WindowEvent e)
            {System.exit(0);}
         public void windowDeiconified(WindowEvent e) {
            demo.start(); }
         public void windowIconified(WindowEvent e) {
            demo.stop(); }
      });
      f.add(demo);
      f.pack();
      f.setSize(new Dimension(640,480));
      f.show();
      demo.start();
   }
}
```

LISTING *Program to Draw Random Animated Ellipses. (continued)*
18.2

19

Parametric Cubic Curves

W hen you want to draw a smooth curve of some unusual shape that can't be represented by a circle, ellipse or a standard conic section, you may find yourself resorting to representing the curve by a large number of short straight line segments as described in Chapter 13 or using the *GeneralPath* class described in Chapter 16. These methods worked well as long as you could define your curve with some form of mathematical formula. They are less than ideal if you take a curve from a piece of graph paper and try to extract from it enough points to completely define the curve. You are likely to find yourself storing a whole lot of point data and even then it is sometimes difficult to produce a curve with a smooth and finished look. This chapter, therefore, will be devoted to looking at some mathematical expressions that you can use to define smooth curves of unusual shapes by specifying just a few control points.

Parametric Cubic Polynomials

A more compact representation of a curve and one that is easier to manipulate is obtained by using equations that are of a higher degree than linear. It turns out that the cubic equations are most often used, because second-degree equations do not provide enough flexibility in the representation of curves, and higher-order equations tend to introduce unwanted wiggles that are hard to control. Given that we want to use cubic equations, we have several options, but all except one have their inherent drawbacks. If we try to use an explicit function, such as $y = f(x)$, we cannot get multiple values of y for a single value of x, which necessitates multiple expressions when multiple values are wanted, such as for representing circles or ellipses. Furthermore, explicit functional representation is not rotationally invariant, so that rotation requires a lot of complicated variations. If we try to use an implicit function of the form $f(x,y) = 0$, we may have limited ourselves to a single value or we may get multiple results when we want only one. Furthermore, there can be difficulties in joining curve segments together. All of these problems can be overcome by using parametric representation of the form $x = x(t)$, $y = y(t)$. In particular, to define a curve segment $B(t) = (x(t), y(t))$ we have expressions of the form

$$x(t) = a_x t^3 + b_x t^2 + c_x t + d_x$$
$$y(t) = a_y t^3 + b_y t^2 + c_y t + d_y$$

(Eq. 19-1)

where $0 \leq t \leq 1$ (t is in the interval between 0 and 1). The points (a_x, a_y), (b_x, b_y), (c_x, c_y), and (d_x, d_y) determine the shape and location of the curve.

The Bezier Curve

While the expressions of Equation 19-1 are guaranteed to produce a curve, we have no idea of how to choose the coefficients to get a curve of a desired shape. To make the cubic parametric curves manageable, we need to impose some constraints on the control points. One set of curves that does this is the *Bezier* curves. The Bezier curve was developed in the early 1970s by Pierre Bezier, who was attempting to use computers to design automobiles. In this chapter we're only going to look at Bezier curves in two dimensions, but the same techniques can easily be extended to three dimensions to generate pleasingly curved three-dimensional shapes for automobiles or boats.

The Bezier curve has four control points: (x_1, y_1), (x_2, y_2), (x_3, y_3), and (x_4, y_4). The curve must begin at the control point (x_1, y_1) and end at the control point (x_4, y_4). At control point (x_1, y_1) the tangent to the curve is the line between (x_1, y_1) and (x_2, y_2). At control point (x_4, y_4) the tangent to the curve is the line between (x_4, y_4) and (x_3, y_3).

Mathematics of the Bezier Curve

In order to proceed further with the Bezier curve, we must know the relation between the coefficients in Equation 19-1 and the four control points just given. For the *x* components, the equations are

$$a_x = -x_1 + 3x_2 - 3x_3 + x_4 \qquad \text{(Eq. 19-2)}$$

$$b_x = 3x_1 - 6x_2 + 3x_3 \qquad \text{(Eq. 19-3)}$$

$$c_x = -3_1 + 3x_2 \qquad \text{(Eq. 19-4)}$$

$$d_x = x_1 \qquad \text{(Eq. 19-5)}$$

We can write a general equation for the Bezier curve as follows:

$$p(u) = \sum_{i=o}^{n} a_i C_{(n,i)} t^i (1-t)^{n-t} \qquad \text{(Eq. 19-6)}$$

The coefficient $C_{(n,i)}$ is the binomial coefficient, so Equation 19-6 can also be written in the form

$$p(t) = \sum_{i=o}^{n} \frac{n!}{i!(n-i)!} a_i t^i (1-t)^{n-t} \qquad \text{(Eq. 19-7)}$$

These two equations give the Bezier curve for any desired value of *n*, where *n* is the number of control points that directly influence the shape of the curve; in most cases we use only four control points. The four control point case can be written in matrix notation like this:

$$p(t) = \begin{bmatrix} t^3 & t^2 & t & 1 \end{bmatrix} \begin{bmatrix} -1 & 3 & -3 & 1 \\ 3 & -6 & 3 & 0 \\ -3 & 3 & 0 & 0 \\ 1 & 0 & 0 & 0 \end{bmatrix} \begin{bmatrix} q_1 \\ q_2 \\ q_3 \\ q_4 \end{bmatrix}$$

(Eq. 19-8)

In the last three equations, *p* is a point on the Bezier curve, *t* is a variable that moves uniformly over the interval 0 to 1, assuming as many values as the number of points on the Bezier curve that you wish to plot, and *q* is the column vector consisting of the four control points.

The Bezier Curve Program

We're now ready to do some programming using Bezier curves. There are several different algorithms we can use to do this. We're going to look at a problem that involves a direct application of the mathematics given in the last section. One important use of Bezier curves is in the design of type fonts for reproducing text on a computer printer. Adobe and other companies that sell a variety of type font software rely heavily on Bezier curves to define the shape of each character in each different type face. We're going to set up a program that creates the letters *A*, *B*, and *C* using a combination of straight lines and Bezier curves. The program is shown in Listing 19.1. To enable you to see any differences that occur when you change from one method of generating Bezier curves to another, we're going to make use of four buttons to allow you to select any one of four different methods. Each time you select a new method, the graphic will be redrawn using that method. To do this, we're going to have four classes: *LiteralCanvas*, *ForwardCanvas*, *deCasteljauCanvas*, and *BernsteinCanvas*.

First, let's look at the principal class, *BezierAlpha1*. We begin by defining four buttons. Then we set up the display title. Next, we add the window listener to determine when we wish to terminate the program. We now create a *tabs* object of class *Panel*. We then create each of the four button objects, give each a title, set up an action listener for it, and add it to the *tabs* panel. Finally, we add the *tabs* panel to the north (top) of our default *Border* layout. We then turn to how we are going to display the four Bezier techniques. We start by creating a new object called *cards*, which is part of the *Panel* class. We then set up

```
/*
   BezierAlpha1.java
   ABC with Various kinds of Bezier Curve Generators
*/

import java.awt.*;
import java.awt.event.*;
import java.awt.geom.GeneralPath;

public class BezierAlpha1 extends Frame implements ActionListener
{
   public BezierAlpha1()
   {
      Button button1, button2, button3, button4;
      setTitle("Creating Letters Using Bezier Curves");
      addWindowListener(new DWAdapter());

      tabs = new Panel();
      button1 = new Button("Literal Method");
      button1.addActionListener(this);
      tabs.add(button1);
      button2 = new Button("Forward Difference Method");
      button2.addActionListener(this);
      tabs.add(button2);
      button3 = new Button("deCasteljau Method");
      button3.addActionListener(this);
      tabs.add(button3);
      button4 = new Button("Bernstein Method");
      button4.addActionListener(this);
      tabs.add(button4);
      add("North", tabs);
      cards = new Panel();
      layout = new CardLayout();
      cards.setLayout(layout);
      cards.add("Literal Method", new LiteralCanvas());
      cards.add("Forward Difference Method", new
         ForwardCanvas());
      cards.add("deCasteljau Method", new
      deCasteljauCanvas());
      cards.add("Bernstein Method", new
         BernsteinCanvas());
      add("Center", cards);
   }

   public void actionPerformed(java.awt.event.ActionEvent
      evt)
   {
      layout.show(cards, evt.getActionCommand());
   }
```

LISTING *Program to Draw A, B, and C Using Bezier Curves. (continues)*

19.1

```
   class DWAdapter extends WindowAdapter
   {
      public void windowClosing(WindowEvent event)
      {
         System.exit(0);
      }
   }

   public static void main(String[] args)
   {
      Frame f = new BezierAlpha1();
      f.setSize(640, 500);
      f.show();
   }

   private Panel cards;
   private Panel tabs;
   private CardLayout layout;
}

class LiteralCanvas extends Panel
{
   int level = 0;

   LiteralCanvas()
   {
   }

   public void paint(Graphics g)
   {
      Graphics2D g2 = (Graphics2D) g;
      g2.setRenderingHint(RenderingHints.KEY_ANTIALIASING,
         RenderingHints.VALUE_ANTIALIAS_ON);
      g2.setRenderingHint(RenderingHints.KEY_RENDERING,
         (RenderingHints.VALUE_RENDER_QUALITY));
      GeneralPath a1 = new GeneralPath(0);
      GeneralPath a2 = new GeneralPath(0);
      GeneralPath a3 = new GeneralPath(0);
      GeneralPath b1 = new GeneralPath(0);
      GeneralPath b2 = new GeneralPath(0);
      GeneralPath b3 = new GeneralPath(0);
      GeneralPath c1 = new GeneralPath(0);
      int col, row;
      double scale;

      g2.translate(0, -80);
      g2.scale(.36, .36);
      a1.moveTo(70, 818);
      drawBezier(g2, a1, 70, 802, 118, 802, 132, 770,
```

LISTING *Program to Draw A, B, and C Using Bezier Curves. (continues)*
19.1

```
        130, 760);
a1.lineTo(351, 250);
a1.lineTo(367, 250);
a1.lineTo(340, 380);
drawBezier(g2, a1, 180, 750, 180, 790, 232, 802,
    242, 802 );
a1.lineTo(241, 818);
a1.closePath();
g2.fill(a1);
a2.moveTo(220, 640);
a2.lineTo(230, 600);
a2.lineTo(440, 600);
a2.lineTo(452, 640);
a2.lineTo(230, 640);
a2.closePath();
g2.fill(a2);
a3.moveTo(436, 818);
drawBezier(g2, a3, 436, 802, 470, 802, 495, 770,
    478, 720);
a3.lineTo(340, 380);
a3.lineTo(367, 250);
drawBezier(g2, a3, 570, 750, 586, 770, 595, 802,
    655, 802);
a3.lineTo(650, 818);
a3.lineTo(436, 818);
a3.closePath();
g2.fill(a3);

g2.translate(620, 250);
b1.moveTo(72, 818);
drawBezier(g2, b1, 70, 802, 118, 802, 138, 790,
    153, 740);
drawBezier(g2, b1, 152, 330, 150, 310, 100, 270,
    72, 278);
b1.lineTo(72, 262);
b1.lineTo(230, 262);
b1.lineTo(230, 818);
b1.closePath();
g2.fill(b1);
b2.moveTo(230, 262);
drawBezier(g2, b2, 310, 262, 540, 280, 510, 520,
    310, 540);
b2.lineTo(230, 540);
b2.lineTo(230, 500);
drawBezier(g2, b2, 230, 500, 510, 511, 510, 280,
    200, 300);
b2.closePath();
g2.fill(b2);
b3.moveTo(230, 816);
```

LISTING *Program to Draw A, B, and C Using Bezier Curves. (continues)*
19.1

```
            drawBezier(g2, b3, 350, 816, 600, 808, 600, 535,
                350, 535);
            b3.lineTo(230, 535);
            b3.lineTo(230, 550);
            drawBezier(g2, b3, 300, 550, 520, 550, 520, 788,
                300, 788);
            b3.lineTo(230, 790);
            b3.closePath();
            g2.fill(b3);

            g2.translate(500, 361);
            c1.moveTo(592, 440);
            drawBezier(g2, c1, 581, 440, 60, -90, 40, 1120,
                590, 680);
            c1.lineTo(590, 680);
            drawBezier(g2, c1, 605, 690, 100, 1180, -160, 100,
                500, 300);
            drawBezier(g2, c1, 500, 300, 530, 310, 580, 280,
                568, 250);
            c1.lineTo(580, 250);
            c1.closePath();
            g2.fill(c1);
        }

    void drawBezier(Graphics2D g, GeneralPath pol, int x1,
        int y1, int x2, int y2, int x3, int y3, int x4,
        int y4)
    {
        int col, row;
        double t;
        for (t=0.0; t<=1.0; t+= 0.02)
        {
            col=(int)((1-t) * (1-t) * (1-t) * x1 + 3 * t *
                (t-1) * (t-1) * x2 + 3 *t *t * (1-t) * x3
                + t * t * t * x4);
            row=(int)((1-t) * (1-t) * (1-t) * y1 + 3 * t *
                (t-1) * (t-1) * y2 + 3 *t *t * (1-t) * y3
                + t * t * t * y4);
            pol.lineTo(col,row);
        }
    }
}

class ForwardCanvas extends LiteralCanvas
{
    ForwardCanvas()
    {
    }
```

LISTING *Program to Draw A, B, and C Using Bezier Curves. (continues)*
19.1

```
    void drawBezier(Graphics2D g, GeneralPath pol, int x1,
        int y1, int x2, int y2, int x3, int y3, int x4,
        int y4)
    {
        int i, col, row;
        double t, x, y, deltax, deltay, deltasqx,
            deltasqy, deltacubex, deltacubey;
        x = x1;
        deltax = .000008 * (x4 - x1 + 3 * x2 - 3 * x3) +
            .0004 * (3 * x1 - 6 * x2 + 3 * x3) + .02 * (3
            * x2 - 3 * x1);
        deltasqx = .000048 * (x4 - x1 + 3 * x2 - 3 * x3) +
            .0008 * (3 * x1 - 6 * x2 + 3 * x3);
        deltacubex = .000048 * (x4 - x1 + 3 * x2 - 3 *
            x3);
        y = y1;
        deltay = .000008 * (y4 - y1 + 3 * y2 - 3 * y3) +
            .0004 * (3 * y1 - 6 * y2 + 3 * y3) + .02 * (3
            * y2 - 3 * y1);
        deltasqy = .000048 * (y4 - y1 + 3 * y2 - 3 * y3) +
            .0008 * (3 * y1 - 6 * y2 + 3 * y3);
        deltacubey = .000048 * (y4 - y1 + 3 * y2 - 3 *
            y3);
        for (i=1; i<=50; i++)
        {
            x += deltax;
            deltax += deltasqx;
            deltasqx += deltacubex;
            y += deltay;
            deltay += deltasqy;
            deltasqy += deltacubey;
            pol.lineTo((int)x, (int)y);
        }
    }
}

class deCasteljauCanvas extends LiteralCanvas
{
    deCasteljauCanvas()
    {
    }

    void drawBezier(Graphics2D g, GeneralPath pol, int x1,
        int y1, int x2, int y2, int x3, int y3, int x4,
        int y4)
    {
        int level =0;
        drawBez(g, pol, level, x1, y1, x2, y2, x3, y3,
            x4, y4);
```

LISTING *Program to Draw A, B, and C Using Bezier Curves. (continues)*
19.1

```
      }

   void drawBez(Graphics2D g, GeneralPath pol, int level,
      int x1, int y1, int x2, int y2, int x3, int y3,
      int x4, int y4)
   {
      int col, row;
      double t, tx1, tx2, tx3, tx4, tx5, ty1, ty2, ty3,
         ty4, ty5, tx6, ty6;
      if (level > 4)
      {
         pol.lineTo(x1, y1);
         pol.lineTo(x2, y2);
         pol.lineTo(x3, y3);
         pol.lineTo(x4, y4);
         return;
      }
      tx1 = (x1 + x2) / 2.0;
      ty1 = (y1 + y2) / 2.0;
      tx2 = (x2 + x3) / 2.0;
      ty2 = (y2 + y3) / 2.0;
      tx3 = (x3 + x4) / 2.0;
      ty3 = (y3 + y4) / 2.0;
      tx4 = (tx1 + tx2) / 2.0;
      ty4 = (ty1 + ty2) / 2.0;
      tx5 = (tx2 + tx3) / 2.0;
      ty5 = (ty2 + ty3) / 2.0;
      tx6 = (tx4 + tx5) / 2.0;
      ty6 = (ty4 + ty5) / 2.0;

      drawBez(g, pol, ++level, x1, y1, (int)tx1,
         (int)ty1, (int)tx4, (int)ty4, (int)tx6,
         (int)ty6);
      drawBez(g, pol, level, (int)tx6, (int)ty6,
         (int)tx5, (int)ty5, (int)tx3, (int)ty3, x4,
         y4);
   }
}

class BernsteinCanvas extends LiteralCanvas
{
   BernsteinCanvas()
   {
   }
   void drawBezier(Graphics2D g, GeneralPath pol, int x1,
      int y1, int x2, int y2, int x3, int y3, int x4,
      int y4)
   {
```

LISTING *Program to Draw A, B, and C Using Bezier Curves. (continues)*
19.1

```
     int col, row, i, j, k;
     double t, x, y, b;
     double [] xp = new double[4];
     double [] yp = new double[4];

     xp[0] = x1;
     yp[0] = y1;
     xp[1] = x2;
     yp[1] = y2;
     xp[2] = x3;
     yp[2] = y3;
     xp[3] = x4;
     yp[3] = y4;
     for (t=0.0; t<=1.0; t+= 0.02)
     {
        x = 0.;
        y = 0.;
        for (j=0; j<4; j++)
        {
           b = 1.0;
           for (k=3; k>j; k—)
              b*= k;
           for (k=3-j; k>1; k—)
              b /= k;
           for (i=1; i<=j; i++)
              b *= t;
           for (i=1; i<=3-j; i++)
              b *= (1-t);
           x += xp[j]*b;
           y += yp[j]*b;
        }
        pol.lineTo((int)x, (int)y);
     }
   }
}
```

LISTING *Program to Draw A, B, and C Using Bezier Curves. (continued)*
19.1

a *Card layout* called *layout*. We then set up four cards, each being given a title representing one of the four Bezier methods and each using a new object whose class type is one of the four mentioned previously. The *cards* panel is added to the center of the default *Border* display, causing the first card to be displayed initially.

Now let's look at the *paint* method of the *LiteralCanvas* class. We are going to draw three large filled letters, *A, B,* and *C.* To do this, we first draw a very large representation of each letter on graph paper. We are going to take coordinates from this graph paper, assuming that the top left corner of the graph paper is the origin and that positive values of *x* go to the right and positive values of *y* toward the bottom. The coordinates we get from the graph paper do not necessarily represent the actual size or position that we want for each character on the display. However, we can easily modify the size with the new Java 2D *scale* command and we can change the position by the new Java 2D *translate* command. Remember that if you use these commands to modify the coordinate system, you need to take the current values into consideration when you use the commands to modify the coordinate system again. We are going to trace around the letter to create one or more *GeneralPath* objects that will be filled to create the letter. We would like to get by with one *GeneralPath* object, but often the shape of a letter is so complex that we can't make just one closed object that can be filled satisfactorily. Look at the letter shape and determine how to break it up into several parts, each of which makes a good closed *GeneralPath* object, if this appears to be necessary. Now, suppose we start with a point on the letter outline, which is the start of a straight line. We specify the coordinates of the point at the beginning of this line and add it to our first polygon. As we move around the letter outline, this is all we have to do as long as we encounter only straight lines. When we come to a curve, we need to use the method *drawBezier*. The first two parameters passed to this method are the name of the *Graphics* object we are using and the name of the *GeneralPath* object. Next come the *x* and *y* coordinates of each of the four control points. The first control point is the endpoint of the last straight line we encountered before the curve. The fourth control point is the endpoint of the curve. If you really want to be critical about your curve, you can determine the tangent lines to the curve at the beginning and endpoints and determine where the second and third control points need to be to establish the proper tangents. It's usually easier to take a reasonable guess at the location of these two control points and then modify them as necessary after viewing the resulting curve. You continue this process of specifying straight lines and curves until you've completed one of your polygons and then call the *fill* method. Once you have done this for all of the *GeneralPath* objects needed for a letter and for all of the letters you're going to display, your *paint* method is complete. Figure 19.1 shows the result of running the program.

If you end up with something that doesn't look much like what you wanted, here's how to go about troubleshooting. First, you will want to change all *fill* statements to *draw* statements. This will enable you to draw just the outline of a letter, rather than filling it in, and will make it easier to identify sources of trouble. There are really only two kinds of trouble that you can have. First, you

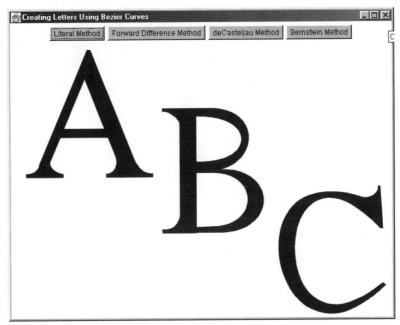

FIGURE   *Letters A, B, and C Drawn with Literal Bezier Curves.*
19.1

may have misread some coordinates from your graph paper. Second, you may not have properly located the second and third control points of one of your Bezier curves. If, when you draw the character in outline, it is still too messed up to be able to identify critical points, comment out all but the first two or three points. Run the program and see if these are okay. If straight lines or Bezier curve endpoints are in the wrong place, recheck their coordinates from the graph and correct as necessary. If a Bezier curve doesn't have the shape you want, change the locations of the second and third control points until the curve shape is satisfactory. (Be sure to keep a record of every change you make so that you don't find yourself retracing the same ground several times.) After you get a small part of the polygon looking okay, restore a few more lines of code to draw a few more line segments and fix these. Continue in this way until the outline of each polygon is correct; then try filling the polygons.

The LiteralCanvas Class

The *paint* method just described used numerous calls to *drawBezier* to generate curved portions of the figure. To see how this is done for the literal Bezier curve let's look at the method *drawBezier* under the *LiteralCanvas* class. We are computing over an interval of 0.0 to 1.0 using a *for* loop. At each iteration, the value of the parameter t is increased by a step of 0.02. This gives you 50 points over the curve, which should be enough to draw a smooth curve, even for fairly large curves. For small curves, this step size may result in a number of superimposed points, which doesn't really do any harm except to make the computer work harder. You can modify this step size to meet your own requirements. The mathematics for computing the values of *row* and *col* comes directly from Equation 19-3. You can verify it, if you are interested. At the end of each iteration of the *for* loop, the coordinates of the calculated point are added to the polynomial that was passed to the method.

The *ForwardCanvas* Class

The next method we're going to use to generate Bezier curves is the forward difference method. We set up our *ForwardCanvas* class to be an extension of the *LiteralCanvas* class, so that it inherits all of that class's methods. In particular, the same long *paint* method is used to paint the three large characters on the screen. However, we override the *drawBezier* method with a new one that draws Bezier curves using the forward difference method.

Suppose we have a function $f(t)$ that we are going to evaluate in equal steps of length δ over the interval from $n=0$ to $n\delta=1$. The forward difference for each step is

$$\Delta(t) = f(t + \delta) - f(t) \qquad \text{(Eq. 19-9)}$$

For the third degree (cubic) polynomial whose components were given in Equation 19-1, we have

$$f(t) - at^3 + bt_2 + ct + d \qquad \text{(Eq. 19-10)}$$

from which we can obtain the forward difference

$$\Delta f(t) = 3a\delta t^2 + (3a\delta^2 + 2b\delta)t + a\delta^3 + b\delta^2 + c\delta \qquad \text{(Eq. 19-11)}$$

To simply further, we take another forward difference, this time for $\Delta(\Delta(ft))$, which we call $\Delta^2 f(t)$. This is found to be

$$\Delta^2 f(t) = 6a\delta^2 t + 6a\delta^3 + 2b\delta^2 \qquad \text{(Eq. 19-12)}$$

which can be rewritten using the index n as

$$\Delta^2 f_n - \Delta f_{n+1} - \Delta f_n \qquad \text{(Eq. 19-13)}$$

We need one more forward difference

$$\Delta^3 f(t) = \Delta(\Delta^2 f(t)) = 6a\delta^3 \qquad \text{(Eq. 19-14)}$$

In terms of the index n we have

$$\Delta^2 f_{n+1} = \Delta^2 f_n + \Delta^3 f_n = \Delta^2 f_n + 6a\delta^3 \qquad \text{(Eq. 19-15)}$$

Now all we need are the initial values. We'll give these both in terms of the generic cubic equation and in terms of the four Bezier control points. They are

$$f_0 = d = q_1 \qquad \text{(Eq. 19-16)}$$

$$\Delta f_0 = a\delta^3 + b\delta^2 + c\delta = (-q_1 + 3q_2 - 3q_3 + q_4)\delta^3 + \\ (3q_1 - 6q_2 + 3q_3)\delta^2 + (-3q_1 + 3q_2)\delta \qquad \text{(Eq. 19-17)}$$

$$\Delta^2 f_0 = 6a\delta^3 + 2b\delta^2 = 6(-q_1 + 3q_2 - 3q_3 + q_4)\delta^3 + \\ 2(3q_1 - 6q_2 + 3q_3)\delta^2 \qquad \text{(Eq. 19-18)}$$

$$\Delta^3 f_0 = 6a\delta^3 = 6(-q_1 + 3q_2 - 3q_3 + q_4)\delta^3 \qquad \text{(Eq. 19-19)}$$

We can now incorporate this information into the new *drawBezier* method for the *ForwardCanvas* class. For each set of operations that required 14 multiplications and 9 additions with the literal method, we need only 3 additions with the forward difference method, resulting in a substantial increase in speed. This method begins by setting the initial values for *x*, *deltax*, *deltasqx*, and *deltacubex*, and the corresponding *y* variables. Although a number of mathematical operations are required for these initializations, they only need to occur once for each Bezier curve generated, rather than having to be repeated for each iteration of the *for* loop. The *for* loop then performs a few simple operations to create each point on the Bezier curve. The points are added to the polygon passed to *drawBezier*.

The deCasteljauCanvas Class

The deCasteljau method is a geometric technique that gives the same results as the literal method, but is much faster. It is comparable to the forward difference method in its speed. The *deCasteljauCanvas* class is also a class that inherits all of the characteristics of the *LiteralCanvas*, class but differs that the *drawBezier* method is overridden with a new one using the deCasteljau method. The process used by this new method is a recursive one. We start with the four Bezier control points a1, a2, a3, and a4. We then find the midpoints t1, t2, and t3 of the first three sides of the box defined by the four control points. In other words, t1 is halfway between a1 and a2, t2 is halfway between a2 and a3, and t3 is halfway between a3 and a4. Then we find three more midpoints: t4 is halfway between t1 and t2, t5 is halfway between t2 and t3, and t6 is halfway between t4 and t5. We now establish two new quadrilaterals. The first consists of the four points b1=a1, b2=t1, b3=t4, and b4=t6. These are the control points for a new Bezier curve. The second consists of the four points c1=t6, c2=t5, c3=t3, and c4 = a4. We now repeat this process with the first new quadrilateral (b1, b2, b3, b4) yielding the quadrilaterals d1, d2, d3, d4, and e1, e2, e3, e4. Repeating the process with the second new quadrilateral (c1, c2, c3, c4) gives two more quadrilaterals: f1, f2, f3, f4 and g1, g2, g3, g4. These are shown in Figure 19.2. This same procedure can be repeated recursively as many times as needed to give a smooth representation of the Bezier curve. During the recursive process, we would like to use the deCasteljau version of *drawBezier* to do all of the recursive actions, but this won't work, because we need to add a parameter containing the current level to permit the recursive action to stop at the correct time. So we make the *drawBezier* method have the same parameters as for the other Bezier classes. The method then initializes an integer *level* object to 0 and then calls *drawBezier*, which contains all of the statements that would normally be in the *drawBezier* method and has all of the same parameters passed to it, but also the *level* parameter. You'll note that the method contains all of the mathematics to create two lines from the line passed to it. Then, at the end, we increment *level* and call *drawBezier* twice, once for

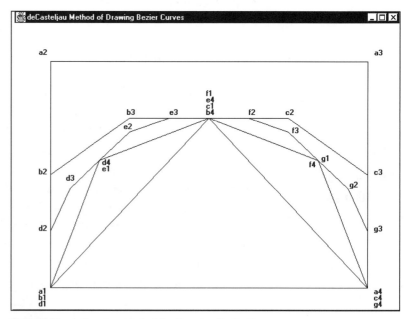

FIGURE *The deCasteljau Method for Drawing Bezier Curves.*
19.2

each of the to lines. On each of these calls, the line passed two it is replaced by two lines and the *drawBezier* method is again called twice to operate on the new lines. This process continues until *level* reaches the prespecified setting, at which time the new line coordinates are set to the *GeneralPath* object and the method terminates.

The BernsteinCanvas Class

The *BernsteinCanvas* class also inherits the characteristics of the *LinearCanvas* class. Again, the *drawBezier* method is overridden, with the new method drawing Bezier curves using Bernstein polynomials. This method is a little faster than the literal method but much slower than the other two methods just described. This method, however, not only works with four control points, but also can be extended to any number of control points by simply increasing the upper limit of the second *for* loop that iterates over the control points without any other major changes in the code. We'll see how this works in the next section. For now, let's look at how a four control point version works. You'll note that there are four *for* loops over *i* and *k* that generate a weighting function for each control point. Each control point is multiplied by its weighting function and the results (for each coordinate) are summed to give the coordinates of a point on the Bezier curve. You can go through the mathematics to show that this is the same as the literal method; when you run the program you'll see that the results are the same for the Bernstein and literal methods.

Bezier Curves with Java 2D

In the preceding program, we used some of the Java 2D features to create our own Bezier curves using four different methods of generation. However, the *GeneralPath* class of Java 2D has a method that will generate Bezier curves faster and more simply than any home-grown techniques. Instead of using the *GeneralPath* method *lineTo(x, y)*, which draws a line from the current position to the location (x, y), we use the method *curveTo(x1, y1, x2, y2, x3, y3)*. This draws a Bezier curve from the current position to the location (x3, y3), with (x1, y1) and (x2, y2) as the control points for the Bezier curve. Listing 19.2 is a program to draw the letters *A, B,* and *C* with this method.

```
/*
   BezierAlpha1. ava
   ABC with Various kinds of Bezier Curve Generators
*/

import  ava.awt.*;
import  ava.awt.event.*;
import  ava.awt.geom.GeneralPath;

public class BezierAlpha2 extends Frame
{
    public BezierAlpha2()
    {
        setTitle("Creating Letters Using Bezier
Curves");
        addWindowListener(new DWAdapter());
    }

    public void paint(Graphics g)
    {
        Graphics2D g2 = (Graphics2D) g;

g2.setRenderingHint(RenderingHints.KEY_ANTIALIASING,
        RenderingHints.VALUE_ANTIALIAS_ON);

g2.setRenderingHint(RenderingHints.KEY_RENDERING,
        (RenderingHints.VALUE_RENDER_QUALITY));
        GeneralPath a1 = new GeneralPath(0);
        GeneralPath a2 = new GeneralPath(0);
        GeneralPath a3 = new GeneralPath(0);
        GeneralPath b1 = new GeneralPath(0);
        GeneralPath b2 = new GeneralPath(0);
        GeneralPath b3 = new GeneralPath(0);
        GeneralPath c1 = new GeneralPath(0);
        double scale;

        g2.translate(0, -60);
        g2.scale(.36, .36);
        a1.moveTo(70, 818);
        a1.lineTo(70, 802);
        a1.curveTo(118, 802, 132, 770, 130, 760);
        a1.lineTo(351, 250);
        a1.lineTo(367, 250);
        a1.lineTo(340, 380);
        a1.lineTo(180, 750);
        a1.curveTo(180, 790, 232, 802, 242, 802 );
        a1.lineTo(241, 818);
        a1.closePath();
        g2.fill(a1);
```

LISTING *Program to Draw A, B, and C Using Bezier Curves. (continues)*
19.2

```
a2.moveTo(220, 640);
a2.lineTo(230, 600);
a2.lineTo(440, 600);
a2.lineTo(452, 640);
a2.lineTo(230, 640);
a2.closePath();
g2.fill(a2);
a3.moveTo(436, 818);
a3.lineTo(436, 802);
a3.curveTo(470, 802, 495, 770, 478, 720);
a3.lineTo(340, 380);
a3.lineTo(367, 250);
a3.lineTo(570, 750);
a3.curveTo(586, 770, 595, 802, 655, 802);
a3.lineTo(655, 818);
a3.closePath();
g2.fill(a3);

g2.translate(620, 250);
b1.moveTo(72, 818);
b1.curveTo(118, 802, 138, 790, 153, 740);
b1.lineTo(152, 330);
b1.curveTo(150, 310, 100, 270, 72, 278);
b1.lineTo(72, 262);
b1.lineTo(230, 262);
b1.lineTo(230, 818);
b1.closePath();
g2.fill(b1);
b2.moveTo(230, 262);
b2.curveTo(540, 280, 510, 520, 310, 540);
b2.lineTo(230, 540);
b2.lineTo(230, 500);
b2.curveTo(510, 511, 510, 280, 200, 300);
b2.lineTo(230, 262);
b2.closePath();
g2.fill(b2);
b3.moveTo(230, 816);
b3.curveTo(600, 808, 600, 535, 350, 535);
b3.lineTo(230, 535);
b3.lineTo(230, 550);
b3.curveTo(520, 550, 520, 788, 300, 788);
b3.lineTo(230, 790);
b3.closePath();
g2.fill(b3);

g2.translate(500, 361);
c1.moveTo(592, 440);
c1.curveTo(60, -90, 40, 1120, 590, 680);
c1.lineTo(590, 680);
```

LISTING *Program to Draw A, B, and C Using Bezier Curves. (continues)*
19.2

```
        c1.curveTo(100, 1180, -160, 100, 500, 300);
        c1.curveTo(530, 310, 580, 280, 568, 250);
        c1.lineTo(580, 250);
        c1.lineTo(592, 440);
        g2.fill(c1);
    }

    class DWAdapter extends WindowAdapter
    {
        public void windowClosing(WindowEvent event)
        {
            System.exit(0);
        }
    }

    public static void main(String[] args)
    {
        Frame f = new BezierAlpha2();
        f.setSize(640, 500);
        f.show();
    }

    private Panel cards;
    private Panel tabs;
    private CardLayout layout;
}
```

LISTING *Program to Draw A, B, and C Using Bezier Curves. (continued)*
19.2

Animated Bezier Curves

Listing 19.3 is a program that creates three filled Bezier curves that change in shape and position on the screen. You need to look closely at the way that the *Demo* class implements *Runnable* and how *start, stop, run, step* and *init* are implemented as they are key to the changing action of the three Bezier curve figures through the repeated running of a *thread*. The *drawDemo* is the method that actually draws an instance of the figures. We first initialize *Demo* by defining three *gradient* objects of class *GradientPaint*, using them to initialize three *fillPaint* objects that determine the filling color of the figures, and defining three *drawPaint* objects, each initialized with a different color, that determine the color of the lines that outline the figures. The *drawDemo* method uses two *for* loops. The outer loop (index *j*) loops once for each figure to be displayed; the inner loop (index *i*) loops over six pairs of coordinates that create each figure. The outer loop begins by initializing variables that contain the last and first points of the Bezier curve and the midpoint between them. It also sets up the *GeneralPath* object for the figure. It then sets up the starting point for the figure at the midpoint. The inner loop determines the two control points and the endpoint for the Bezier curve and calls the *curveTo* method to create the curve. When the inner loop is finished, we call *closePath* to close the figure and then set the color for the outer line, the color for the fill, and the style of the outer line (solid). The outer line is then drawn and the figure is then filled.

Each time *thread* runs, the *step* method modifies all of the points that make up the definition of each figure. Basically, a point has an associated delta added to it. This goes on until the point reaches the bounds of the display, at which time the direction of the motion and the delta value are changed. The method *reset* is used to change all of the point locations and delta values when the *paint* method indicates that such a change is necessary. The overall result of all this is that a display is produced that contains three constantly changing figures. A snapshot of this display is shown in Plate 11.

```
/*
   AnimBez5. ava
   Animated Bezier Curves
*/

import   ava.awt.*;
import   ava.awt.event.*;
import   ava.awt.image.BufferedImage;
import   ava.awt.geom.GeneralPath;
import   avax.swing.*;

public class AnimBez5 extends JApplet
{
   Demo demo;

   public void init()
   {
      getContentPane().add(demo = new Demo());
   }

   public void start()
   {
      demo.start();
   }

   public void stop()
   {
      demo.stop();
   }
```

LISTING *Program to Generate Animated Bezier Curves. (continues)*
19.3

```java
public class Demo extends JPanel implements Runnable
{
   private Thread thread;
   private BufferedImage bimg;
   protected BasicStroke solid = new BasicStroke(10.0f,
      BasicStroke.CAP_BUTT, BasicStroke.JOIN_ROUND);
   private float animpts[][] = new float[3][12];
   private float deltas[][] = new float[3][12];
   protected Paint fillPaint[] = new Paint[3];
   protected Paint drawPaint[] = new Paint[3];
   protected GradientPaint gradient[] = new
      GradientPaint[3];
   protected BasicStroke stroke;

   public Demo()
   {
      gradient[0] = new GradientPaint(0, 0,
         Color.red,320,240, Color.yellow);
      fillPaint[0] = gradient[0];
      drawPaint[0] = Color.blue;
      gradient[1] = new GradientPaint(0,0,Color.blue,
         320,240,Color.orange);
      fillPaint[1] = gradient[1];
      drawPaint[1] = Color.green;
      gradient[2] = new GradientPaint(0,0,Color.blue,
         320,240,Color.red);
      fillPaint[2] = gradient[2];
      drawPaint[2] = new Color(200, 0, 200);
      stroke = solid;
   }

   public void reset(int w, int h)
   {
      for (int  =0;  <3;  ++)
      {
         for (int i = 0; i < 12; i += 2)
         {
            animpts[ ][i + 0] = (float) (Math.random() *
               w);
            animpts[ ][i + 1] = (float) (Math.random() *
               h);
            deltas[ ][i + 0] = (float) (Math.random() *
               6.0 + 4.0);
            deltas[ ][i + 1] = (float) (Math.random() *
               6.0 + 4.0);
            if (animpts[ ][i + 0] > w / 2.0f)
            {
               deltas[ ][i + 0] = -deltas[ ][i + 0];
            }
```

LISTING *Program to Generate Animated Bezier Curves. (continues)*
19.3

```
                    if (animpts[ ][i + 1] > h / 2.0f)
                    {
                        deltas[ ][i + 1] = -deltas[ ][i + 1];
                    }
                }
            }
        }

    public void step(int w, int h)
    {
        for (int  =0;   <3;   ++)
        {
        for (int i = 0; i < 12; i += 2)
        {
            float newpt = animpts[ ][i] + deltas[ ][i];
            if (newpt <= 0)
            {
                newpt = -newpt;
                deltas[ ][i] = (float) (Math.random() * 4.0
                    + 2.0);
            } else if (newpt >= w)
            {
                newpt = 2.0f * w - newpt;
                deltas[ ][i] = - (float) (Math.random() *
                    4.0 + 2.0);
            }
            animpts[ ][i] = newpt;
            newpt = animpts[ ][i+1] + deltas[ ][i+1];
            if (newpt <= 0)
            {
                newpt = -newpt;
                deltas[ ][i+1] = (float) (Math.random() *
                    4.0 + 2.0);
            } else if (newpt >= h)
            {
                newpt = 2.0f * h - newpt;
                deltas[ ][i+1] = - (float) (Math.random() *
                    4.0 + 2.0);
                }
                animpts[ ][i+1] = newpt;
            }
        }
    }

    public void drawDemo(int w, int h, Graphics2D g2)
    {
        float prevx, prevy, curx, cury, midx, midy;

        GeneralPath gp[] = new GeneralPath[3];
```

LISTING *Program to Generate Animated Bezier Curves. (continues)*

19.3

```
     for (int  =0;   <3;   ++)
     {
        prevx = animpts[ ][10];
        prevy = animpts[ ][11];
        curx = animpts[ ][0];
        cury = animpts[ ][1];
        midx = (curx + prevx) / 2.0f;
        midy = (cury + prevy) / 2.0f;
        gp[ ] = new GeneralPath(
           GeneralPath.WIND_NON_ZERO);
        gp[ ].moveTo(midx, midy);
        for (int i = 2; i <= 12; i += 2)
        {
           float x1 = (midx + curx) / 2.0f;
           float y1 = (midy + cury) / 2.0f;
           prevx = curx;
           prevy = cury;
           if (i < 12)
           {
              curx = animpts[ ][i + 0];
              cury = animpts[ ][i + 1];
           } else
           {
              curx = animpts[ ][0];
              cury = animpts[ ][1];
           }
           midx = (curx + prevx) / 2.0f;
           midy = (cury + prevy) / 2.0f;
           float x2 = (prevx + midx) / 2.0f;
           float y2 = (prevy + midy) / 2.0f;
           gp[ ].curveTo(x1, y1, x2, y2, midx, midy);
        }
        gp[ ].closePath();
        g2.setPaint(drawPaint[ ]);
        g2.setStroke(stroke);
        g2.draw(gp[ ]);
        g2.setPaint(fillPaint[ ]);
        g2.fill(gp[ ]);
     }
  }

  public void paint(Graphics g)
  {
     Dimension d = getSize();
     step(d.width, d.height);
     Graphics2D g2 = null;
     if (bimg == null || bimg.getWidth() != d,width ||
        bimg.getHeight() != d.height)
     {
```

LISTING *Program to Generate Animated Bezier Curves. (continues)*
19.3

```
            bimg = (BufferedImage) createImage(d.width,
                d.height);
            reset(d.width, d.height);
        }
        g2 = bimg.createGraphics();
        g2.setBackground(getBackground());
        g2.clearRect(0, 0, d.width, d.height);
        g2.setRenderingHint(RenderingHints.KEY_ANTIALIASING,
            RenderingHints.VALUE_ANTIALIAS_ON);
        drawDemo(d.width, d.height, g2);
        g2.dispose();
        if (bimg != null)
        {
            g.drawImage(bimg, 0, 0, this);
        }
    }

    public void start()
    {
        thread = new Thread(this);
        thread.setPriority(Thread.MIN_PRIORITY);
        thread.start();
    }

    public synchronized void stop()
    {
        thread = null;
    }

    public void run()
    {
        Thread me = Thread.currentThread();
        while (thread == me)
        {
            repaint();
            try
            {
                thread.sleep(10);
            } catch (Exception e) { break; }
            }
            thread = null;
        }
    }

    public static void main(String argv[])
    {
        final AnimBez5 demo = new AnimBez5();
        demo.init();
        Frame f = new Frame("Animated Bezier Curves");
```

LISTING *Program to Generate Animated Bezier Curves. (continues)*
19.3

```
        f.addWindowListener(new WindowAdapter() {
           public void windowClosing(WindowEvent e)
           {System.exit(0);}
           public void windowDeiconified(WindowEvent e)
           { demo.start(); }
           public void windowIconified(WindowEvent e)
           { demo.stop(); }
        });
        f.add(demo);
        f.pack();
        f.setSize(new Dimension(640,480));
        f.show();
        demo.start();
    }
}
```

LISTING *Program to Generate Animated Bezier Curves. (continued)*
19.3

Bezier Curves with Many Control Points

Thus far, we have restricted ourselves to the case where the Bezier curve is solely defined by four control points. We made more complex figures by combining individual Bezier curves, each of which was generated using four control points. Since we know location of the endpoints and the direction that the curve is taking at each endpoint, it is easy to make the curves fit together well. Another approach is to use many control points to generate a complex Bezier curve. Each control point is weighted so that only those control points nearest the point on the Bezier curve that is currently being generated actually contribute to determining the point's location. A program to do this is given in Listing 19.4. In the *paint* method, we simply define an object *Bez* of class *Bezier*, set up eight control points, set the parameter *last* to indicate that array member 7 contains the last control point, and then call the method *drawBezier*. There is no limit to the number of control points that can be used with this technique. coordinates and one for the *y*. We have arbitrarily defined the *Bezier* class to have the coordinates of twenty control points in two arrays, one for the *x* coordinates. You can change the array sizes to any number you want. Now, if you look at the method *drawBezier* in the *Bezier* class, you'll observe that it is just the same as the drawing method used for the *Bernstein* program, except that the for loop over *j* iterates from 0 to last instead of from 0 to 3. This enables all of the control points to contribute their weighted values. Figure 19.3 shows the result of running the program. The eight control points are shown as small filled circles.

```
/*
   BezierCurves. ava
   Using Bezier Curves with Many Control Points
*/

import  ava.awt.*;
import  ava.util.*;
import  ava.awt.event.*;
import  ava.awt.geom.GeneralPath;
import  ava.awt.geom.Ellipse2D;

class Bezier
{
    int last = 7;
    int[] xpoint = {300, 320, 320, 120, 120, 410, 380,
        520};
    int[] ypoint = {240, 240, 360, 360, 40, 90, 240, 240};

    void drawBezier(Graphics g)
    {
        double interval, x, y, blend, t;
        int c, i,   , h, k, m;

        Graphics2D g2 = (Graphics2D) g;
        g2.setRenderingHint(RenderingHints.KEY_ANTIALIASING,
            RenderingHints.VALUE_ANTIALIAS_ON);
        g2.setRenderingHint(RenderingHints.KEY_RENDERING,
            (RenderingHints.VALUE_RENDER_QUALITY));
        GeneralPath p = new GeneralPath(0);
        p.moveTo(xpoint[0], ypoint[0]);
        for (t=0.0; t<=1.0; t+=0.01)
        {
            x = y = 0.0;
            for ( =0;   <=last;   ++)
            {
                blend = 1.0;
                for (k=last; k> ; k—)
                {
                    blend *= k;
                    blend /= (k- );
                }
                for (i=1; i<= ; i++)
                    blend *= t;
                for (i=1; i<= last- ; i++)
                    blend *= (1.0 - t);
                x += xpoint[ ]*blend;
                y += ypoint[ ]*blend;
            }
```

LISTING *Program to Draw a Bezier Curve Using Many Control Points. (continues)*
19.4

```
            p.lineTo((int)x, (int)y);

        }
            p.lineTo(xpoint[7], ypoint[7]);
            BasicStroke bs;
        bs = new BasicStroke(3.0f);
        g2.setStroke(bs);
        g2.draw(p);
        }
    }

    class BezierCanvas extends Canvas
    {
        Bezier Bez = new Bezier();
        BezierCanvas()
        {
        }

        public void paint(Graphics g)
        {
            int i,  , x, y, diameter1, diameter2, width;
                Graphics2D g2 = (Graphics2D) g;
            g2.setRenderingHint(RenderingHints.KEY_ANTIALIASING,
                RenderingHints.VALUE_ANTIALIAS_ON);
            g2.setRenderingHint(RenderingHints.KEY_RENDERING,
                (RenderingHints.VALUE_RENDER_QUALITY));
            Bez.drawBezier(g);
            g2.fill(new Ellipse2D.Float(295, 235, 10, 10));
            g2.fill(new Ellipse2D.Float(315, 235, 10, 10));
            g2.fill(new Ellipse2D.Float(315, 355, 10, 10));
            g2.fill(new Ellipse2D.Float(115, 355, 10, 10));
            g2.fill(new Ellipse2D.Float(115, 35, 10, 10));
            g2.fill(new Ellipse2D.Float(405, 85, 10, 10));
            g2.fill(new Ellipse2D.Float(375, 235, 10, 10));
            g2.fill(new Ellipse2D.Float(515, 235, 10, 10));
            g.drawString("p1",295, 227);
            g.drawString("p2",315, 227);
            g.drawString("p3",315, 347);
            g.drawString("p4",115, 347);
            g.drawString("p5",115, 27);
            g.drawString("p6",405, 77);
            g.drawString("p7",375, 227);
            g.drawString("p8",515, 227);
        }
    }

    class BezierCurves extends Frame
    {
        public BezierCurves()
```

LISTING *Program to Draw a Bezier Curve Using Many Control Points. (continues)*
19.4

```
    {
        super("A Bezier Curve with Multiple Control Points");
    setBackground(Color.white);
    setLayout( new BorderLayout());
    add("Center", new BezierCanvas());
    setSize(640, 480);
    show();
    WindowListener lis = new WindowAdapter()
    {
        public void windowClosing(WindowEvent e)
        {
            System.exit(0);
        }
    };
    addWindowListener(lis);
    }

    public static void main(String args[])
    {
        BezierCurves f = new BezierCurves();
    }
}
```

LISTING 19.4 *Program to Draw a Bezier Curve Using Many Control Points. (continued)*

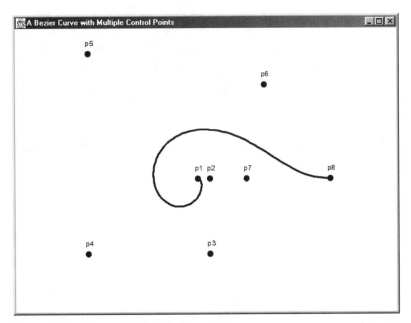

FIGURE 19.3 *Bezier Curve with Multiple Control Points.*

The B-Spline Curve

Originally, a *spline* was a flexible metal strip used in drafting to lay out curved surfaces. Weights were attached to the spline to pull it in various directions. The spline and its weights could be moved around on the drawing board while maintaining the same complex curved shape. The mathematical equivalent of a spline, the *B-Spline,* is a cubic polynomial that has one more degree of continuity than the Bezier curve and therefore is inherently smoother. It would be a better choice if it were as easy to use. Unfortunately, however, the *B-Spline* curve does not pass through the beginning and ending control points, making it much more difficult to select the proper control points for a desired curve. It is possible to repeat the first and last control points several times, and thus bring the beginning and ending points of the curve nearer to the first and last control points, but this isn't a very satisfactory solution. To see what we're up against, take a look at Figure 19.4, which attempts to use the same control points to generate the letters *A, B,* and *C* with *B-Spline* curves.

FIGURE *Attempt to Draw Letters A, B, and C with B-Spline Curves.*
19.4

The following matrix equation gives a B-Spline representation using four control points:

$$p(t) = \begin{bmatrix} t^3 & t^2 & t & 1 \end{bmatrix} \begin{bmatrix} -1 & 3 & -3 & 1 \\ 3 & -6 & 3 & 0 \\ -3 & 0 & 3 & 0 \\ 1 & 4 & 1 & 0 \end{bmatrix} \begin{bmatrix} q_1 \\ q_2 \\ q_3 \\ q_4 \end{bmatrix}$$

(Eq. 19-20)

Converting Bezier Points to B-Spline Control Points

If you want to switch from Bezier curves to B-Spline curves to get some extra smoothness and you are working with four control points, there is a direct conversion that can be applied to the Bezier control point values to obtain the B-spline control points that will yield the same curve. It is given by the following equation:

$$\begin{bmatrix} p_1 \\ p_2 \\ p_3 \\ p_4 \end{bmatrix} = \begin{bmatrix} 6 & -7 & 2 & 0 \\ 0 & 2 & -1 & 0 \\ 0 & -1 & 2 & 0 \\ 0 & 2 & -7 & 6 \end{bmatrix} \begin{bmatrix} q_1 \\ q_2 \\ q_3 \\ q_4 \end{bmatrix}$$

(Eq. 19-21)

where the qs are Bezier control points and the ps are B-Spline control points. Listing 19.5 is the familiar program to draw the letters A, B, and C. It differs from the previous programs in that it uses the method *drawBSpline* of the class *BSpline* to draw the curved parts of the letters. At the beginning of this method, you'll observe that there are eight equations to convert from the four control points that are passed to the method (which are the same Bezier control points that we have been using) to the corresponding B-Spline control points. The equations are derived from the matrix Equation 19-21, which you can verify mathematically if you so desire. These equations are followed by the *for* loop that iterates over the interval of 0.0 to 1.0 for t. Within this loop, the expressions from Equation 19-20 are used to find the points on the B-Spline curve.

```
/*
   BSplineAlpha.java
   ABC with B Spline Curves
*/

import java.awt.*;
import java.util.*;
import java.awt.event.*;
import java.awt.geom.GeneralPath;

class BSpline
{
   void drawBSpline(Graphics2D g, GeneralPath pol,
      int x1, int y1, int x2, int y2, int x3, int y3,
      int x4, int y4)
   {
      int col, row, i;
      int xp1, yp1, xp2, yp2, xp3, yp3, xp4, yp4;
      double t;

      xp1 = 6*x1 - 7*x2 + 2*x3;
      xp2 = 2*x2 - x3;
      xp3 = -x2 + 2*x3;
      xp4 = 2*x2 - 7*x3 + 6*x4;
      yp1 = 6*y1 - 7*y2 + 2*y3;
      yp2 = 2*y2 - y3;
      yp3 = -y2 + 2*y3;
      yp4 = 2*y2 - 7*y3 + 6*y4;

      for (t=0.0; t<=1.0; t+= 0.02)
      {
         col = (int)(((1-t)*(1-t)*(1-t)*xp1 + (3*t*t*t
            - 6 * t*t + 4) * xp2 + (-3*t*t*t + 3 * t*t
            + 3*t + 1) * xp3 + t*t*t*xp4)/6);
         row = (int)(((1-t)*(1-t)*(1-t)*yp1 + (3*t*t*t
            - 6 * t*t + 4) * yp2 + (-3*t*t*t + 3 * t*t
            + 3*t + 1) * yp3 + t*t*t*yp4)/6);
         pol.lineTo(col,row);
      }
   }
}

class BSplineCanvas extends Canvas
{
   BSplineCanvas()
   {
   }

   public void paint(Graphics g)
```

LISTING *Program to Draw A, B, and C with B-Spline Curves. (continues)*
19.5

```
{
    BSpline B = new BSpline();
    Graphics2D g2 = (Graphics2D) g;
    g2.setRenderingHint(RenderingHints.KEY_ANTIALIASING,
        RenderingHints.VALUE_ANTIALIAS_ON);
    g2.setRenderingHint(RenderingHints.KEY_RENDERING,
        (RenderingHints.VALUE_RENDER_QUALITY));
    GeneralPath a1 = new GeneralPath(0);
    GeneralPath a2 = new GeneralPath(0);
    GeneralPath a3 = new GeneralPath(0);
    GeneralPath b1 = new GeneralPath(0);
    GeneralPath b2 = new GeneralPath(0);
    GeneralPath b3 = new GeneralPath(0);
    GeneralPath c1 = new GeneralPath(0);
    int col, row, x, y;
    double scale;

    col = 70;
    row = 818;
    g2.translate(0, -80);
    g2.scale(.36, .36);
    a1.moveTo(col, row);
    B.drawBSpline(g2, a1, 70, 802, 118, 802, 132,
        770, 130, 760);
    col = 351;
    row = 250;
    a1.lineTo(col, row);
    col = 367;
    a1.lineTo(col, row);
    col = 340;
    row = 380;
    a1.lineTo(col, row);
    B.drawBSpline(g2, a1, 180, 750, 180, 790, 232,
        802, 242, 802);
    col = 241;
    row = 818;
    a1.lineTo(col, row);
    g2.fill(a1);
    col = 220;
    row = 640;
    a2.moveTo(col, row);
    col = 230;
    row = 600;
    a2.lineTo(col, row);
    col = 440;
    a2.lineTo(col, row);
    col = 452;
    row = 640;
    a2.lineTo(col, row);
```

LISTING *Program to Draw A, B, and C with B-Spline Curves. (continues)*
19.5

```
xcol = 230;
row = 640;
a2.lineTo(col, row);
g2.fill(a2);
col = 436;
row = 818;
a3.moveTo(col, row);
B.drawBSpline(g2, a3, 436, 802, 470, 802, 495,
    770, 478, 720);
col = 340;
row = 380;
a3.lineTo(col, row);
col = 367;
row = 250;
a3.lineTo(col, row);
B.drawBSpline(g2, a3, 570, 750, 586, 770, 595,
    802, 655, 802);
col = 650;
row = 818;
a3.lineTo(col, row);
col = 436;
a3.lineTo(col, row);
g2.fill(a3);

g2.translate(583, 305);
xcol = 72;
row = 818;
b1.moveTo(col, row);
B.drawBSpline(g2, b1, 70, 802, 118, 802, 138, 790,
    153, 740);
B.drawBSpline(g2, b1, 152, 330, 150, 310, 100,
    270, 72, 278);
col = 72;
row = 262;
b1.lineTo(col, row);
col = 230;
b1.lineTo(col, row);
row = 818;
b1.lineTo(col, row);
g2.fill(b1);
col = 230;
row = 262;
b2.moveTo(col, row);
B.drawBSpline(g2, b2, 310, 262, 540, 280, 510,
    520, 310, 540);
col = 230;
row = 540;
b2.lineTo(col, row);
row = 500;
```

LISTING *Program to Draw A, B, and C with B-Spline Curves. (continues)*
19.5

```
      b2.lineTo(col, row);
      B.drawBSpline(g2, b2, 230, 500, 510, 511, 510,
         280, 200, 300);
      col = 230;
      row = 262;
      b2.lineTo(col, row);
      g2.fill(b2);
      col = 230;
      row = 816;
      b3.moveTo(col, row);
      B.drawBSpline(g2, b3, 350, 816, 600, 808, 600,
         535, 350, 535);
      col = 230;
      row = 535;
      b3.lineTo(col, row);
      col = 230;
      row = 550;
      b3.lineTo(col, row);
      B.drawBSpline(g2, b3, 300, 550, 520, 550, 520,
         788, 300, 788);
      col = 230;
      row = 790;
      b3.lineTo(col, row);
      col = 230;
      row = 816;
      b3.lineTo(col, row);
      g2.fill(b3);

      g2.translate(442, 350);
      col = 592;
      row = 440;
      c1.moveTo(col, row);
      B.drawBSpline(g2, c1, 581, 440, 60, -90, 40, 1120,
         590, 680);
      col = 590;
      row = 680;
      c1.lineTo(col, row);
      B.drawBSpline(g2, c1, 605, 690, 100, 1180, -160,
         100, 500, 300);
      B.drawBSpline(g2, c1, 500, 300, 530, 310, 580,
         280, 568, 250);
      col = 580;
      row = 250;
      c1.lineTo(col, row);
      col = 592;
      row = 440;
      c1.lineTo(col, row);
      g2.fill(c1);
   }
```

LISTING *Program to Draw A, B, and C with B-Spline Curves. (continues)*
19.5

```
}

class BSplineAlpha extends Frame
{
    public BSplineAlpha()
    {
        super("Creating Letters with B Spline Curves");
        setBackground(Color.white);
        setLayout( new BorderLayout());
        add("Center", new BSplineCanvas());

        setSize(640, 480);
        show();
        WindowListener lis = new WindowAdapter()
        {
            public void windowClosing(WindowEvent e)
            {
                System.exit(0);
            }
        };
        addWindowListener(lis);
    }

    public static void main(String args[])
    {
        BSplineAlpha f = new BSplineAlpha();
    }
}
```

LISTING *Program to Draw A, B, and C with B-Spline Curves. (continued)*
19.5

B-Spline Curves with Many Control Points   Listing 19.6 gives a program that will draw a B-Spline curve using eight control points. The same control points are used that were used to draw a corresponding curve with Bezier curves. The resulting curve is shown in Figure 19.5. Note that the curve is dramatically different from the Bezier curve with the same control points as shown in Figure 19.5. Again, there is a mathematical relationship that makes it possible to obtain the B-Spline control points from the corresponding Bezier control points, but by the time we have an 8 × 8 or larger matrix, things become rather cumbersome. If you need to work with this type of B-Spline curve, it's probably better to find the proper control points experimentally.

```
/*
   BSplineCurve.java
   Using B-Spline Curve with Multiple Control Points
*/

import java.awt.*;
import java.util.*;
import java.awt.event.*;
import java.awt.geom.GeneralPath;
import java.awt.geom.Ellipse2D;

class BSplines
{
   int last = 7;
   int[] xpoint = {300, 320, 320, 120, 120, 410, 380, 520};
   int[] ypoint = {240, 240, 360, 360, 40, 90, 240, 240};

   void drawBSpline(Graphics2D g2)
   {
      double x, y, t;
      int i;

      GeneralPath p = new GeneralPath(0);
      for (i=0; i<last-2 ; i++)
      {
         for (t=0.0; t<=1.0; t+=0.01)
         {
            x = (1-t)*(1-t)*(1-t)*xpoint[i] + (3*t*t*t
               - 6 * t*t + 4) * xpoint[i+1] +
               (-3*t*t*t + 3 * t*t + 3*t + 1)
               * xpoint[i+2] + t*t*t*xpoint[i+3];
            y = (1-t)*(1-t)*(1-t)*ypoint[i] + (3*t*t*t
               - 6 * t*t + 4) * ypoint[i+1] +
               (-3*t*t*t + 3 * t*t + 3*t + 1)
               * ypoint[i+2] + t*t*t*ypoint[i+3];
            if (t == 0.)
               p.moveTo((float)(x/6), (float)(y/6));
            else
               p.lineTo((float)(x/6), (float)(y/6));
         }
         BasicStroke bs;
         bs = new BasicStroke(3.0f);
         g2.setStroke(bs);
         g2.draw(p);
      }
   }
}

class BSplineCanvas extends Canvas
```

LISTING *B-Spline Curve Using Multiple Control Points. (continues)*
19.6

```
{
    BSplines BSp = new BSplines();
    BSplineCanvas()
    {
    }

    public void paint(Graphics g)
    {
        int i, j, x, y, diameter1, diameter2, width;

        Graphics2D g2 = (Graphics2D) g;
        g2.setRenderingHint(RenderingHints.KEY_ANTIALIASING,
            RenderingHints.VALUE_ANTIALIAS_ON);
        g2.setRenderingHint(RenderingHints.KEY_RENDERING,
            (RenderingHints.VALUE_RENDER_QUALITY));
        BSp.drawBSpline(g2);
        g2.fill(new Ellipse2D.Float(295, 235, 10, 10));
        g2.fill(new Ellipse2D.Float(315, 235, 10, 10));
        g2.fill(new Ellipse2D.Float(315, 355, 10, 10));
        g2.fill(new Ellipse2D.Float(115, 355, 10, 10));
        g2.fill(new Ellipse2D.Float(115, 35, 10, 10));
        g2.fill(new Ellipse2D.Float(405, 85, 10, 10));
        g2.fill(new Ellipse2D.Float(375, 235, 10, 10));
        g2.fill(new Ellipse2D.Float(515, 235, 10, 10));
        g.drawString("p1",295, 227);
        g.drawString("p2",315, 227);
        g.drawString("p3",315, 347);
        g.drawString("p4",115, 347);
        g.drawString("p5",115, 27);
        g.drawString("p6",405, 77);
        g.drawString("p7",375, 227);
        g.drawString("p8",515, 227);
    }
}

class BSplineCurve extends Frame
{
    public BSplineCurve()
    {
        super ("A B Spline Curve with Multiple Control Points");
        setBackground(Color.white);
        setLayout( new BorderLayout());
        add("Center", new BSplineCanvas());
        setSize(640, 480);
        show();
        WindowListener lis = new WindowAdapter()
        {
            public void windowClosing(WindowEvent e)
            {
```

LISTING *B-Spline Curve Using Multiple Control Points. (continues)*
19.6

```
            System.exit(0);
        }
    };
    addWindowListener(lis);
}

public static void main(String args[])
{
    BSplineCurve f = new BSplineCurve();
}
}
```

LISTING *Spline Curve Using Multiple Control Points. (continued)*
19.6

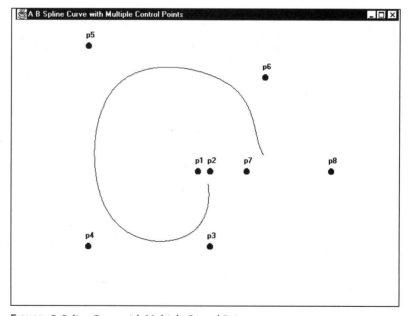

FIGURE *B-Spline Curve with Multiple Control Points.*
19.5

20

Three-Dimensional Modeling

A t the time the first edition of this book was written, Java had no tools available for drawing three-dimensional figures. We devoted one whole chapter to creating classes and methods for producing vectors and matrices and performing the various mathematical operations upon them, such as addition, subtraction, dot products, cross products, and so forth. Java 2 now has a class called *vecMath* that handles all these operations, so you no longer need to create your own methods. We devoted another chapter to creating three-dimensional objects and scenes, making heavy use of vector operations. The technique we used was to define each solid as a collection of facets, each of which was a quadrilateral. If the surface of the solid was curved, we'd try to use a sufficient number of quadrilaterals so that the fact that we were approximating a curved surface by a collection of flat surfaces was not noticeable. Each generic solid was defined so as to fit in a box that was + or − 1 unit in each direction and centered at the origin. Then we set up a *transform* vector to enlarge, move, and rotate the solid as required, with vectors.

Java now has a package of 3D graphics classes and methods that perform all these operations and more. This package can provide on any Java-compatible platform the high-end graphics features that used to be available only on high-priced graphics workstations. The Java 3D API makes it possible to describe large virtual worlds that can be rendered very efficiently. The package was developed through the joint efforts of Intel Corporation, Silicon Graphics, Apple Computer, and Sun Microsystems, giving it a wide degree of acceptance across the industry. It can do everything that we did in our previous chapter on Java three-dimensional graphics programming and more, and do it faster and easier. Java 3D is not part of the Java 2 package, but is readily available, both on the CD-ROM accompanying this book and from the Sun Microsystems Java site on the Web. Once you run the Java 3D unpacking program, it incorporates all parts of the Java 3D package into the appropriate directories and subdirectories of your Java 2 installation and you are ready to create three-dimensional universes.

The downside of this is that the size and complexity of the Java 3D package makes it hard to understand and there is no really complete documentation that explains how to use every capability that is available. The book *The Java 3D API Specification* by Henry Sowizral, Kevin Rushforth and Michael Deering is basically a listing of Java 3D classes, methods and passed parameters; it is 482 pages long. This is available from most bookstores that have a good stock of computer books, or from *amazon.com*. It can also be downloaded from the Java Website if you have enough patience. Obviously we can't begin to provide a full description in a single chapter of this book. Instead, what we're going to do is describe a couple of simple three-dimensional programs. Once you become familiar with these, you'll have an idea of how to develop your own Java 3D programs. If you need to do something that isn't covered in these programs, there is usually a way to do it; you just have to search through the long list of classes and methods.

The Painter's Algorithm

When we have a scene comprised of several solid objects and attempt to reproduce it on a two-dimensional viewing screen, we may have several surfaces that are at different depths in the three-dimensional original but appear at the same place on the two-dimensional viewing screen. If you are attempting to place all these objects on the screen yourself, you'll need to have some way of determining which of these surfaces is actually seen by the viewer. One way of doing this is to use what is called the *painter's algorithm*. This simply says that we first draw the farthest object on the screen, then the next farthest, and so forth until the closest object is drawn last. Then nearer objects correctly cover or partially cover farther ones, and the resulting picture appears realistic, as if we were viewing an actual three-dimensional scene. This can get a little complicated, especially when objects have complex shapes and are entwined with each other. Fortunately, Java 3D takes care of all this internally; all you have to do is specify objects and their locations and Java 3D takes care of the rest.

The *Earth.java* Program

Listing 20.1 is a program to display a rotating earth. Let's begin by looking at the packages that are imported at the beginning of the program. The packages *javax.media.j3d.** and *javax.vecmath.** are needed to perform the mathematical and other operations required to manipulate the three-dimensional objects. The package *com.sun.j3d.utils.universe.** provides the tools to create the virtual universe in which our three-dimensional scene will exist. The packages *com.sun.j3d.utils.geometry.Primitive* and *com.sun.j3d.utils.geometry.Sphere* are used to create and manipulate the sphere object. The package *com.sun.j3d.utils. image.TextureLoader* is used to read the graphic image from the data files and wrap it around the sphere.

Now let's look at the end of the program where we create the constructor for the *Earth* class. This begins by setting up a *Border* layout. We then create an object *c* of class *Canvas3D*. We add this to the center of the display. We now create an object *scene* of class *BranchGroup* and fill it by calling the method *createSceneGraphic,* which we'll describe later. We pass the object *c* to this method. Now we are ready to create our universe. First we create an object *u* of

```
/*
   Earth.java
   Program to display rotating earth
*/

import java.applet.Applet;
import java.awt.BorderLayout;
import java.awt.event.*;
import com.sun.j3d.utils.applet.MainFrame;
import com.sun.j3d.utils.geometry.Primitive;
import com.sun.j3d.utils.geometry.Sphere;
import com.sun.j3d.utils.universe.*;
import com.sun.j3d.utils.image.TextureLoader;
import javax.media.j3d.*;
import javax.vecmath.*;

public class Earth extends Applet
{
    public BranchGroup createSceneGraph(Canvas3D c)
    {
        BranchGroup objRoot = new BranchGroup();
        BoundingSphere bounds =
            new BoundingSphere(new Point3d(0.0,0.0,0.0),
            100.0);
        Color3f bgColor = new Color3f(0.05f, 0.05f, 0.2f);
        Background bg = new Background(bgColor);
        bg.setApplicationBounds(bounds);
        objRoot.addChild(bg);

        Color3f lColor1 = new Color3f(0.7f, 0.7f, 0.7f);
        Vector3f lDir1 = new Vector3f(-1.0f, -0.5f,
            -1.0f);
        Color3f alColor = new Color3f(0.2f, 0.2f, 0.2f);
        Color3f black = new Color3f(0.0f, 0.0f, 0.0f);
        Color3f white = new Color3f(1.0f, 1.0f, 1.0f);

        AmbientLight aLgt = new AmbientLight(alColor);
        aLgt.setInfluencingBounds(bounds);
        DirectionalLight lgt1 = new DirectionalLight(lColor1, lDir1);
        lgt1.setInfluencingBounds(bounds);
        objRoot.addChild(aLgt);
        objRoot.addChild(lgt1);
        Appearance app = new Appearance();
        TextureLoader tex = new TextureLoader("earth.jpg",
            this);
        app.setTexture(tex.getTexture());
        app.setMaterial(new Material(white, black, white,
            white, 1.0f));
        objRoot.addChild(createObject(app,.5, 0.0, 0.0));
```

LISTING *Program to Create Solid Objects. (continues)*
20.1

```
         objRoot.compile();
         return objRoot;
   }

   private Group createObject(Appearance app, double
      scale, double xpos, double ypos)
   {
         Transform3D t = new Transform3D();
         t.set(scale, new Vector3d(xpos, ypos, 0.0));
         TransformGroup objTrans = new TransformGroup(t);
         TransformGroup spinTg = new TransformGroup();
         spinTg.setCapability (TransformGroup.ALLOW_TRANSFORM_WRITE);
         spinTg.setCapability (TransformGroup.ALLOW_TRANSFORM_READ);
         Primitive obj = null;
         obj = (Primitive) new Sphere(1.0f,
            Sphere.GENERATE_NORMALS |
            Sphere.GENERATE_TEXTURE_COORDS, 28, app);
         spinTg.addChild(obj);
         Alpha rotationAlpha = new Alpha(-1,
            Alpha.INCREASING_ENABLE, 0, 0, 50000, 0, 0,
            0, 0, 0);
         RotationInterpolator rotator =
            new RotationInterpolator(rotationAlpha,
            spinTg);
         BoundingSphere bounds =
            new BoundingSphere(new Point3d(0.0,0.0,0.0),
            100.0);
         rotator.setSchedulingBounds(bounds);
         objTrans.addChild(rotator);
         objTrans.addChild(spinTg);
         return objTrans;
   }

   public Earth()
   {
         setLayout(new BorderLayout());
         Canvas3D c = new Canvas3D(null);
         add("Center", c);
         BranchGroup scene = createSceneGraph(c);
         SimpleUniverse u = new SimpleUniverse(c);
         u.getViewingPlatform( ).setNominalViewingTransform();
         u.addBranchGraph(scene);
   }

   public static void main(String[] args)
   {
         new MainFrame(new Earth(), 700, 700);
   }
}
```

LISTING *Program to Create Solid Objects. (continued)*
20.1

class *SimpleUniverse*. We then create the default viewing platform by calling the method *getViewingPlatform*. This completes the *Earth* constructor.

Now let's take a look at the method *createSceneGraph*. This begins by creating an object *objRoot* of class *BranchGroup*. We next set up an object *bounds* of class *BoundingSphere*. Two parameters are used in initializing this object; the first is a vector that represents the center point of the sphere and the second is the radius of the sphere. This object represents the limits within which various portions of the scene must be contained. It is not the sphere that is to be drawn in the display. Note that we are using a normalized coordinate system throughout the Java 3D package. The center of the universe is at (0.0, 0.0, 0.0). The *x* coordinate is negative to the left of the center and positive to the right, reaching maximum values of -1.0 and +1.0. Similarly, values of the *y* coordinate are negative as one moves from the center toward the bottom of the screen and positive as one moves from the center toward the top. Again, values of the *z* coordinate are negative toward the observer and positive away from the observer.

We now turn our attention to the background. We first create a color object *bgColor* of class *Color3F* and initialize it with a dark blue color. We then create an object *bg* of class *Background* and initialize it with the color *bgColor*. We use the method *setApplicationBounds* to set the bounds for the background and then add the background as a child to *objRoot*.

Now we turn to the matter of lighting. We set up two lighting colors, the objects *lColor1* and *alColor*, both of class *Color3F*. The first is the color for the directional lighting and is nearly white. The second is the ambient lighting, the light that is received by the object in the absence of any other illumination. We also create a vector object *lDir1* that defines the position of the directional light source. It is at the left front, about one quarter of the way up. Now we generate an ambient light object *aLgt* of class *AmbientLight* and initialize it with the color *alColor*. We use the *setInfluencingBounds* method to establish bounds for this lighting. Similarly, we generate a directional light source object *lgt1* of class *DirectionalLight* and initialize it with the color *lColor1*. We again use the *setInfluencingBounds* method to establish bounds for this lighting. We then make each light source a child of *objRoot*.

Our next concern is the texture that is to appear on the sphere that we are going to generate. We first set up an object *app* of class *Appearance*. Next we set up an object *tex* of class *TextureLoader*, initializing this with the name of the file *earth.jpg*. This is a flat earth map from one of the Java demos. It must be in the same subdirectory as our *Earth* program. Figure 20.1 is a picture of this map. We next use the *getTexture* method to put the file contents into *tex* and then the *setTexture* method to move it into *app*.

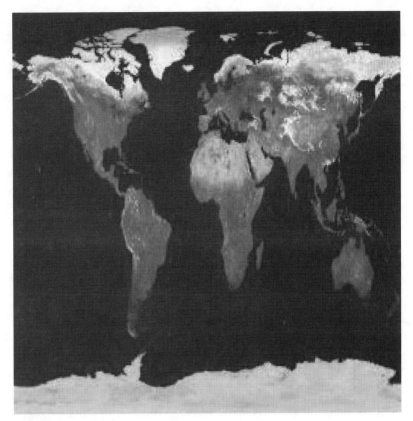

FIGURE   *Flat Earth Map.*
20.1

We now call the method *createObject* to create the sphere object that we want to display. The parameters passed to this method are *app*, which defines the appearance of the object (the texture applied or color); *scale*, which determines the object size; and the *x* and *y* coordinates of the object's position. The method returns an object of class *TransformGroup*, which we set to be a child of *objRoot*. This is the last object to be added to *objRoot*.

We then run *objRoot.compile()* to optimize our whole scene.

The *createObject* method begins by defining an object *t* of class *Transform3D*. We then set the size of this object by calling the method *set* and passing it the parameters *scale* (for defining the size) and a *Vector3D* object, which defines the object's position. The components of this vector are the *x* and *y* coordinates passed to the *createObject* method and 0.0 for the *z* coordinate. Next we create an object *objTrans* of class *TransformGroup* to which we pass the object *t*. We also create another *TransformGroup* object called *spinTg*. We then use the *setCapability* method twice to allow *spinTg* to have read and write capabilities. Next, we define an object *obj* of class *Primitive*. We set this object up to create a sphere. The parameters that are passed to this sphere are the scale factor (1.0 in our case), flags that allow the object to generate normals and texture coordinates, the number of divisions (which determines the resolution of the sphere—we are using 28), and the appearance (*app*). We then add *obj* as a child to *spinTg*.

We are now going to provide the earth with the capability of rotating on its axis. First, we need an object that provides a changing value between 0.0 and 1.0 over time. To do this, we create an object *rotationAlpha* of class *Alpha*. This class has the following parameters:

```
public Alpha(int loopCount, int mode, long triggerTime,
   long phaseDelayDuration, long
   increasingAlphaDuration, long
   increasingAlphaRampDuration,long AlphaAtOneDuration,
   long decreasingAlphaDuration, long
   decreasingAlphaRampDuration, longAlphaAtZeroDuration)
```

The first parameter, *loopCount,* specifies how many loops *Alpha* shall perform before it stops. We set this to –1, which causes *Alpha* to cycle continuously. The next parameter, *mode*, we set to *INCREASING_ENABLE*, which causes *Alpha* to begin by increasing from 0.0 to 1.0. Alternately we could have set it to *DECREASING_ENABLE* to allow *Alpha* to change in direction in the opposite direction, or we could *OR* these two to allow movement in both directions. The only other parameter that we are concerned with is *increasingAlphaDuration*. This parameter is the number of milliseconds that it takes for *Alpha* to complete one full cycle from 0.0 to 1.0. When we use *Alpha* to control rotation, this parameter will determine the rate at which rotation occurs. If you don't like the rate at which the rotation of the earth occurs in this example program, you can modify this parameter to get a speed that pleases you. The other parameters are mostly concerned with setting up acceleration parameters if you don't want *Alpha* to change at a constant rate. Constant rotation is fine for this example, so we just fill the other parameters with zeroes.

Now that we have the *rotationAlpha* parameter pinned down, we are ready to install the rotation software. We begin by creating an object *rotator* of class *RotationInterpolator.* We only need to pass two parameters to this object: the *rotationAlpha* parameter, which controls motion around the y axis, and *spinTg*, which is the target object for the rotation. What if you don't want to rotate around the *y* axis? There is another form of the *RotationInterpolator* method that allows you to enter a new object of the class as one of the parameters. You can rotate the coordinate system of this object and your rotation will then take place around the y axis of this new coordinate system rather than your original one. Now, to finish off with our rotation enabling, we set up a new bounding sphere and set the bounds for *rotator*. We then add *rotator* as a child of *objTrans* to control rotation, and *spinTg* as a child of *objTrans* to create the object that is rotated.

A snapshot of the resulting display (with North and South America facing the viewer) is shown in Plate 15. Observe how simply we were able to wrap the flat world map around the sphere to create a world globe. If you run the program, you'll also be able to observe how simple it is to produce a display with a rotating object.

The *Solid4* Class

Listing 20.2 is a program to create a display of a number of rotating three-dimensional objects. This program is somewhat more complex than the previous one, except for the fact that it does not use textures on the objects themselves. If you look at the beginning of the program, you'll observe that there are a number of additional packages that are imported. These supply capabilities for generating other objects that weren't included in the previous program.

```
/*
   Solid4. ava
   Three Dimensional Figures
*/

import  ava.applet.Applet;
import  ava.awt.BorderLayout;
import  ava.awt.event.*;
import  ava.awt.GraphicsConfiguration;
import com.sun. 3d.utils.applet.MainFrame;
import com.sun. 3d.utils.geometry.Primitive;
import com.sun. 3d.utils.geometry.Sphere;
import com.sun. 3d.utils.geometry.Cone;
import com.sun. 3d.utils.geometry.Cylinder;
import com.sun. 3d.utils.universe.*;
import com.sun. 3d.utils.image.TextureLoader;
import com.sun. 3d.utils.geometry.ColorCube;
import  avax.media. 3d.*;
import  avax.vecmath.*;

public class Solid4 extends Applet
{
```

LISTING *Program to Create Rotating Three-Dimensional Objects. (continues)*
20.2

```java
    private BranchGroup createSceneGraph()
    {
        // Create the root of the branch graph
        BranchGroup ob Root = new BranchGroup();

        // Create a bounds for the background and lights
        BoundingSphere bounds =
            new BoundingSphere(new Point3d(0.0,0.0,0.0),
            100.0);

        // Set up the background
        TextureLoader bgTexture = new
            TextureLoader("background. pg", this);
        Background bg = new
            Background(bgTexture.getImage());
        bg.setApplicationBounds(bounds);
        ob Root.addChild(bg);

        // Set up the global lights
        Color3f lColor1 = new Color3f(0.7f, 0.7f, 0.7f);
        Vector3f lDir1 = new Vector3f(-1.0f, -1.0f,
            -1.0f);
        Color3f alColor = new Color3f(0.2f, 0.2f, 0.2f);

        AmbientLight aLgt = new AmbientLight(alColor);
        aLgt.setInfluencingBounds(bounds);
        DirectionalLight lgt1 = new
            DirectionalLight(lColor1, lDir1);
        lgt1.setInfluencingBounds(bounds);
        ob Root.addChild(aLgt);
        ob Root.addChild(lgt1);
        // Create a bunch of ob ects with a behavior and // add them into
    the scene graph.

        Appearance ap1 = new Appearance();
        Appearance ap2 = new Appearance();
        Appearance ap3 = new Appearance();
        Appearance ap4 = new Appearance();
        Appearance ap5 = new Appearance();
        Appearance ap6 = new Appearance();
        Appearance ap7 = new Appearance();
        Color3f black = new Color3f(0.0f, 0.0f, 0.0f);
        Color3f white = new Color3f(1.0f, 1.0f, 1.0f);
        Color3f ob Color = new Color3f(0.0f, 0.0f, 0.8f);
        ap1.setMaterial(new Material(ob Color, black,
            ob Color, white, 80.0f));
        ob Root.addChild(createOb ect(4, ap1, 0.2, -.6,
            -.5, 0.0));
        ob Color = new Color3f(0.8f, 0.0f, 0.0f);
```

LISTING *Program to Create Rotating Three-Dimensional Objects. (continues)*
20.2

```
        ap2.setMaterial(new Material(ob Color, black,
           ob Color, white, 80.0f));
        ob Root.addChild(createOb ect(0, ap2, 0.25, -.33,
           -.1, 0.38));
        ob Color = new Color3f(0.8f, 0.8f, 0.0f);
        ap3.setMaterial(new Material(ob Color, black,
           ob Color, white, 80.0f));
        ob Root.addChild(createOb ect(4, ap3, 0.2, -.2,
           -.5, 0.0));
        ob Color = new Color3f(0.0f, 0.8f, 0.0f);
        ap4.setMaterial(new Material(ob Color, black,
           ob Color, white, 80.0f));
        ob Root.addChild(createOb ect(4, ap4, 0.2, -.47,
           -.5, -0.5));
        ob Color = new Color3f(0.0f, 0.8f, 0.8f);
        ap5.setMaterial(new Material(ob Color, black,
           ob Color, white, 80.0f));
        ob Root.addChild(createOb ect(1, ap5, 0.2, .5,
           -.5, 0.0));
        ob Color = new Color3f(0.8f, 0.8f, 0.8f);
        ap6.setMaterial(new Material(ob Color, black,
           ob Color, white, 80.0f));
        ob Root.addChild(createOb ect(2, ap6, 0.2, .95,
           -.5, -.75));
        ob Root.addChild(createOb ect(3, ap7, 0.2, .3,
           -.5, -.7));

        // Let Java 3D perform optimizations on this scene // graph.
        ob Root.compile();
        return ob Root;
    }

    private Group createOb ect(int type, Appearance app,
        double scale, double xpos, double ypos, double
        zpos)
    {

        // Create a transform group node to scale and
        // position the ob ect.
        Transform3D t = new Transform3D();
        t.set(scale, new Vector3d(xpos, ypos, zpos));
        TransformGroup ob Trans = new TransformGroup(t);

        // Create a second transform group node and
        // initialize it to the identity. Enable the
        // TRANSFORM_WRITE capability so that
        // our behavior code can modify it at runtime.
        TransformGroup spinTg = new TransformGroup();
        spinTg.setCapability(
```

LISTING *Program to Create Rotating Three-Dimensional Objects. (continues)*

20.2

```
            TransformGroup.ALLOW_TRANSFORM_WRITE);
      Primitive ob  = null;
      switch (type)
      {
         case 0:
            ob  = (Primitive) new Sphere(1.0f,
               Sphere.GENERATE_NORMALS, 28,
                  app);
               ob .setAppearance(app);
               spinTg.addChild(ob );
            break;
         case 1:
            ob  = (Primitive) new Cone();
               ob .setAppearance(app);
               spinTg.addChild(ob );
            break;
         case 2:
            ob  = (Primitive) new Cylinder();
               ob .setAppearance(app);
               spinTg.addChild(ob );
            break;
         case 3:
            spinTg.addChild(new ColorCube(1.0));
            break;
         case 4:
            Shape3D shape = new Tetrahedron();
            shape.setAppearance(app);
            spinTg.addChild(shape);
      }

      // Create a simple shape leaf node and set the // appearance

      Alpha rotationAlpha = new Alpha(-1,
         Alpha.INCREASING_ENABLE,
         0, 0,5000, 0, 0, 0, 0, 0);

      RotationInterpolator rotator =
         new RotationInterpolator(rotationAlpha,
         spinTg);

      BoundingSphere bounds =
         new BoundingSphere(new Point3d(0.0,0.0,0.0),
         100.0);

      rotator.setSchedulingBounds(bounds);

   // Add the behavior and the transform group to the // ob ect
      ob Trans.addChild(rotator);
      ob Trans.addChild(spinTg);
```

LISTING *Program to Create Rotating Three-Dimensional Objects. (continues)*
20.2

```
      return ob Trans;
   }

   public Solid4()
   {
      setLayout(new BorderLayout());
      Canvas3D c = new Canvas3D(null);
      add("Center", c);

      // Create a simple scene and attach it to the // virtual universe
      BranchGroup scene = createSceneGraph();
      SimpleUniverse u = new SimpleUniverse(c);

      // This will move the ViewPlatform back a bit so // the ob ects in
the scene can be viewed.
      u.getViewingPlatform(
      ).setNominalViewingTransform();
      u.addBranchGraph(scene);
   }

   // The following allows Solid4 to be run as an
   // application as well as an applet

   public static void main(String[] args)
   {
      new MainFrame(new Solid4(), 640, 480);
   }
}
```

LISTING *Program to Create Rotating Three-Dimensional Objects. (continued)*

20.3

If you look at the end of the program, you'll see that the code for the *Solid4* constructor sets up the virtual universe in exactly the same way as was done for *Earth* in the previous program.

As with the previous program, we have near the beginning of the program the definition of the method *createSceneGraph*. Now let's take a look at the method *createSceneGraph*. This begins by creating an object *objRoot* of class *BranchGroup*. We next set up an object *bounds* of class *BoundingSphere*. Two parameters are used in initializing this object: the first is a vector that represents the center point of the sphere, and the second is the radius of the sphere. We now turn our attention to the background. We first set up the object *bgTexture* of class *TextureLoader* and initialize it with the name of the graphics file *background.jpg*. We made this file by combining the ground of a photograph with a Java demo picture of the sky with clouds. The previous program just assigned a color to the background. In this program we create the background object *bg* of class *Background* by getting the *bgTexture* picture instead of assigning a color. We use the method *setApplicationBounds* to set the bounds for the background and then add the background as a child to *objRoot*.

Now we turn to the matter of lighting. This works just the same way as the previous program, creating an ambient light source and a directional light source, except that the position of the directional light source has been moved somewhat. We use the *setInfluencingBounds* method to establish bounds for the ambient lighting and again use it to establish bounds for this lighting. We then make each light source a child of *objRoot*.

Next, we need to set up objects *ap1* through *ap7* of class *Appearance* to control the color of our scene objects. Then for each object that appears in the picture, we first set up the object *objColor* with the desired color. We then set up the appearance object with the *setMaterial* method, passing to it values for the ambient color, the emissive color, the diffuse color, the specular color, and the shininess. For each object to be drawn we then call the *createObject* method (described later) passing it the type parameter, the appearance parameter, the scale parameter, and the three coordinates of the object's position. The method returns an object of class *TransformGroup*, which we set to be a child of *objRoot*. We then run *objRoot.compile()* to optimize our whole scene.

The *createObject* method begins by defining an object *t* of class *Transform3D*. We then set the size and location of this object by calling the method *set* and passing it the parameters *scale* (for defining the size) and a *Vector3D* object, which defines the object's position. The components of this vector are the coordinates passed to the *createObject* method. Next we create an object *objTrans* of class *TransformGroup* to which we pass the object *t*. We also create another *TransformGroup* object called *spinTg*. We then use the *setCapability* method twice to allow *spinTg* to have write capability. Next, we define an object *obj* of class *Primitive*. Then we enter a *switch* statement, which uses the parameter *type* to determine what kind of object we shall create. Case 0 creates a sphere. The parameters that are passed to this sphere are the scale factor (1.0 in our case), a flag that allows the object to generate normals, the number of divisions (which determines the resolution of the sphere—we are using 28), and the appearance (*app*). We then add *obj* as a child to *spinTg*. All other cases work in essentially the same way except for case 4. You may have wondered what happens if the shape you want to create is one that is not in the Java 3D package. Case 4 is an example of this. We want a tetrahedron, so we create it as a separate class and then add it to the scene as shown in case 4. The remainder of this method sets up to permit rotation of each object in exactly the same way as was done with the previous program.

The tetrahedron class code is shown in Listing 20.3. This program was created by Sun Microsystems as part of one of the Java 3D demonstrations. You can see how each of the faces of the tetrahedron is defined and combined to define the solid.

```
/*
 * @(#)Tetrahedron.java 1.6 98/02/20 14:29:42
 *
 * Copyright (c) 1996-1998 Sun Microsystems, Inc. All Rights Reserved.
 *
 * Sun grants you ("Licensee") a non-exclusive, royalty free, license to
use,
 * modify and redistribute this software in source and binary code form,
 * provided that i) this copyright notice and license appear on all
copies of
 * the software; and ii) Licensee does not utilize the software in a
manner
 * which is disparaging to Sun.
 *
 * This software is provided "AS IS," without a warranty of any kind.
ALL
 * EXPRESS OR IMPLIED CONDITIONS, REPRESENTATIONS AND WARRANTIES,
INCLUDING ANY
 * IMPLIED WARRANTY OF MERCHANTABILITY, FITNESS FOR A PARTICULAR PURPOSE
OR
 * NON-INFRINGEMENT, ARE HEREBY EXCLUDED. SUN AND ITS LICENSORS SHALL
NOT BE
 * LIABLE FOR ANY DAMAGES SUFFERED BY LICENSEE AS A RESULT OF USING,
MODIFYING
 * OR DISTRIBUTING THE SOFTWARE OR ITS DERIVATIVES. IN NO EVENT WILL SUN
OR ITS
 * LICENSORS BE LIABLE FOR ANY LOST REVENUE, PROFIT OR DATA, OR FOR
DIRECT,
 * INDIRECT, SPECIAL, CONSEQUENTIAL, INCIDENTAL OR PUNITIVE DAMAGES,
HOWEVER
 * CAUSED AND REGARDLESS OF THE THEORY OF LIABILITY, ARISING OUT OF THE
USE OF
 * OR INABILITY TO USE SOFTWARE, EVEN IF SUN HAS BEEN ADVISED OF THE
 * POSSIBILITY OF SUCH DAMAGES.
 *
 * This software is not designed or intended for use in on-line control
of
 * aircraft, air traffic, aircraft navigation or aircraft
communications; or in
 * the design, construction, operation or maintenance of any nuclear
 * facility. Licensee represents and warrants that it will not use or
 * redistribute the Software for such purposes.
```

LISTING *Program to Create Tetrahedron Class. (continues)*
20.3

```
*/

import javax.media.j3d.*;
import javax.vecmath.*;

public class Tetrahedron extends Shape3D {
   private static final float sqrt3 = (float) Math.sqrt(3.0);
   private static final float sqrt3_3 = sqrt3 / 3.0f;
   private static final float sqrt24_3 = (float) Math.sqrt(24.0) / 3.0f;

   private static final float ycenter = 0.5f * sqrt24_3;
   private static final float zcenter = -sqrt3_3;

   private static final Point3f p1 = new Point3f(-1.0f, -ycenter, -
zcenter);
   private static final Point3f p2 = new Point3f(1.0f, -ycenter, -
zcenter);
   private static final Point3f p3 =
   new Point3f(0.0f, -ycenter, -sqrt3 - zcenter);
   private static final Point3f p4 =
   new Point3f(0.0f, sqrt24_3 - ycenter, 0.0f);

   private static final Point3f[] verts = {
   p1, p2, p4, // front face
   p1, p4, p3, // left, back face
   p2, p3, p4, // right, back face
   p1, p3, p2, // bottom face
   };
   private Point2f texCoord[] = {
      new Point2f(0.0f, 0.0f),
   new Point2f(1.0f, 0.0f),
      new Point2f(0.5f, sqrt3 / 2.0f),
   };

   public Tetrahedron() {
   int i;

   TriangleArray tetra = new TriangleArray(12, TriangleArray.COORDINATES
|
      TriangleArray.NORMALS | TriangleArray.TEXTURE_COORDINATE_2);

   tetra.setCoordinates(0, verts);
      for (i = 0; i < 12; i++) {
         tetra.setTextureCoordinate(i, texCoord[i%3]);
      }

   int face;
   Vector3f normal = new Vector3f();
   Vector3f v1 = new Vector3f();
```

LISTING *Program to Create Tetrahedron Class. (continues)*
20.3

```
    Vector3f v2 = new Vector3f();
    Point3f [] pts = new Point3f[3];
    for (i = 0; i < 3; i++) pts[i] = new Point3f();

    for (face = 0; face < 4; face++) {
       tetra.getCoordinates(face*3, pts);
       v1.sub(pts[1], pts[0]);
       v2.sub(pts[2], pts[0]);
       normal.cross(v1, v2);
       normal.normalize();
       for (i = 0; i < 3; i++) {
       tetra.setNormal((face * 3 + i), normal);
       }
    }
    this.setGeometry(tetra);
    this.setAppearance(new Appearance());
    }
}
```

LISTING *Program to Create Tetrahedron Class. (continued)*
20.3

A snapshot of the resulting display is shown in Plate 16. You really need to run the program to see the display in action. The three tetrahedrons are rotating and the sphere is balanced on top of them and rotating also. All the other objects in the display are also rotating. This is most obvious with the color cube, which shows the different colors on its faces as it rotates.

21

More Advanced Web Pages

In Chapter 12 you learned how to create your own simple Web page and put it on the Web. Here, we're going to look at a few more advanced topics in Web page creation. We've created a sample Web page to illustrate these topics. The *HTML* file that drives the applet is shown in Listing 21.1, and the Java program listing for the applet in Listing 21.2.

```
<APPLET CODE="DoublePage.class" WIDTH=300 HEIGHT=200
</APPLET>
```

LISTING *HTML Listing for Double Web Page Program.*
21.1

```
/*
   DoublePage. ava
   Program to Generate Two Web Pages
*/

import   ava.awt.*;
import   ava.applet.*;
import   ava.util.*;
import   ava.awt.event.*;
import   ava.net.*;
import   ava.io.*;

public class DoublePage extends Applet implements
   ActionListener
{
   Button tip;
   Button lair;
   Label label;
   Page tipPro;
   DPage Dragon;

   public DoublePage()
   {
      setLayout(new BorderLayout());
      add("North",label = new Label
         ("Select Page for Display!",Label.CENTER));
      add("West",tip = new Button("Graphics Tip"));
      add("East",lair = new Button("Dragon's Lair"));
      tip.addActionListener(this);
      lair.addActionListener(this);
```

LISTING *Sample Program to Create Two Web Pages. (continues)*
21.2

```
    }

    public void actionPerformed( ava.awt.event.ActionEvent
        evt)
    {
        if (evt.getActionCommand().equals ("Graphics Tip"))
            tipPro = new Page();
        if (evt.getActionCommand().equals
            ("Dragon's Lair"))
            Dragon = new DPage();
    }

    class Page extends Frame
    {
        Image pic1, pic2;

        public Page()
        {
            addWindowListener(new WindowAdapter()
            {
                public void windowClosing(WindowEvent e)
                {
                    dispose();
                }
            });
                setSize(640,480);
                show();
        }

        public void paint(Graphics g)
        {
            pic1 = getImage(getDocumentBase(),
                "Aspen2. pg");
            pic2 = getImage(getCodeBase(), "Aspen40. pg");
            Font f = new Font("TimesRoman", Font.BOLD, 24);
            g.setFont(f);
            g.drawString("A Graphics Tip",230,50);
            g.drawString("By Roger T. Stevens",200,75);
        Font f1 = new Font("TimesRoman", Font.PLAIN, 14);
            g.setFont(f1);
            g.drawString("Have you ever been told that if you convert a
JPEG graphics file to another format for editing and", 20, 100);
            g.drawString("then convert it back to JPEG again and repeat
this several times, the accumulated loses of the JPEG ", 20, 115);
            g.drawString("conversions will leave your picture unuseable?
This is simply not true. True, the first JPEG", 20, 130);
            g.drawString("conversion causes some loss of detail, but
succeeding conversions cause no additional losses because", 20, 145);
```

LISTING *Sample Program to Create Two Web Pages. (continues)*
21.2

```
        g.drawString("the algorithm attempts to remove the very same
detail that was already removed by the first conversion." , 20, 160);
        g.drawString("That detail is already gone. Nothing else is
removed. To demonstrate this, I took a BMP graphics file", 20, 175);
        g.drawString("and converted it to JPEG. The resulting picture
is shown below on the left. I then converted this file",20,190);
        g.drawString("back to BMP format and then converted back to
JPEG again and repeated this process 20 times. The", 20, 205);
        g.drawString("JPEG picture is shown below on the right. As you
can see, there is no discernible difference in quality",20,220);
        g.drawString("after 20 JPEG conversions.",20,235);
        g.drawImage(pic1, 0, 240, this);
        g.drawImage(pic2, 320, 240, this);
    }
  }

  class DPage extends Frame implements ActionListener
  {
    Panel panel;
    private TitleCanvas2 canvas1;
    Button send;
    TextField nameField = new TextField();
    TextField streetField = new TextField();
    TextField cityField = new TextField();
    TextField stateField = new TextField();
    TextField zipField = new TextField();
    Dragon2 dragon;

    public DPage()
    {
        setLayout(new GridLayout(3,1));
        canvas1 = new TitleCanvas2();
        add(canvas1);
        dragon = new Dragon2(panel);
        add(dragon);
        add(addressDialog());
        dragon.start();
        addWindowListener(new WindowAdapter()
        {
           public void windowClosing(WindowEvent e)
           {
              dispose();
           }
        });
        setSize(640,480);
        show();
        send.addActionListener(this);
    }
```

LISTING *Sample Program to Create Two Web Pages. (continues)*

21.2

```
   public void AddressData(String sdata)
{

    String hostname = "webname.com";
    String script = "/cgi-bin/mailto.pl";
    int port = 80;
    Socket s = null;
    System.out.println(sdata);
    try
    {

        s = new Socket(hostname, port);
        DataOutputStream os = new
           DataOutputStream(s.getOutputStream());
        os.writeBytes("POST " + script
           + " HTTP/1.0\r\n"
              + "Content-type: application/octet- stream\r\n"
           + "Content-length: "
           + sdata.length() + "\r\n\r\n");
        os.writeBytes(sdata);
        os.close();
    }
    catch (Exception e)
    {
        System.out.println("Error " + e);
        if (s != null)
            try
    {
        s.close();
    }
    catch (IOException ex)
    {
    }
    }
}

private Panel addressDialog()
{

    GridBagLayout gbl = new GridBagLayout();
    Panel p = new Panel();
    p.setLayout(gbl);
    GridBagConstraints gbc = new
       GridBagConstraints();
    gbc.fill = GridBagConstraints.BOTH;
    gbc.weightx = 100;
    gbc.weighty = 100;
    gbc.anchor = GridBagConstraints.CENTER;
    add(p, new Label
```

LISTING *Sample Program to Create Two Web Pages. (continues)*

21.2

```
            ("Please enter your name and address: "),
          gbl, gbc, 0, 0, 5, 1);
       gbc.anchor = GridBagConstraints.WEST;
       add(p, new Label("Name"), gbl, gbc, 0, 1,
          1, 1);
       add(p, nameField, gbl, gbc, 1, 1, 3, 1);
       add(p, new Label(" "), gbl, gbc, 4, 1,
          1, 1);
       add(p, new Label("Street"), gbl, gbc, 0, 2,
          1, 1);
       add(p, streetField, gbl, gbc, 1, 2, 3, 1);
       add(p, new Label(" "), gbl, gbc, 4, 2,
          1, 1);
       add(p, new Label("City"), gbl, gbc, 0, 3,
          1, 1);
       add(p, cityField, gbl, gbc, 1, 3, 3, 1);
       add(p, new Label(" "), gbl, gbc, 4, 3,
          1, 1);
       add(p, new Label("State"), gbl, gbc, 0, 4,
          1, 1);
       add(p, stateField, gbl, gbc, 1, 4, 1, 1);
       add(p, new Label("
          Zip"), gbl, gbc, 2, 4, 1, 1);
       add(p, zipField, gbl, gbc, 3, 4, 1, 1);
       add(p, new Label(" "), gbl, gbc, 4, 4,
          1, 1);
       gbc.fill = GridBagConstraints.NONE;
       add(p, send = new Button("Send"), gbl, gbc,
          1, 5, 1, 1);
       return p;
    }

    public void
       actionPerformed( ava.awt.event.ActionEvent evt)
    {
       String data;
       data = nameField.getText() + "\n"
          + streetField.getText() + "\n"
          + cityField.getText() + " "
          + stateField.getText() + " "
          + zipField.getText() + "\n\n";
       AddressData(data);
    }

    private void add(Container p, Component c,
       GridBagLayout gbl, GridBagConstraints gbc,
       int x, int y, int w, int h)
    {
       gbc.gridx = x;
```

LISTING *Sample Program to Create Two Web Pages. (continues)*
21.2

```
        gbc.gridy = y;
        gbc.gridwidth = w;
        gbc.gridheight = h;
        gbl.setConstraints(c, gbc);
        p.add(c);
    }
}

class TitleCanvas2 extends Canvas
{

    public void paint(Graphics g)
    {
        String s1 = "Welcome to the";
        String s2 = "Dragon's Lair!";
        int swidth;
            Font f = new Font("TimesRoman", Font.BOLD,
                36);
            g.setFont(f);
            FontMetrics fm = g.getFontMetrics(f);
            swidth = fm.stringWidth(s1);
            g.drawString(s1, (640 - swidth)/2, 40);
            swidth = fm.stringWidth(s2);
            g.drawString(s2, (640 - swidth)/2, 90);
        }
    }

    class Dragon2 extends Canvas implements Runnable
    {

        Dragon2(Panel c)
        {
        }

        public void run()
        {
            repaint();
        }
    }

    public void start()
    {
        if (runner == null)
        {
            runner = new Thread(this);
            runner.start();
        }
    }

    private Thread runner;
```

LISTING *Sample Program to Create Two Web Pages. (continues)*
21.2

```java
public void paint(Graphics g)
{
    double deltaX, deltaY, P, Q, XMax, YMax, Xmin,
        YMin,X, Y, Xsquare, Ysquare, Ytemp, temp_sq,
        temp_xy;
    int i,   , mincol, maxcol, maxrow, max_iterations
        = 512, row, col, index=0;
    Color dcolor;
    Color color[] = new Color[16];
    color[0] = Color.black;
    color[1] = new Color(0, 0, 170);
    color[2] = new Color(255, 85, 0);
    color[3] = new Color(255, 255, 85);
    color[4] = new Color(255, 170, 0);
    color[5] = new Color(255, 0, 85);
    color[6] = new Color(170, 85, 0);
    XMax = 1.4;
    XMin = -.4;
    YMax = .8;
    YMin = -.8;
    Q = 0.967049;
    P = 1.65;
    maxcol = 320;
    maxrow = 160;
    mincol = 160;
    deltaX = (XMax - XMin)/(maxcol);
    deltaY = (YMax - YMin)/(maxrow);
    for ( =0;   <8;   ++)
    {
        for (col=0; col<=maxcol; col++)
        {
            for (row=0; row<=maxrow; row+=8)
            {
                X = XMin + col * deltaX;
                Y = YMax - (row +   ) * deltaY;
                Xsquare = 0;
                Ysquare = 0;
                i = 0;
                while ((i<max_iterations) &&
                    ((Xsquare + Ysquare) < 4.0))
                {
                    Xsquare = X*X;
                    Ysquare = Y*Y;
                    temp_sq = Ysquare - Xsquare;
                    temp_xy = X*Y;
                    temp_xy += temp_xy;
                    Ytemp = Q*(temp_sq + X)-
                        P*(temp_xy - Y);
                    X = P*(temp_sq + X)
```

LISTING *Sample Program to Create Two Web Pages. (continues)*
21.2

```
                        + Q*(temp_xy - Y);
                Y = Ytemp;
                i++;
                }
                if (i >= max_iterations)
                    dcolor = color[((int)((Xsquare
                        + Ysquare)*6))%6 + 1];
                else
                    dcolor = Color.black;
                g.setColor(dcolor);
                g.drawLine(col+mincol, row+j,
                    col+mincol, row+7);
            }
        }
      }
     }
    }
   }
```

LISTING *Sample Program to Create Two Web Pages. (continued)*
21.2

Multiple Web Pages

In many cases, you will want to have more than one display screen available at your Web page site. There are many ways to do this, including chaining together a number of Java applets with intervening sections of *HTML* language. Since this is primarily a Java book, our sample program in Listing 21.2 uses a single Java applet to do the job. You'll remember that an *HTML* program such as that shown in Listing 21.1 is needed to activate the applet, which is run either through Java's *AppletViewer* program or through your Web browser. The *HTML* program includes *Height* and *Width* parameters that establish the size of the applet window that is to be created. The window that we create, however, is used only to allow the user to select one of two available Web pages. If you look at the beginning of the *DoublePage* program, you'll see that we create a window using the *Border* layout. We put the heading "Select Page for Display!" at the north or top side of the window, the "Graphics Tip" button at the west or left side, and the "Dragon's Lair" button at the east, or right edge. We include listeners to detect when either button is clicked and an *actionPerformed* method that creates a new *Page* object or a new *Dpage* object, depending upon which button was clicked.

The *Page* class is almost the same as the applet program in Chapter 20—there are a few differences in string placing. *Page* is an extension of *Frame* rather than *Applet*. This permits us to control the size of the new window that is to be created with a *setSize* statement rather than having to pass size parameters through the *HTML* program. We make the window large; it therefore covers the original page option window. The constructor for *Page* includes a *windowListener* that detects a window closing action (clicking the mouse on the x at the top right corner of the display). When this action occurs, the *dispose* method shuts down the window and the original page selection display is revealed.

The *Dpage* class creates the second Web page. The *Dpage* constructor sets up a window layout of the grid type having three equal sized rectangles stacked vertically. Each of these is created in a different way. The first, *canvas1*, is created by the *paint* method of the *TitleCanvas2* class when this object is instantiated. The second is created by the *run* method of the class *Dragon2*. The third section of the window is created by the method *addressDialog*.

The TitleCanvas2 Class	The *TitleCanvas2* class is used to create the title that occupies the top third of the second Web page. These two lines of type are centered to make up the title. This is done in the *paint* method. First, this method sets up a Times Roman font in 36-point size and sets the font metrics. It determines the width of each string, subtracting that from the width of the applet line, and then choosing half of the remaining available space to determine the beginning of each text string. This results in each string being centered. In Windows 95 or 98, you can resize the applet by clicking and dragging the mouse on one of the window sides or by clicking the small square at the top right of the window. It's best not to do these things if you want the applet to keep the title centered, since the change in applet width is not reported back to the program. The method *drawString* is then used to draw the first string at the proper place on the screen with the proper horizontal starting point specified for the string so that it will be centered horizontally in the applet. The same procedure is then used with the second title string.
What's the Best Way to Draw a Graphic?	Our first Web page was characterized by two photographs that were stored as *JPEG* graphics files. In that case, we didn't have much choice; the graphics files had to be stored along with the Java class file and had to be downloaded by your browser before you could view the completed Web page. You probably noticed, if you downloaded this page from the Web, that the text appeared quite quickly and then there was a significant lapse of time before the pictures appeared. One commonly used way of making this situation better is to have the original text page include boxes for the graphics, possibly with a text string

telling what the box will contain. Thus the whole page downloads quite quickly, and while you are reading it, the pictures will download and fill the boxes more slowly. If you decide you don't need to see the whole graphics, you can continue on without waiting for a full download.

In the second of our two Web pages we are going to make use of a graphic that can be generated by code included in the applet. Now, you are faced with two choices. You can create the graphic offline and store it a graphics file. Then you can download it from your Web page to the user, paying the penalty of whatever length of time is required for the download. This depends on the size of the graphics file; you might want to use some form of image compression to speed things up. However, you also have the option of downloading the code that creates the graphic and then using this code to generate the graphic locally. This may be much faster. It all depends upon how much complicated mathematics is required to create each pixel. Our second graphics page uses this second method.

The *Dragon2* Class

The *Dragon2* class is used to draw a fractal dragon, point by point, at the center of the applet. This may take a long time, even with a fast computer. The first thing to consider is that if you use the ordinary technique of having a *Dragon* class that is an extension of the *Panel* or *Canvas* class and draws the dragon in its *paint* method, you will be unable to access the rest of the applet while the dragon is being drawn. You'll see later that we're going to ask the user to type in his name and address. Now suppose he would like to do this before the dragon has been completely drawn. With the ordinary technique, he just can't. First, he can't move the cursor or access the keyboard while the dragon is being drawn, and second, the panel for entering the name and address doesn't even appear until the dragon is complete. To avoid these problems, we've chosen to generate the dragon graphic in a completely separate thread from the rest of the page. With things set up in this way, the user will be able to enter his name and address, make corrections in it, send it to the originating Website, or exit the applet altogether before the dragon drawing portion of the program has been finished. *Dragon2* is an extension of class *Canvas* and it has the added qualification *implements Runnable*. The *paint* method performs the actual creation of the dragon graphic. Normally, there is a *start* method that begins the instantiation of a *Dragon2* object by running *paint*, but in this case, we override the *start* method with a new one that simply sets up a new thread and starts it if it is not already running. We also have a new *run* method that simply repaints the screen, running in the independent thread. This does a much better job of updating the dragon when necessary, but unfortunately we don't have full control of how various threads are interacting. The result is that although we can write our name and address while the dragon is being drawn, the characters that we type in are not necessarily echoed to the screen until the dragon is finished. So this isn't a perfect solution to our problem. Now let's look at the *run* method. We begin by defining an array of colors and assigning the values we need to draw the dragon to the first seven colors in the array. We then set up the *x* and *y* limits for the dragon display and the proper values for *Q* and *P* that will make the fractal look like a dragon. We then set up the parameters *maxcol* and *maxrow* to determine the size of the dragon in the window, and *mincol*, which is used to position the dragon in the center of the display. The parameters *deltax* and *deltay* are the changes required for *x* and *y* for each increase of one column or row. We could now go through the mathematics for calculating each point of the dragon, using a pair of nested *for* loops to first go down each row and then move over column by column until the entire dragon was plotted. If we did this, the user would see the dragon appear a little bit at a time until eventually the picture was complete. Usually, however, when we put a graphic on a Web page, we want to give the user an overall idea of the picture as soon as possible and then fill in the detail later. To do this, we add a third *for* loop that iterates from 0 through 7. At the first iteration, we plot only every eighth row of picture data and draw a line of the selected color from that point down to where the next picture element begins. This all gets done in about one-eighth of the time required to paint the entire picture, but leaves out a lot of detail. On the next iteration of the third *for* loop, we begin one row lower and paint a line one pixel shorter for each picture element that we are calculating. This leaves each point that we originally computed plus some new lines to fill up the picture. This process is repeated until, after eight iterations, the entire picture is displayed. The mathematics of computing the pixels is fairly straightforward. Almost any book on fractals will explain it in detail if you are interested. As for the colors, every point where we went through the maximum number of iterations without the function blowing up is drawn in black. If the function blows up before the maximum number of iterations is reached, we draw the point in a color that corresponds to the number of iterations that have taken place before a test function exceeded a specified threshold. One final thing; if we had been using the *paint* function as we have in all our previous graphics programs, the *Graphics* object would have been properly eliminated by the garbage collector in Java after we were finished with it. This isn't true when we've constructed a graphics object as we did for this class, so we have to use the *dispose* method to make sure no traces of the *Graphics* object are left.

The *addressDialog* Method

The *addressDialog* method returns a *Panel* that fills the bottom third of the Web page. It provides labels indicating where the user's name, street address, city, state, and zip code are to be entered and text fields where this data can be entered. The *GridBagLayout* type of layout is used. You can refer to Chapter 4 to see how the constraints are used to obtain the desired layout. Note also that we have overwritten the *add* method that is ordinarily used to add the component to the panel. The new version of *add* sets the values of four constraints that need to be specified for each component of the panel, and then adds the component to the panel. This turns out to make the coding a lot simpler than if we included all the constraint settings in the *addressDialog* method.

Returning Data to the Originating Site

Figure 21.1 shows how the Web page appears in black and white. In addition to what has been described thus far, there is one more operation necessary to make the Web page complete. When the user has finished entering his name and address, it needs to be transferred back to the originating Website. This operation is performed by two additional methods. You'll note that on the Web page we've included a button marked *Send*. When the user clicks on this button, an *action* event occurs, which is processed by the method *action*. This method starts with an *if* statement that returns the event for further processing except when the *Send* button was clicked. In this case, the name and address data from the various text fields is read into a string called *data* with appropriate

FIGURE *Final Web Page.*
21.1

carriage returns and spaces inserted where needed. The method then calls the method *AddressData*, passing the *data* string to it.

Assuming the user is connected to a Web server, there is a standard way for you to interface with that server through a *Common Gateway Interface (CGI)*. To use this, you need to know the name of the Web server and the port to which it should send the information. Since you're writing this Web page for transmission to users through your server, you should know this information. For the example program, we've called the server *webname.com* and assumed the use of port 80. Change these as required. Next, we've printed out the data using *System.out.println*. This is only used to show you that the data is indeed there if you're using *AppletViewer* to look at the Web page. Ordinarily it may be omitted. We then enter a *try* section, which first looks for a socket connection to the server. An output stream is then set up with the server. The proper header is sent to it, followed by the content type and content length and finally the name and address data. The stream is then closed. In case of any errors, the *catch* section reports the error and then closes down the connection.

You've now seen how to create a Web page and permit the user to interact with it. Using Java, you can elaborate on it to make any kind of Web page and interact in whatever way you require for your application.

CHAPTER

22

Commercial Java Packages

In Chapter 2, we described how to use the Java Developers Kit, the Windows Notepad editor, and a DOS window to compile and run a simple Java program. Using this approach, let's go over what's involved with more complicated Java programs. Suppose we first just consider stand-alone Java applications. Suppose you have a window containing the Notepad editor, in which you've written a Java program that will be displayed in a window. First, you have to save this program as a file to which you assign a name having the extension *java*. Next, you switch to your DOS window and set the default directory to be the one containing your Java program file. Then type the line:

```
javac yourname.java
```

where *yourname* is the name you assigned to the file. The file will then be compiled and either you'll get some error messages if there are mistakes in the file, or you'll just get a new instance of the prompt legend. If there are errors, you'll want to return to the Notepad window and make some corrections. Then save the file again and compile again. Once the program compiles correctly, you need to type:

```
java yourname
```

which runs the compiled program. Note that when compiling, you need to include both the file name and the extension *java* but that when you're running the program, you don't include any extension. (The file that is being run is *yourname.class* but Java takes care of handling the extension without you supplying it. If you do add the extension, Java will try to include it twice and the program will not run). Java will now create a window and run the program in it.

You may remember that our first Java programs used the command *System.out.println();* to display information on the DOS window, but that when we made a Java program that created a window, we needed to use graphics commands to display data in the newly created window. When debugging a complicated program, it is convenient to display debugging statements with *System.out.println();*. Such statements do not interfere with the display that you are trying to draw in the newly created window, but can be read by shifting to the DOS window.

If you're going to create a Java applet rather than a stand-alone application, you need to have a principle class that is an extension of the *Applet* class and you need to eliminate the *main* method that is part of every stand alone application. You create this program from your editor and then compile it from the DOS window as before. You now also need an *HTML* program. It usually has the name of your *Applet* class followed by the extension *html.* You run this applet by typing a line such as

```
Appletviewer Yourname.html
```

The *HTML* program contains as a minimum the name of the applet to be run and the width and height parameters of the window to be created.

The WinEdit Editor

You may well decide that the Notepad editor is too rudimentary and that you would rather edit your Java programs with something more sophisticated. There is a shareware editor that is ideal for creating Java programs. It is called *WinEdit.* Version 96u of this program is included on the CD-ROM. There is a later version than this, but it would not run on my installation of Windows 98. The program is available from

Wilson WindowWare Inc.
2701 California Avenue SW
Suite 212
Seattle, WA 98116

Unfortunately, if you want to continue to use WinEdit after the trial period, the company expects you to send them $99.95, which is a little pricey for a shareware product. Nevertheless, you might want to try this program and you might just like it well enough to buy it.

Microsoft Visual J++

Microsoft Visual J++ 6.0 is a commercial Java system that ties together Sun's Java Developers Kit with an editor and capabilities for easily compiling and editing Java programs. It also provides extensive support for Java Beans and Java Swing. Visual J++ includes software that is particularly oriented toward efficient use with Windows 95/98. If you use this, your program may not run on platforms not using Windows. This feature is the issue in a lawsuit between Sun Microsystems and Microsoft, so if you take advantage of it, you are in danger of being unable to use your program at some time in the future. You can, however, use Visual J++ to produce pure Java code. Let's suppose you are going to create a stand-alone Java application. Table 22-1 compares the steps required to do this with the Java Developers Kit and an ASCII editor with the steps needed to produce the same application with Visual J++.

The amount of work you have to do is about the same in either system. The main difference is that you don't have to switch between windows with Visual J++.

One important eccentricity of Visual J++ is that only one class in your program can be preceded by the word *public* and that is the principal class whose name is identical to the file name in a case-sensitive fashion. If you try to compile and run any of the programs in this book with Visual J++ and the program has more than one *public* class, you'll get a compiler error. This is unlike the Java Developers Kit, which will allow several *public* classes in a program.

We chose the *ViewPic* program from Chapter 9 to test out Visual J++, since the *FileDialogFilter* didn't work with the Java Developers Kit. We wanted to see if Microsoft had fixed this problem, but they had not. So to make the filter work in either case you have to use Java Swing components. The internal workings of the Java compiler and interpreter in this regard seem to be identical with Sun's. Otherwise, the program ran fine.

Now suppose you want to create a Java applet with Visual J++. You create a program in the same way as in Table 22-1. As with the Java Developers Kit, you need to have the principal class an extension of class *Applet* and you need to eliminate the *main* method. When you get to the point where the table tells you to select the radio button, you select "Browser" instead of "Stand-alone interpreter". If you don't have an *HTML* file, Visual J++ will create one for you. The name of this file may be somewhat obscure. Also, if you are passing parameters to the applet through the HTML file, you won't be able to use Visible J++ to automatically create an HTML file, since it creates a barebones file with no parameters passed. Instead, you'll have to write your own HTML file. Visual J++ uses the Microsoft Internet Explorer to process and display the applet, rather than the *AppletViewer* program. This gives you a little more flexibility and comes closer to allowing you to see how the applet actually appears on the Net; at least for systems using Microsoft's browser.

We noted earlier that it was convenient to include debugging statements in a program that would be displayed on the DOS window without affecting the window created by the Java program. You can't do this with Visual J++ because the DOS window disappears before the program has run and cannot be recovered. In this aspect, the original JDK technique is far superior.

The full Professional version of Visual J++ lists for $549. Thus, unless you are heavy into commercial Java programming, it is not a desirable option. There is also a standard edition that is available for $109. Since Visual J++ has a built-in editor, the low-priced version may be as good a buy as going out and paying $99 for an editor to edit the free Java programs.

Table 21-1.   Creating a Java Standalone Application.

Java Developers Kit and ASCII Editor	MicroSoft Visual J++
	Close any existing project by choosing Close Workspace from the File menu.
Open your editor and start a new text file.	Choose New from the File menu and then select Text File.
Type in the code for your Java program.	Type in the code for your Java program.
From the File menu choose Save.	From the File menu choose Save.
Save with the file name corresponding to your principal class with the extension *Java*. (If you're using the Windows Notepad, it may automatically save the file with the extension *Txt* and you'll have to leave the editor and change it.	Save with the file name corresponding to your principal class with the extension *Java*.
Set up a DOS window by selecting Start/ Programs/MSDOS Prompt.	From the Build menu, select Build followed by your program name. A dialog box appears asking if you want to create a default workspace.
Type *javac* followed by the name of your file (including the *java* extension).	Click Yes. Visual J++ creates a default workspace and builds the application.
Type *java* followed by your program name (without the extension).	From the Build menu choose Execute. The information for Running Class dialog box appears. Type your file name without the extension. Select the radio button "Stand-alone interpreter" and then click OK.
The application runs.	The application runs.

Symantec Visual Café

Symantec Corp.'s Visual Café 3.0a is the newest in a line of integrated Java program development tools. It is supposed to have visual interfaces that enable you to do Java programming better and faster with less programming knowledge and to be a powerful tool for corporate Java developers. You can also plug different versions of Java into Visual Café, including Java 2. The price you pay for this is $799, which may rule it out for many who are not doing full-time Java programming. Previous versions of Café, when installed, have added lines to the *autoexec.bat* program that force all Java compiling and interpreting to be done by Café. On the contrary, Visual J++ is self-contained so that you can create a Java program with Visual J++ and then compile and run it either with the JDK or with Visual J++. This might be a very useful thing to do if you want to make sure that your new program is fully compatible with the latest Sun version of Java.

Appendix

About the CD-ROM

The programs on the CD-ROM are designed to be run on a PC that is running Windows 95 or Windows 98. If you have a MacIntosh, you can download the Mac version of Java and use it to compile the programs in this book, but you won't be able to use the CD-ROM, which is in PC format. The CD-ROM contains the following directories:

JAVA

This directory contains the file **jdk12-win32.exe**. Java and all Java-based trademarks and logos are trademarks or registered trademarks of Sun Microsystems, Inc. in the United States and other countries. You need to transfer the file to a directory on your hard drive and then run it to automatically expand and properly locate the files for Java Developers' Kit version 1.2. This is the latest version of Java that was released just before this book was going to print. All the programs in this book were created using Java version 1.2.

The directory also contains the file **jdk12-doc.zip,** which contains the documentation for the JDK version 1.2. You'll need to transfer the file to your hard drive, but you don't need to unzip it. Any browser or explorer that can handle zipped files will automatically let you view a desired file in unzipped format.

JAVABOOK

This directory consists of four subdirectories that contain the data from this book. They are:

FIGURES — This subdirectory contains all of the monochrome figures used in the book. They are in Windows bitmapped (BMP) file format.

PLATES   This subdirectory contains graphics files for all of the color plates used in the book in Windows bitmapped (BMP) format.

PROGRAMS   This subdirectory contains all of the programs used throughout the book in both source code and compiled versions.

WORDDOCS   This subdirectory contains all of the text used in the book in Microsoft Word format.

Graphics Workshop

This directory contains the file **gwsp20.exe**. When you run this program, it will self- install Graphics Workshop Professional, a shareware product of Alchemy Mindworks. The program allows you to view and manipulate a wide variety of graphics file formats and change one to another. It also includes a lite version of the GIF Construction Server, which allows you to create GIF graphics files, including animated ones. The Graphics Workshop Professional software included with this publication is provided as shareware for your evaluation. If you try this software and find it useful, you are requested to register it as discussed in its documentation and in the About screen of the application. The publisher of this book has not paid the registration fee for this software.

VPIC

This directory contains the file **vpic61.zip,** a DOS program for displaying many different types of graphics files in any desired graphics mode and converting from one graphic format to another. After unzipping the file, see the file *Readme.1st* for further instructions. VPIC is provided as shareware for your evaluation. If you try this software and find it useful, you are requested to register it as discussed in its documentation and in the About screen of the application. The publisher of this book has not paid the registration fee for this software.

WINEDIT

This directory contains the file **we99a32i.zip,** an excellent editor for producing Java source files You need to transfer this file to your hard drive and then unzip it with *PKUNZIP* or *WINZIP*. You can then install **WinEdit,** an excellent programmer's editor by Wilson WindowWare Inc. The WinEdit software included with this publication is provided as shareware for your evaluation. If you try this software and find it useful, you are requested to register it as discussed in its documentation and in the About screen of the application. The publisher of this book has not paid the registration fee for this software.

Programmer's File Editor	This directory contains the file **pfe0701i.zip,** an excellent editor for producing Java source files. You need to transfer this file to your hard drive and then unzip it with *PKUNZIP* or *WINZIP*. This is a much less fancy and more basic editor than WinEdit, but it is free.
AnfyJava	This directory contains a number of Java applets that are suitable for use in generating your own Web pages. The source code for these is not available, but enough options are provided so that you can tailor them for most applications.

Index

Sun Microsystems, Inc.
Binary Code License Agreement

READ THE TERMS OF THIS AGREEMENT AND ANY PROVIDED SUPPLEMENTAL LICENSE TERMS (COLLECTIVELY "AGREEMENT") CAREFULLY BEFORE OPENING THE SOFTWARE MEDIA PACKAGE. BY OPENING THE SOFTWARE MEDIA PACKAGE, YOU AGREE TO THE TERMS OF THIS AGREEMENT. IF YOU ARE ACCESSING THE SOFTWARE ELECTRONICALLY, INDICATE YOUR ACCEPTANCE OF THESE TERMS BY SELECTING THE "ACCEPT" BUTTON AT THE END OF THIS AGREEMENT. IF YOU DO NOT AGREE TO ALL THESE TERMS, PROMPTLY RETURN THE UNUSED SOFTWARE TO YOUR PLACE OF PURCHASE FOR A REFUND OR, IF THE SOFTWARE IS ACCESSED ELECTRONICALLY, SELECT THE "DECLINE" BUTTON AT THE END OF THIS AGREEMENT.

1. LICENSE TO USE. Sun grants you a non-exclusive and non-transferable license for the internal use only of the accompanying software and documentation and any error corrections provided by Sun (collectively "Software"), by the number of users and the class of computer hardware for which the corresponding fee has been paid.

2. RESTRICTIONS. Software is confidential and copyrighted. Title to Software and all associated intellectual property rights is retained by Sun and/or its licensors. Except as specifically authorized in any Supplemental License Terms, you may not make copies of Software, other than a single copy of Software for archival purposes. Unless enforcement is prohibited by applicable law, you maynot modify, decompile, reverse engineer Software. You acknowledge that Software is not designed or licensed for use in on-line control of aircraft, air traffic, aircraft navigation or aircraft communications; or in the design, construction, operation or maintenance of any nuclear facility. Sun disclaims any express or implied warranty of fitness for such uses. No right, title or interest in or to any trademark, service mark, logo or trade name of Sun or its licensors is granted under this Agreement.

3. LIMITED WARRANTY. Sun warrants to you that for a period of ninety (90) days from the date of purchase, as evidenced by a copy of the receipt, the media on which Software is furnished (if any) will be free of defects in materials and workmanship under normal use. Except for the foregoing, Software is provided "AS IS". Your exclusive remedy and Sun's entire liability under this limited warranty will be at Sun's option to replace Software media or refund the fee paid for Software.

4. DISCLAIMER OF WARRANTY. UNLESS SPECIFIED IN THIS AGREEMENT, ALL EXPRESS OR IMPLIED CONDITIONS, REPRESENTATIONS AND WARRANTIES, INCLUDING ANY IMPLIED WARRANTY OF MERCHANTABILITY, FITNESS FOR A PARTICULAR PURPOSE, OR NON-INFRINGEMENT, ARE DISCLAIMED, EXCEPT TO THE EXTENT THAT THESE DISCLAIMERS ARE HELD TO BE LEGALLY INVALID.

5. LIMITATION OF LIABILITY. TO THE EXTENT NOT PROHIBITED BY LAW, IN NO EVENT WILL SUN OR ITS LICENSORS BE LIABLE FOR ANY LOST REVENUE, PROFIT OR DATA, OR FOR SPECIAL, INDIRECT, CONSEQUENTIAL, INCIDENTAL OR PUNITIVE DAMAGES, HOWEVER CAUSED REGARDLESS OF THE THEORY OF LIABILITY, ARISING OUT OF OR RELATED TO THE USE OF OR INABILITY TO USE SOFTWARE, EVEN IF SUN HAS BEEN ADVISED OF THE POSSIBILITY OF SUCH DAMAGES. In no event will Sun's liability to you, whether in contract, tort (including negligence), or otherwise, exceed the amount paid by you for Software under this Agreement. The foregoing limitations will apply even if the above stated warranty fails of its essential purpose.

6. Termination. This Agreement is effective until terminated. You may terminate this Agreement at any time by destroying all copies of Software. This Agreement will terminate immediately without notice from Sun if you fail to comply with any provision of this Agreement. Upon Termination, you must destroy all copies of Software.

7. Export Regulations. All Software and technical data delivered under this Agreement are subject to US export control laws and may be subject to export or import regulations in other countries. You agree to comply strictly with all such laws and regulations and acknowledge that you have the responsibility to obtain such licenses to export, re-export, or import as may be required after delivery to you.

8. U.S. Government Rights. If Software is being acquired by or on behalf of the U.S. Government or by a U.S. Government prime contractor or subcontractor (at any tier), then the Government's rights in Software will be only as set forth in this Agreement; this is in accordance with 48 CFR 227.7201 through 227.7202-4 (for Department of Defense (DOD) acquisitions) and with 48 CFR 2.101 and 12.212 (for non-DOD acquisitions).

9. Governing Law. Any action related to this Agreement will be governed by California law and controlling U.S. federal law. No choice of law rules of any jurisdiction will apply.

10. Severability. If any provision of this Agreement is held to be unenforceable, this Agreement will remain in effect with the provision omitted, unless omission would frustrate the intent of the parties, in which case this Agreement will immediately terminate.

11. Integration. This Agreement is the entire agreement between you and Sun relating to its subject matter. It supersedes all prior or contemporaneous oral or written communications, proposals, representations and warranties and prevails over any conflicting or additional terms of any quote, order, acknowledgment, or other communication between the parties relating to its subject matter during the term of this Agreement. No modification of this Agreement will be binding, unless in writing and signed by an authorized representative of each party.

For inquiries please contact: Sun Microsystems, Inc. 901 San Antonio Road, Palo Alto, California 94303

JAVA™ 2 SDK, STANDARD EDITION, V 1.2.1
SUPPLEMENTAL LICENSE TERMS

These supplemental terms ("Supplement") add to the terms of the Binary Code License Agreement (collectively the "Agreement"). Capitalized terms not defined herein shall have the same meanings ascribed to them in the Agreement. The Supplement terms shall supersede any inconsistent or conflicting terms in the Agreement above, or in any license contained within the Software.

1. Limited License Grant. Sun grants to you a non-exclusive, non-transferable limited license to use the Software without fee for evaluation of the Software and for development of Java™ applets and applications provided that you: (i) may not re-distribute the Software in whole or in part, either separately or included with a product; and (ii) may not create, or authorize your licensees to create additional classes, interfaces, or subpackages that are contained in the "java" or "sun" packages or similar as specified by Sun in any class file naming convention. Refer to the Java Runtime Environment Version 1.2.1 binary code license (http://java.sun.com/products/jdk/1.2/jre/index.html) for the availability of runtime code which may be distributed with Java applets and applications.

2. Java Platform Interface. In the event that Licensee creates an additional API(s) which: (i) extends the functionality of a Java Environment; and, (ii) is exposed to third party software developers for the purpose of developing additional software which invokes such additional API, Licensee must promptly
publish broadly an accurate specification for such API for free use by all developers.

3. Trademarks and Logos. Licensee acknowledges as between it and Sun that Sun owns the Java trademark and all Java-related trademarks, logos and icons including the Coffee Cup and Duke ("Java Marks") and agrees to comply with the Java Trademark Guidelines at http://www.sun.com/policies/trademarks.

4. Source Code. Software may contain source code that is provided solely for reference purposes pursuant to the terms of this Agreement.